# Gender and Development in India

# Gender and Development in India

## Current Issues

U. Kalpagam

RAWAT PUBLICATIONS

Jaipur • New Delhi • Bangalore • Hyderabad • Guwahati

ISBN 978-81-316-0470-0





*Published by*
Prem Rawat for **Rawat Publications**
Satyam Apts, Sector 3, Jawahar Nagar, Jaipur 302 004 (India)
Phone: 0141 265 1748/7006 Fax: 0141 265 1748
E-mail: info@rawatbooks.com
Website: www.rawatbooks.com

*New Delhi Office*
4858/24, Ansari Road, Daryaganj, New Delhi 110 002
Phone: 011 2326 3290

Also at *Bangalore, Hyderabad* and *Guwahati*

Typeset by Rawat Computers, Jaipur
Printed at Chaman Enterprises, New Delhi

# Contents

# Preface

My long-standing interest on women's issues and development has resulted in my reflections on these issues. Requests to write for seminars/conferences resulted in some papers that served as the first draft of some of the chapters of the book. The perspective of this book draws from the acknowledged position of scholars and activists in the field of gender and development studies that it is imperative to assess the development processes from the vantage point of poor women in developing countries. This perspective foregrounds issues of power, inequality, marginalization and social justice, and leads to an interrogation of the structural and social dynamics of poverty and inequality, power asymmetries and exclusionary mechanisms that are in operation.

In my endeavours, I have received support and encouragement from Jaya Arunachalam, President of Working Women's Forum (India), Chennai whose commitment to the causes of women's movement has always been inspiring. All my other friends at Working Women's Forum (India) have over the years cheerfully assisted me in numerous ways. I wish to thank Sudersena, Asha and Nandini who have been partners in many of the studies. Data collection for the chapter on "ICT and Women in the Informal Sector" was done by R. Asha and S. Nandini, and for the chapter on social security was done by Sudersena of Working Women's Forum (India). They deserve perhaps more than this acknowledgement of thanks. The respondents in the studies did so even if they did not fully comprehend it, in the hope that they and those like them may stand to gain from these studies. I offer my thanks to all of them. I also thank Ankita Yadav for providing some research assistance in this work.

# 1

# Gender and Development

## Interrogating Current Issues

Development discourses of globalization, liberalization and human development that have come to occupy the centre stage in the last twenty years or so have also caused a shift in the perspective on issues relating to women and development in India. Globalization has ushered in a new model of corporate capitalism in which multinational corporates and the growing internationalized Indian corporates all seek to redefine a borderless national space of capital accumulation. Such a model of corporate globalization has opened up new opportunities of employment both within and outside the country for some and has stimulated new desire for affluent middle-class lifestyles emulating those of the West. Thus, the transformation of the urban landscape with shopping malls, McDonaldś and KFC outlets, advertisements of Western branded products are all part of this phenomenon. This process of corporate globalization necessitated the liberalization of the economy by which the market forces are allowed to operate in a free and unhindered manner. Development policies of the earlier decades sought to promote import-substitution industrialization, mixed economy of public and private sectors, and planned development through various forms of state interventions in the pricing and allocation of resources. The economic reform programmes of the last two decades sought to remove these state-induced distortions in the markets and to let markets function within the new regulatory frameworks. It was reckoned that such a model of corporate globalization required healthy, educated and skilled labour force which the developing countries with mass poverty, illiteracy and low health status everywhere cannot supply in the long run to sustain this model of corporate globalization. It is also evident that this process of economic globalization is the new form of uneven development which even as it stimulates economic growth of global, regional and national economies, and creates new opportunities for many but not all, it is also more likely to engender both old and new disparities and inequalities in access to resources, incomes and assets, opportunities and lifestyle changes. The United Nations set the "Millennium Development Goals" (MDGs) in human development targets so that nations and the global community do not lose their focus and commitment on poverty reduction and improvement of the living standards of a vast majority of the poor around the world. Human development thus entered the development discourse in the last two decades with its associated implications for development policies, interventions and practices.

These recent developments have had a significant impact on labour in India in terms of employment, wages and incomes, poverty and vulnerabilities, and human development issues relating to health, education and skill acquisition. Women too have been impacted by these developments in their multiple roles as workers and care-givers. With the changes in the roles of the developmental state in India, the period has also witnessed the growing influence of the civil society organizations and strengthening of decentralized democracy. These changes have brought about a change in the perspectives on gender and development at the level of practice. After traversing the path of women's equality and the role of the welfare state to promote such measures to attain equality, the period of the 70s and 80s saw efforts at integrating women in the development process (known as the WID approach). Poor women became the central focus and the state, bureaucracy, scholars, activists and development practitioners all sought to ensure that development interventions, especially poverty alleviation measures included poor women and female-headed households. This integrationist WID approach left unquestioned the development strategy itself which in its conception, intervention and target approach had built-in biases against the excluded groups (Kabeer, 1994). The development process and its outcomes were determined by power and dominance both in the echelons of development bureaucracy and at the local levels. Interrogating the social structures of power and dominance led feminist scholars to the understanding that gender was a social construct and that gender was also a social relation of power and dominance, much like other social relations. Gender relation is one component in the matrix of social power relationships that determine and are determined by institutional processes and outcomes, and everyday life experiences. Gender-power relationships constitute women's and men's subjectivities. Gender and development (GAD) perspective evolved out of this understanding, and development strategies for women informed by this perspective adopted transformative approaches seeking to alter the nature of power relationships in ways that could be more favourable to women in general and poor women in particular (Kalpagam, 1994; Murthy, 2001). New approaches and concepts emerged from this understanding such as the process of "gender planning" and "strategic and practical gender needs" (Moser, 1993).

When the structural adjustment policies (SAP) began to roll out in many developing economies in the 90s of the last century based on the wisdom of what has come to be known as "the Washington consensus" which contained the World Bank and IMF ideas and prescriptions on neoliberalism, many economists of feminist orientation sought to work with GAD perspectives within the World Bank in its many projects worldwide. If earlier in the 70s USAID did much to popularize the WID approaches worldwide, in the 90s the World Bank and other international donor agencies succeeded in transferring the GAD perspectives in useful modular formats that could be used for project evaluations worldwide with some modifications to account for local details and particulars. The modular formatting sought to inquire into gender-based division of labour and with whom the decision-making powers rested as regards household and family life among others. These undoubtedly are valid in all contexts, but a true GAD approach that acknowledges gender-power relations as one component of social power relations has to cognize these others social structures of power and their articulation with gender relations in a processual and dynamic framework. This implies that the political economy analysis and gender analysis have to be integrated.

The intellectual antecedents of the GAD perspective are firmly located in the various ideologies and politics of Marxist and socialist feminism, and based on the worldwide feminist activism of increasing women's awareness and consciousness of the causes of their subordinate status which by the 70s of the last century was a significant force to reckon with in many developed Western societies and in those ex-colonial countries that had forged ahead in their nationalist movements to overthrow the colonial rule (Jayawardene, 1986). The women's movement and the nationalist movement in countries like India were aligned and worked in tandem for both the nation's and women's freedom, even if not all the women were encompassed in it (Roy, 2005; Chaudhuri, 2010). The politics of the women's movement everywhere was geared towards transformation and emancipation. However, the popularizing of the GAD approach in modular formats unwittingly succeeded in wresting it from its antecedent ideological and political basis.

As the decade of the 90s progressed, we were soon engulfed by the discourse of women's "empowerment". The GAD approach vanished with its perspective, opening the way for a more plural and depoliticized women's "empowerment" discourse. No doubt, the word "empowerment" does contain the word "power" in it, and therefore it may appear that "women's empowerment" refers to making women more powerful or make women possess more power. This is a gross simplification of how gender-power relations were sought to be cognized and the transformative strategies that were encouraged under the GAD perspective. This simplified empowerment perspective was thus shorn of any ideological or political grounding and became acceptable and popular to different stakeholders and agents with diverse political orientations thus making the site of women's empowerment a pluralistic one with its associated advantages and disadvantages.

Globalization has altered the terrain of development interventions. With the role of the state in its welfare and developmental roles being restricted and yet looked upon to provide safety nets for the emergent vulnerabilities induced by the market, the Indian state has clearly gone ahead in associating civil society organizations as partners in the domain of development interventions. India's 10th Five-Year Plan (2002–2007) document states that with "the acceptance of market liberalism and globalization it is expected that the state yields to the market and the civil society in many areas where it had a direct but distortionary and inefficient presence … It also includes the role of the state as a development catalyst where, perhaps, civil society has better institutional capacity. At the same time, with the growth of markets and the presence of an aware and sensitive civil society, many developmental functions as well as functions that provide stability to the social order have to be progressively performed by the market and civil society organizations" (2002: 181). This era has also witnessed a remarkable growth of the civil society organizations engaging with various issues of development practice and informed by a variety of ideological and political orientations.

With the institutionalization of the civil society organizations in this space of interventions, the empowerment perspective became acceptable to work with for the very diverse groupings of the civil society organizations. With the state's approach of women's empowerment as spelt out and with the modular format of GAD perspective on empowering women in the development process, the diverse civil society organizations in the field of women's development interventions could all now articulate the discourse of "women's empowerment" even if their understanding and approaches were ideologically and politically different. Many in the women's movement feel that this homogenizing discourse of women's empowerment has served to dilute the radical political perspective of the autonomous women's movement that had earlier emphasized on social transformation and emancipation. True, even earlier there were women's groups associated with political parties that had varying ideologies and goals, and they too had always been considered part of the women's movement in the country. However, feminism then was largely viewed as a transformative approach, meant to transform both women's lives and the society they live in.

Globalization has also brought in the corporate sector as a player in the terrain of the development interventions. By encouraging what has come to be known as "Corporate Social Responsibility" (CSR), corporates are now engaging in a variety of development interventions. These no doubt are well-intentioned efforts but they do ideologically support the system that benefits them, that allows them to make profits out of which a small percentage is allocated for development activities signifying their social responsibility. They are therefore for the status quo even if their efforts alleviate poverty and may provide health and education benefits to some. Global examples of corporate philanthropy such as Microsoft's Bill Gates and Warren Buffet have been actively exhorting Indian corporates some of whom are now growing rich as fast as those in the developed world to give back a substantial part of their assets to the society. Even the Indian government has made it mandatory in the Union Budget 2010 to contribute to CSR. Corporate Social Responsibility has also played a part in the growth of the civil society organizations through the availability of its funding.

With so many diverse players in the terrain of women's development interventions, it is not surprising that the "empowerment" perspective seems to have caught the imagination of all. Scholars may be engaged in debates of what empowerment means. But out there in the arena of development practice, each player adopts a perspective on empowerment of women that is suitable for their goals and mission. No doubt, all efforts and actions do have some relevance to the people at whom they are aimed. A gross categorization of the ideological positions would be of those who think that alleviation of global mass poverty and decent life options cannot be achieved under the present model of capitalist globalization and that an alternative economic system at global and national levels that factors in the various issues of sustainability can only realize the goal. Some others think that such a radical transformation of bringing in an alternate economic system is only a utopian ideal, and history has taught us that those efforts had failed. For these people, a more pragmatic approach of working within the system to secure welfare gains for the poor is the only meaningful strategy. Some feminist scholars today think that the women's movement has relied far too much on the state as an ally to deliver welfare gains and that in the present context of market liberalism the women's movement needs to strategically reposition itself to leverage the market for securing welfare gains and equity for women (Phadke, 2003).

Women's empowerment as understood by all these different agents involves a minimal set of capabilities and entitlements so that poor women can access better living conditions, improved health and education status, greater autonomy in decision-making and fulfilment of their roles as wives, mothers and workers under non-oppressive conditions. For instance, there is likely to be unanimity among them that domestic violence should be curbed, but there may not be consensus among them of how family roles can be restructured or household tasks distributed among male and female members. Similarly, they may all agree on the notion that a decent living wage is a woman's right, but they may not all agree that waged work outside the home is better than piece-rated home-based work. It appears that the empowerment perspective has been able to hold out an open umbrella for many to stand under it and with a possible likelihood of consensus on certain core issues of women's empowerment, although such a consensus is not really required for each of them to function within the newly redefined space.

Some of the core issues relevant to the empowerment of poor women in the current context of globalization and liberalization are employment and livelihood security issues, availability and access to a wide range of social protection measures and issues of governance. Each of these issues is fraught with a number of challenges that we seek to interrogate here.

**Employment and Livelihood Issues**

The factors that determine women's involvement in the labour force have been well analysed in the literature on labour markets. It is evident that most women combine housework and caring roles in conjunction with economic work which could be home-based economic work or waged work outside. The impact of globalization and liberalization on women has been to increase their workload (Ghosh, 2009) across the whole spectrum of the working population in India. Inflationary trends in the economy and rising aspirations of a consumerist culture that is evident in the growing demand for commodities such as colour TVs, mixers and grinders, fans, etc., as also evident from the freebies offered by the political parties during election time indicate that this desire for goods is not restricted to a growing urban middle class alone. Women of the working class and poor women also consider these consumer gadgets as reducing drudgery like their middle class counterparts. Women and especially younger women members of the working class families now seek work and work longer hours to secure incomes to buy these goods to ease their everyday lives. But the availability of employment for women has been restricted and there is also unevenness in the availability of jobs across regions and between rural and urban areas. The majority of women find jobs in the informal sector and studies indicate that in some regions there is now, on account of the overall economic growth in the last couple of years, a greater regularity of low-paying informal sector jobs for women. Even with new investments on account of globalization, the economy is still on the path of jobless growth. While open unemployment for younger women is around 15% in urban areas and around 6% in rural areas, concealed unemployment (which refers to women willing to work if work is provided to them but is not in the labour force seeking work) is very high. It is necessary to understand why employment creation is faltering and the impact on old employment and the kinds of new employment that are being created as a consequence of globalization and liberalization.

The general perception is that liberalization of the economy has opened up a range of employment opportunities for young women in the IT sector, export units such as garments and electronics, the urban retail sector, hospitality services and so on. Studies also indicate that young women working in these sectors do enjoy a feeling of liberation and some autonomy, but many also do not have the needed control over the earnings, face increasing insecurities living in hostile urban settings with poor residence facilities and so on (Chhachhi, 1999; Jeyaranjan and

Swaminathan, 1999; Unni and Bali, 2002; Mazumdar, 2007). Such employment opportunities are not available in rural areas and many young rural women are increasingly migrating to urban centres for such employment. The majority of rural women everywhere face bleak employment prospects in the non-farm sector. Given this scenario, it is not surprising that microfinance to promote entrepreneurship especially among women has been seen as a panacea for the ills on the employment front.

Microfinance was used successfully by a number of women's organizations to mobilize and empower women until recently, the most well-known organizations are Working Women's Forum (India) and SEWA (Ahmedabad) both of which started their activities in the late 70s of the last century and achieved quite a bit as to become role models. Simultaneously, from around the early 80s, Grameen Bank doing the same in Bangladesh gained wide international repute. The initiatives in India were based on a model of group lending to help informal sector workers from the clutches of moneylenders who were charging very high interest rates. Although one of the factors that motivated the nationalization of banks in the late 60s was to extend credit and banking services to the vast majority in the rural areas, financial inclusiveness still remained a far off ideal. Both Working Women's Forum (India) [WWF(I)] and SEWA set up their own co-operative banks and charged interest rates that were governed by the norms for priority sector lending, which bearing an interest subsidy was pegged at around 4% when the banks' lending rate was around 10% or 12%. Seeing the success of these two women's organizations in helping poor women, many small women's groups such as *Pennurimai Iyakkam* (Chennai) in the early 1980s used their influence and negotiated with some banks to give group loans under the differential interest rate scheme. Although this scheme was then available in all nationalized banks, they were reluctant to deal with poor illiterate women and thought that they were not bankable; the idea of group lending was even more suspect. The evidence of low default rates from the successful initiatives soon convinced the government that poor women were in fact bankable.

With the liberalization of the economy, financial inclusiveness as part of an inclusive growth strategy assumed importance and the interest subsidy under the priority sector lending was also withdrawn. With employment growth prospects appearing bleak and the poverty alleviation programmes such as the Integrated Rural Development Programme (IRDP) not achieving significantly much on the ground, the governments realized that promoting self-employment through entrepreneurship could be a strategy that could also stimulate entrepreneurship among poor women, who anyway are self-employed in significant numbers in the informal sector. The state's encouragement for microfinance through its numerous redrafted strategies such as the Swarna Jayanthi Swarojgar Yojana and others fitted well with the neoliberal agendas of rolling back the state's welfare role and let the poor citizens become risk-bearing subjects capable of handling the vagaries of the market. This agenda of promoting entrepreneurship where individuals bear the risks themselves is no doubt attractive to the many new players in the terrain of development interventions. Whereas the earlier women's NGOs had used microcredit as a point of entry to mobilize women to build solidarity groups and promote conscientization about their subordinate status, the new microfinance institutions (MFIs) seek merely to fill in the institutional void for rural credit that still exists after nearly 40 years of bank nationalization. Many of the new MFIs are just a new set of moneylenders, but unlike the traditional moneylenders they articulate a discourse of women's empowerment. Having realized that group lending is less risk free, they have opted for this model of credit lending. Their main goals are only lending and some perhaps do provide guidance in entrepreneurial activities. But much of the onus and responsibility for running the enterprises successfully remains with the groups who are formed as Self Help Groups (SHGs).

The National Bank for Agriculture and Rural Development (NABARD) has been the apex bank that has been funding SHGs through other banks and many NGOs have started the formation of SHGs to help women to access microcredit. These SHGs are small thrift groups that first need to save money before they can access the loan, which is a different approach from WWF (I) lending that seeks to strengthen women's position when they are already pursuing an occupation. The thrift-based SHG model is clearly aimed at women who are housewives who would like to earn some cash income and independence by pursuing an economic activity. While many of these NGOs may be sincere about working towards women's empowerment, each of them have their own ideas of what women's empowerment is and so do the SHGs as well (Burra et al., 2005). The general perception both in the numerous government microcredit programmes and the MFIs is that it is only getting the credit to women, which is necessary for their empowerment and nothing else is required. Once an SHG starts an economic activity it automatically empowers women. These are too simplistic approaches to women's empowerment, but this simplistic perspective has now a wide acceptance.

Globalization and liberalization have also resulted in a deepening and global integration of financial markets. True to the model of corporate globalization and neoliberalism, one well-known MFI in India called *SKS Microfinance* entered the primary market for capital mobilization and then listed itself on the stock market thus trading its shares in the secondary market. As many MFIs are functioning as moneylenders, their clients take multiple and overlapping loans from even multiple MFIs making their debt portfolios so heavy and unviable to repay the loans that are now given at very high interest rates. This default rate increased risk and lowered the MFI share rating resulting in their share prices going down. As clients default, they use strong-arm tactics to retrieve the loans leading to enormous stress for the clients with some women committing suicides (Staff Reporter, 2010a). The irony cannot be lost here – the empowerment perspective leading to corporate gains and women's deaths!

Numerous studies and surveys have revealed many of the problems faced by women SHGs in their enterprise initiatives and have also indicated that microcredit is not a magic solution for poverty alleviation as the progress on that front is tardy and slow (Kabeer, 2001; Kalpana, 2005; Datar and Pawar, 2008; Schenk-Sandbergen, 2008). There is also the view that microcredit is not really targeted at the very poor women for whom wage employment in public works through programmes such as National Rural Employment Guarantee Act (NREGA) is a more advantageous solution. New evidence from long-standing organizations like WWF (I) now indicate that while the majority of the clients may not be the poorest of the poor, yet informal sector workers such as street vendors are not economically well off and the repeated loans they have availed from WWF (I) have undoubtedly improved their earnings from their occupations and have brought about betterment in their lives through improved living conditions, education for children and so on (Azad, 2007). While many are still at the same occupations even after many years of participation in the microcredit scheme suggesting no radical alleviation of poverty, some have undoubtedly scaled up their operation or moved to new lines of activity to be called successful "micro" entrepreneurs. With this broad evidence on hand, is it possible to make a balanced judgement of the microcredit and SHG activities, especially since it has either drawn euphoric praise or been severely condemned?

Clearly, microcredit and SHG movements do have their places to promote self-employment, entrepreneurial initiatives and income generation, but it is necessary to ensure that these are not promoted with the neoliberal ideals and goals of producing risk-bearing citizens to fit the model of corporate globalization (Menon, 2010). Given the problems of financial inclusiveness and the lack of decent living standards for the masses in the country, it is necessary to substantially lower the interest rates for microcredit lending as was done earlier under the differential interest rate scheme for the priority sectors. Some MFI leaders such as Mr Mahajan of Basix think that it is a myth among the middle class and the intelligentsia that MFI interest rates could be brought down to a single-digit figure given the cost of funds that MFIs themselves borrow and the transaction costs in addition. The question that is important to ask is why it is not possible to adopt the earlier policy of low interest rate for priority sector lending, especially since with liberalization economic growth in certain sectors is quite commendable. As far as women's empowerment is concerned, we have already noted that in the pluralistic terrain there would be a variety of players. But it is necessary to regulate MFIs from being a new class of moneylenders and to evolve new formats for women's empowerment that can be replicated across the board based on the experiences and best practices of organizations like WWF (I) and SEWA.

It should also be evident that microcredit for entrepreneurship alone is not sufficient and there has to be robust measures to promote and strengthen wage employment for all women. Capacity building for NGOs, SHGs and MFIs should be undertaken so that they can find innovative ways to strengthen the bargaining capacity of those in wage employment. Both SEWA and WWF (I) do enhance the bargaining capacity of women in both piece-rate and time-rate wage employment.

Clearly, the challenges on the employment front are not all. Capitalist globalization has also engendered widespread livelihood insecurity. Today, we hear so much on land struggles everywhere as farmers' lands are appropriated for mega-urbanization projects or industrialization leading to livelihood insecurities. Tribal and marginalized communities everywhere are threatened by displacement as their traditional resource bases such as forests, water and hills are taken over by predatory profit-oriented forces. This is true across a wide spectrum of traditional occupations. The new employments created by the new urban and industrial projects generally do not benefit those who have been displaced for a variety of reasons, not the least being the lack of skills especially for women. This growth trajectory has instilled vulnerabilities on account of it being an unsustainable growth trajectory. The situation gets worse when we begin to cognize and reckon with the livelihood risks posed by climate change. Merely facing the employment challenges and encouraging the microcredit and SHG movements are not sufficient to address the sustainability issues that threaten livelihoods. The perspective on women's empowerment is yet to fully grapple this issue.

## Social Protection for Women

In recent years, scholars and activists have favoured social protection for women over what was earlier called social security measures (Jhabvala and Subrahmanya, 2000). Social security measures generally include unemployment benefits, healthcare benefits by way of health insurance or access to free or subsidized health facilities, old-age benefits such as pension and other retirement benefits, widows' pension, accident insurance for disability and death, maternity and paternity benefits, insurance for occupational risks and hazards to list the common ones. It was believed that some of these are life-cycle events such as old age and death and some are contingent events that can strike at any time. Based on the Beveridge model of social security in England and adopted as a characteristic feature of all welfare states, it was expected that the state would bear the responsibility of ensuring such adequate measures. In India, planned development only succeeded in introducing some basic social security measures such as retirement benefit and health facility to the organized sector workers. The bulk of the labour force, nearly 93% who work in the unorganized or informal sectors were never covered by the social security measures. The National Commission for Enterprises in the Unorganized Sector (NCEUS, 2008) provides a comprehensive account of all the protective legislation applicable to the unorganized sector workers and the experience of implementation. Some measures were introduced by different state governments based on the sensitivity of the political parties in power to the issue. Tamil Nadu state where the two Dravidian parties have for long been involved in competitive introduction of welfare measures to the poor had instituted old-age pension and widows pension, and over the years have sought to improve its delivery such that presently they receive it at their doorstep every month through the postal system. The poor at whom these limited measures in some states are targeted are anyway employed in the informal sector. But the bulk of the informal sector workers are not covered under any social security measures. In the absence of such state supported measures, informal sector workers are bound in some form of feudal patron-client relationships looking up to landlords, money lenders and employers for support to meet emergent crises in the family such as marriage expenses, sickness and death, and were bound to them by onerous conditions of employment to repay the loans.

The concept of "social protection" has been promoted by the ILO from above and from women's organizations such as SEWA and WWF (I) at the grassroots. Social protection attempts a broader coverage than social security and includes employment and livelihood strengthening as these when weakened accentuate vulnerabilities, especially those of women. Both SEWA and WWF (I) argue that their microcredit group lending is a core aspect of social protection to which they have added on numerous social security measures such as health insurance and even natural disaster insurance in the case of WWF (I). The WWF (I) was able to negotiate with the LIC and later with another private insurance company for micro insurance coverage for health, disability, death, education, disaster, etc. Once these pioneering organizations were able to prove that it is possible to provide some social security measures to the informal sector under the umbrella of microcredit social protection, much interest was evinced by the state and other civil society organizations and community-based organizations. Similar to the subtle transmutation of microcredit group lending to the formation of SHGs as thrift groups, here too the many new players initiating micro insurance are now guided by the neoliberal ideas that full risks be borne by the clients and have therefore adopted a model of beneficiary payment of insurance premiums for micro insurance in small installments both within and outside the SHG framework; these are MFIs in the micro insurance business. It is important to take cognisance of how the empowerment of women is sought to be achieved by making women bear the full risks of contingencies and enable them to make claims out of a commercial insurance scheme that has factored in operational convenience for the clients.

If "better late than never" is a virtuous principle, the state has now stepped in to provide social security to informal sector workers recently. The NCEUS set up by the national government in 2004 has like other earlier commissions recommended social security coverage for agricultural and non-agricultural workers to cover health, life and disability, and old age which will be financed by the National Social Security and Welfare Fund. They have given estimates of the likely costs to the central exchequer which could be reduced by cost sharing with the states and private employers. The Unorganized Sector Worker's Social Security Bill, 2005 was passed by the Indian parliament in December 2008. It seeks to provide social security to 340 million unorganized sector workers including agricultural workers and migrant workers over the following five-year period. It would provide health, life and disability insurance, old-age pension and group accident insurance scheme. Although a good beginning, it still remains a distant dream to provide social protection for all the unorganized sector workers and ensure that it is all effectively implemented. But political commitment can deliver these benefits. Soon after Ms. Jayalalitha took office as the Chief Minister of Tamil Nadu recently, she put into effect her promised freebies and increased the old age and widow's pension from ₹ 500 to ₹ 1,000 per month! For most of the working class poor women, these forms of assistance are small but important, but they all continue to be employed earning some wages as long as their bodies allow them to do so. For many of the old women, it is their daughters who support and stand by them in their old age rather than their husbands or sons.

**Women and Governance**

Governance issues have come to the fore at all levels in recent years, in part because better governance is necessary for the success of corporate globalization and also because in the enfolding of rights-based development, popular expectations from the state have also increased manifold. The popular masses now understand well that unless they can ensure better governance and accountability, their interests and concerns will be bypassed in this era of market-led development. If women's voices have to be heard, it is necessary to redefine governance from a gender perspective which carves out a space for women to voice their concerns (Mukhopadhyay and Meer, 2004).Women's concerns with governance are at two levels – the impact of governance on women and how meaningful participation of women in governance could be ensured. These concerns clearly underline the important roles of women in the public sphere, a sphere which as citizens they share with the men. How effectively these concerns are addressed will also determine the nature of the citizenship and the realizations of their rights and duties as citizens in a democracy.

Regarding the impact of governance on women, certain initiatives have been taken in recent years, which is the outcome of the efforts of lobbying by activists and scholars with the government. With a huge amount of resources being spent by the state through planned development, it became necessary to ensure that such planned efforts do not by-pass women. From the sixth Five-Year Plan onwards, a separate chapter on women was added in the national plan document. Efforts at mainstreaming gender brought forth the establishment of ministries of women at the federal and state levels. By the late 80s, there was general criticism that on account of leakages and corruption only a small fraction of development funds were reaching the targeted groups on the ground. Women activists and scholars were quick to point out that women fared worse than men on this. Since then, the demand for greater accountability and transparency in development governance has been voiced by various civil society organizations. Feminist economists advising in various working groups of the government departments and the Planning Commission pushed for gender audits to find how much of the money spent by various departments and ministries was actually benefiting women. Gender Budgeting Initiative was started as a way of integrating women's interests in the macro-economic policy framework (Dewan and Prabhu, 2009). Until 2005, the budgets of the various ministries were dissected post-facto for its allocations for women-related programmes. For the first time, in 2005, the Ministry of Finance gave a mandate to all the ministries to establish a Gender Budgeting Cell by January 2005. At present, 54 ministries and departments have formed gender budget cells and have provided annual reports and performance budgets highlighting budgetary allocations for women (Dewan, 2005; Patel, 2010). With the passing of the RTI Act in 2005, it has become possible for citizens to seek greater transparency on governance issues. With the media too doing its share in highlighting issues of governance, even illiterate and poor women are becoming aware of their rights and their dues from the state. All this does not mean that the impact of governance on women has radically transformed for the better. But, the framework has been laid for NGOs and CBOs to undertake initiatives to empower women on issues of governance.

Women's participation in development governance has been facilitated by one-third seat reservation in the lower tiers of the decentralized democratic governance – the Gram Panchayats and Nagar Palikas – by the 73rd and 74th amendments to the Indian Constitution, respectively. Over the years, since it became a law, hundreds of thousands of women are participating as elected members in village-level decision-making. Although the patriarchal nature of the society inhibits a large number of these elected women representatives from functioning independently from the male members of the family and are not therefore autonomous, it could be expected that in the long run, with increase in women's education, there is bound to be a significant change. This measure is a very bold and remarkable step in politically empowering grassroots women. No doubt, local-level politics of power and dominance plays a role in whether Dalit women and those from marginalized communities are able to participate as elected representatives. Also, it should be quite obvious that these women can never succeed in getting elected without the support of the male members of their groups. While reports from the field suggest that in certain places Dalit elected women face resistance from the upper castes, the overwhelming evidence is that women have by large become enthusiastic participants in local governance and are able to address practical issues that affect their lives. Some states have now increased the reservation for women from one-third seats to one-half. At the higher levels of democratic governance, a similar proposal of reservation of seats for women was stalled for long by political parties that wanted to protect their caste vote-banks and while it has been accepted in principle, it has not yet been passed into a law. In the mean time, the political landscape of the country is well occupied by a number of articulate and publicly visible women politicians that many may wonder why such a reservation is necessary at all if the political system has been quite receptive to women. But these women politicians who hog the media limelight are few and women elected representatives in the central and state legislatures are generally less than 10–12%, which is very far from the one-third seats that are demanded. Political parties also field only a small percentage of women candidates in elections.

The media has in recent time projected successful women in the corporate sector and in other fields. In spite of their achievements, most of the institutions exhibit male bias. Such male bias is not merely in terms of the number of women at different levels of the work hierarchy, but a male bias in the sense that male thinking, their ideas and attitudes permeate the everyday functioning of the organization such that the organization itself is socialized at all levels into one reproducing a patriarchal culture even if the rules *per se* of the organization have no gender bias. This is an area in which feminist scholars need to engage in their future research. Organizational ethnographies need to be written up so that greater insights and understanding are gleaned about these processes that are at work, of the awareness of women in organizations to the subtle and not-so-subtle processes of exclusion, inferiorizing and domination, and building women's capacities to take on the challenge. Knowledge on how organizations are reproducing patriarchal mindsets is now very sparse unlike that of the household or the state.

## A Preview of the Book

The foregoing has presented some of the current issues on gender and development in India. The various chapters of the book explore empirically the numerous issues that have been identified so far as being the relevant development challenges in the era of globalization that impinge especially on poor women's lives. Chapter 2 examines women's employment and unemployment status in conjunction with their involvement in domestic duties from the latest rounds of the NSS data. Chapter 3 presents evidence from micro-studies as well as ethnography of the impact of liberalization and globalization on women's employment and livelihood highlighting the insecurities and vulnerabilities across sectors and industries. Chapter 4 examines the impact of ICT on women in the informal sector through a survey conducted among rural and urban women. Globalization has been accompanied by revolutionary changes ushered in by information and communication technologies such as computers, worldwide web and mobile phones that have made possible rapid transmission of information across the world bringing with it the possibilities of doing business globally and in new ways. But how ICT development has impacted on the lives and livelihoods of poor women in India is only now being enquired and this chapter provides interesting insights on it. Chapter 5 contributes to the emerging literature on women and climate change. It critically examines the idea of sustainability in the present climate change solutions and argues that only a re-evaluation of the industrial mode of life can bring about a sustainability that does not undermine livelihoods, food security and habitats of poorer non-industrialized communities around the world. It argues that women in pre-modern India had much traditional knowledge on sustainable agricultural and other practices that were undermined by modern industrialization. Chapter 6 discusses the strategies of evolving multiple securities and securing gender needs in the present context of flexiblization, informalization and the pervasive livelihood insecurities. Chapter 7 highlights the social security needs of women workers in the informal sector and argues for an expanded notion of social security. Pointing to some of the difficulties of providing social protection to women workers in the informal sector in varying social contexts, it highlights the strengths and the challenges of the social security programmes of WWF (I). Chapter 8 discusses the nature of systemic exclusion and discrimination that women face in the development process and argues that gender-sensitive grassroots governance under the present system of PRIs is possible only if women gain "voice" and "rights". It requires that synergies be built with Community-Based Organizations (CBOs), NGOs and social movements. The last chapter outlines a perspective for a grassroots feminist theory. It works towards a contextually relevant grassroots feminist theory underlining the importance of incorporating into the framework how the forces of modernity impinge at the grassroots in terms of transformation of desires, needs and resources. Such aspirations of modernity in the present era of globalization sometimes encounter resistance expressed through various forms and discourses of cultural nationalism. The perspective of women's empowerment is thereby challenged and requires constant reiterations through the discourses and practices of the women's movement.

# 2

# Employment, Unemployment and Domestic Work After Liberalization[1]

The employment scenario in the period of globalization has been generally presented optimistically in terms of the new kinds of employment in the emerging sectors such as IT, and pessimistically about many other sectors such as agriculture and the informal sector. Many women in countries of Latin America underwent an intensification of household work during the period of structural adjustment on account of withdrawal of subsidies and paid services that had to be provisioned by women in the household (Sparr, 1994). It is therefore of interest to know and understand the macro situation on women's employment and unemployment in the period since liberalization of the economy from 1991 and to understand the burden of domestic labour on women and the changes if any over the period.

According to the NSS 61st round estimates (2004–2005), there were 408 million workers including about 40 million as subsidiary workers in the usual status of whom 272 million were male workers and 135 million were female workers. Of these, about 318 million were rural workers and 90 million were urban workers. Women workers numbered about 136 million, of whom 116 million were rural workers and 19.7 million were urban workers. Workers as a proportion of population – Work Participation Rates (WPR) by usual status (principal status) – decreased marginally for men over the period from 1993–1994 to 2004–2005 in both rural areas from 53.8% to 53.5%, while in urban areas it increased from 51.3% to 54.1% in the same period. But WPR (usual status-principal) for women in rural areas increased marginally from 23.4% to 24.2% between 1993–1994 and 2004–2005. Urban WPR (usual status-principal) of women increased from 12.1% to 13.5% in the same period. Except the case of rural males, in all other categories there has been a marginal increase in the WPR.

Open unemployment rates (usual, current weekly and current daily rates) for rural men and women have increased over the period 1993–1994 to 2004–2005, with female rates of unemployment being higher than the male rates. While the usual status unemployment rate for rural males was 2.1%, the current daily rate unemployment was 8.0% in 2004–2005, the latter increased from 5.6% in 1993–1994. In the case of rural females, the usual status unemployment rate increased from 1.3% in 1993–1994 to 3.1% in 2004–2005 and the current daily rate unemployment increased from 5.6% to 8.7% over the same period.

Urban unemployment rates are in general higher than the rural rates and higher among urban women than urban men. Over the period 1993–1994 to 2004–2005, the usual status urban unemployment rate for males decreased from 5.4% to 4.4%, the current weekly status unemployment rate remained the same at 5.2%, while the current daily rate unemployment increased from 6.7% to 7.5% suggesting that days of unemployment in a week have increased even if long status unemployment has decreased. Unemployment rates for urban women increased in all categories over the period 1993–1994 to 2004–2005 and remained much higher than men. The usual status unemployment rate of urban women increased from 8.3% in 1993–1994 to 9.1% in 2004–2005, the current weekly unemployment rate increased from 7.9% to 9.0% over the same period and the current daily unemployment rate increased from 10.4% to 11.6% between 1993–1994 and 2004–2005.

**Measurement of Women's Work**

It is widely acknowledged that the NSS coverage of workers in agriculture is more inclusive than the 1991 census. According to the 1991 census, work connotes participation in any economically productive activity. Such participation may be physical or mental in nature, involving not only actual work but also effective supervision and direction of work. It also includes unpaid work on farm or in family enterprise. According to the NSS definition, work implies being engaged in gainful work for pay, profit or family gain, or in other words, that which adds value to the national product. However, activities in agriculture in which part or whole of the agriculture production is used for own consumption and does not go for sale are considered gainful. But processing of primary products for own consumption was not considered as economic activity.

Also the activities relating to the own-account production of fixed assets like construction of own houses, wells and machinery and tools for household enterprise is considered economic activity (NSSO, 2006). The NSS provides better coverage for women in agriculture by including all activities in Division "O" even if carried out for own consumption (agricultural production, hunting, forestry, fishing), while the census considers only "agriculture production".

While retaining the concept of "gainful work", the NSSO has been conscious of the fact that boundaries of productive work are difficult to define, and that there may be a set of borderline activities that persons may engage in, which are in many ways useful to them but do not get counted in the workforce data. It has sought to provide information on these borderline activities through a set of probing questions since the 32nd round (1977–1978). Three groups of borderline activities were identified. First, activities relating to agricultural production, such as maintenance of the kitchen garden, work in the household poultry, dairy and so on, including free collection of agricultural products for household consumption, which were hitherto considered gainful; second, processing of primary products by the household for households' consumption which had not until then been considered gainful and third, other activities for own consumption but resulting in economic benefits to the households, which were again newly recognized as gainful. Two new activity codes (92 & 93) pertaining to "domestic activity" and those combining domestic activity with "free collection of fuel, fodder, etc." for those outside the labour force sought in particular to provide a more disaggregated picture of women's work, especially of those who perceive and declare their main activity as domestic work and hence outside the labour force, but also combine it with some form of gainful activity.

There has been some significant criticism of the NSS methodology as regards measurement of women's work. The NSS surveys canvassed a time-disposition block in its schedule by way of half-day blocks for ascertaining the current weekly and current daily status employment and unemployment. But this time-disposition block was only canvassed to those respondents who had already identified themselves as being engaged in gainful activity. It has been argued convincingly, although quite not successfully, that a majority of women who perceive themselves as being predominantly engaged in "domestic activity" are unlikely to declare as having engaged in any gainful activity. Also, "domestic activity" is itself not disaggregated further into cooking, cleaning and childcare – the three "Cs". Crucial information necessary for planning for women's needs such as time spent on childcare are thus not made available in the NSS. Thus, the NSS procedure of netting was biased against women given the widely prevalent perception biases among them.

Jain (1996) notes based on time allocation studies in Rajasthan and West Bengal that many productive activities that women engage in are lost in the domain of the kitchen and perceived as domestic work. In landed families in West Bengal, while women declared themselves as not being engaged in gainful activities, they were often found during harvest times to be cooking and serving food for farm hands. But in Rajasthan when women work on farms like men during the harvest season, their work gets into the reckoning. She therefore makes a significant conclusion that "the more male-like the activities of females the more likely that it will be measured and noticed" (p. WS 50). Also, women of all age groups seem to weave in and out of the economic and non-economic activities with the same range of "time", measured in hours of involvement per day. It is therefore not surprising that women are perceived and perceive themselves as mainly engaged in domestic activity.

Thus, we note that despite all the attempts to improve the methodology of measuring women's work there are significant gaps. Work that does not render monetary rewards and is non-marketed forms a large and complex set of activities that are difficult to both disaggregate and measure. Also, the intermittency of women's work and their engagement in multiple jobs render it no less difficult to measure. Thus, with money and the market being the yardsticks of value, much of women's work becomes invisible in national and international data systems.

### Women in the Labour Force

In what follows, the latest available statistics (NSS 61st round survey for 2004–2005) on women's employment, unemployment and domestic duties in rural and urban India are analysed and compared with the 55th round for the year 1993–1994.

#### *Age-specific WPR*

Age-specific WPRs of rural women who are principal workers by usual status indicate not surprisingly higher rates in the age groups 15–29 years, 30–44 years and 45–59 years. The rates in 2004–2005 were 28.8% (31.1), 45.8% (42.5) and 44.4% (40.1) (the figures in brackets are the corresponding 1993–1994 figures), which show an increase over the period in the age groups 30–44 years and 45–49 years. The WPR of rural women in the 60 plus age group increased from 14.5% in 1983 to 17.2% in 1993–1994 to 19.7% in 2004–2005. These numbers force upon us the question as to what nearly more than half of the rural women in the ages of 15–59 years really do as they do not seem to be working by usual status. This question becomes even more relevant in the case of urban women where the highest WPR in 2004–2005 was only 25.4% in the 30–44 age group. While WPRs of men are in general much higher than those of women, it is important to note that over 60% of the rural men and 36% of the urban men continue to work beyond 60 years, the corresponding figures for women are much lower.

### *Irregularity of Employment*

It is widely accepted that women suffer greater irregularity and intermittence of employment. The NSSO data capture intermittence of employment through the Current Weekly Status (CWS) and Current Daily Status employment (CDS). Except rural males where both CWS and CDS WPR have decreased even though marginally, for all other categories these rates of employment have increased over the 10-year period of 1993–1994 and 2004–2005. However, the Index of Underemployment [(CWS-CDS)/CWS *100] reveals an increase for all categories except urban women between 1993–1994 and 2004–2005. The increase is quite marked for rural women over the period from 17.8% to 21.45%, while for urban women it has decreased from 13.67% to 12.5%. Although the male rates of underemployment are strikingly lower than those for women, the percentage of underemployment for both rural and urban men have increased over the period and stands at 6.87% for rural men and 3.35% for urban men in 2004–2005. This indicates that while employment rates in terms of Weeks show improvement in most categories, there are fewer days of employment during the week, and hence the extent of underemployment during the week has increased for rural women, once again suggesting a greater degree of intermittence of work.

### *Discouraged Worker Effect*

There is a significant underestimation of women in the urban labour force, although it is also true that urban WPRs for women are in general lower than rural WPRs. Generally, it is believed that the "discouraged worker effect" (i.e., the withdrawal from labour force on account of non-availability of work) operates more strongly in the case of women than in case of men. This is perhaps due to the fact that men are deemed to be heads of the households and responsible for the support of the family, whereas women's earnings are meant to be supplementary to that of men in the household. But, the fact that unemployment rates for women have increased in all categories during the period is likely to be interpreted that the "discouraged worker effect" is perhaps not very strong. Cross-classification of workers by usual status and current weekly status who declared as being not in the labour force gives a better idea of the "discouraged worker" effect.

### *The Effect on Rural Labour Force*

Of those usually employed (principal and subsidiary workers) in 2004–2005, it was found that 2.1% of rural males and 14.7% of rural females were found to be not in the labour force by the current weekly status. This suggests that when women do not have employment in a week they do not seek work or are available for work but remain outside of the labour force. If it is because of the seasonality of agricultural work and the nature of the sexual division of work in agriculture, then the effect is likely to be more or less uniform across regions. But, the state-wise analysis of this data indicates that the percentage of usually employed women who are not in the labour force by current weekly status is above 20% in the states of Chhattisgarh, Jharkhand, Orissa and Madhya Pradesh and Uttar Pradesh (19.5%), and above 15% in Bihar. These are identified as backward states, and it is therefore not surprising that non-availability of work discourages the rural women to move out of the labour force. Assam and Jammu and Kashmir also have above 20% of usually employed women outside of the labour force by current weekly status. Of those usually employed, 4.6% of rural men and 29.6% of rural women are declared to be out of the labour force by current daily status, a much higher figure for rural women than men under the daily status. The problem of rural women being discouraged from seeking work on account of non-availability of work is moderate to severe in most states barring Andhra Pradesh, Maharashtra and Tamil Nadu.

A similar cross-classification of rural men and women employed by the current weekly status shows that 2.7% of rural men and 18.0% of rural women are found to be not in the labour force by current daily status. Clearly, rural women rather than men have the tendency to move out of the labour force when work is not available throughout the week. This tendency is strong in the states of Assam, Bihar, Gujarat, Haryana,

Himachal Pradesh, Jharkhand, Kerala, Mizoram, Nagaland, Orissa, Punjab, Rajasthan, Sikkim, Uttaranchal, Uttar Pradesh, West Bengal, Andaman & Nicobar and Dadra & Nagar Haveli, in all of which 15% of employed women are not in the labour force by the current daily status. It is the non-availability of work opportunities that discourages these rural women from seeking work and hence they remain out of the labour force.

### *The Effect on the Urban Labour Force*

Let us now compare it with the urban scenario. 0.9% of the urban men and 7.1% of the urban women usually employed reported not in the labour force by the current weekly status, while 1.9% of the urban men and 17.1% of the urban women who are usually employed reported not in the labour force by the current daily status. While the urban percentages are much lower than the corresponding rural percentages, there is a higher percentage of urban women reporting not in the labour force than the percentage of urban men. The "discouraged worker effect" among urban women is moderate to strong in the states of Bihar, Chhattisgarh, Haryana, Gujarat, Himachal Pradesh, Jammu & Kashmir, Kerala, Madhya Pradesh, Nagaland, Orissa, Punjab, Rajasthan, Uttaranchal, Uttar Pradesh, West Bengal and Dadra & Nagar Haveli.

Of those employed by the current weekly status, 1.0% urban men and 11.0% urban women reported to be outside of the labour force by daily status. States where more than 10% of the urban women reported outside of the labour force are Assam, Bihar, Gujarat, Haryana, Himachal Pradesh, Jammu & Kashmir, Jharkhand, Kerala, Manipur, Mizoram, Nagaland, Punjab, Rajasthan, Uttar Pradesh and West Bengal. While intermittency of work in agriculture could explain the situation of rural women, intermittence of urban jobs for women comes as a bit of surprise and their discouragement to seek work perhaps because of the non-availability of work indicates urban work scarcity for women.

### *The Status of Women's Employment*

Table 2.1 below presents the distribution of usually employed (principal) by category of employment in India in the period 1993–1994 and 2004–2005. It can be noted that in rural India, self-employment among males and females have increased, the increase being more among the females over the period. At the same time, regular employees in rural India have also increased though marginally. The proportion of casual workers among rural workers have decreased, the decrease among females being from 45.3% in 1993–94 to 38.9% in 2004–2005.

In urban India, Table 2.1 shows that during the period 1993–1994 and 2004–2005, self-employment among males increased by 3%, while regular wage and casual work decreased by nearly 2% each, clearly indicating scarcity of wage work for males in urban India. In the case of females though, casual work percentage has increased marginally with a corresponding marginal decrease in self-employment.

**Table 2.1**

*Distribution of usually employed (principal) by category of employment India – 2004–2005 and 1993–1994*

| | *Rural Male (%)* | *Rural Female (%)* | *Urban Male (%)* | *Urban Female (%)* |
|---|---|---|---|---|
| *61st Round Survey 2004–2005* | | | | |
| Self-Employed | 57.6 | 56.4 | 44.6 | 40.4 |
| Regular Employees | 9.1 | 4.8 | 40.8 | 42.2 |
| Casual Workers | 33.3 | 38.9 | 14.6 | 17.4 |
| *50th Round Survey 1993–1994* | | | | |
| Self-Employed | 56.7 | 51.3 | 41.1 | 41.7 |
| Regular Employees | 8.7 | 3.4 | 42.7 | 42 |
| Casual Workers | 34.6 | 45.3 | 16.2 | 16.3 |

*Source:* NSSO Report No. 515 – *Employment and Unemployment Situation in India,* 2004–2005 (Part I & II), GOI, September 2006.

Workers in self-employment and casual workers provide a rough measure of the size of the informal sector. It was estimated that in 1994, 90.4% of the workforce (comprising main workers only) were in the informal/unorganized sector, while the formal/organized sector has absorbed only 9.6% of the main workforce.

The characteristic features of the structure of the female workforce in the 90s included an increasing feminization of the urban workforce on account of an increased WPR for urban women, a feminization of agriculture on account of an increased share of women workers in the primary sector, rigidities and a declining share for women in rural non-farm employment, decrease in secondary sector employment and an increase in tertiary sector employment for women largely in community and other services. The retrogressive features of the female workforce structure become even starker if the share of women's employment in the organized sector is examined.

Organized sector employment growth even over a 15–year period of 1981–1996 has been abysmal at 1.39%. It has been aptly characterized as witnessing "near jobless growth". But even then it has been a male bastion. Women constitute only 15.8% of the organized sector workers. Srivastava (1999) showed that even though 60% of the women employees in the organized sector are in the public sector, the male-female employment ratio is more adverse in the public sector than in the private sector. A favourable male-female employment ratio in the private sector is compensated by an unfavourable male-female wage ratio in that sector which suggests that more women are occupying the lower rungs of the job hierarchy with low wages.

Mukhopadhyay (1999) showed that the intensity of female employment is much higher in Own-Account Manufacturing Enterprises (OAMEs) which are generally smaller units run primarily on family labour and presumably at low earnings and low productivity levels. She also observed that the incidence of women workers is higher in part-time employment in both Non-Directory Manufacturing Establishments (NDME) and OAMEs in both rural and urban areas. While their reproductive roles and responsibilities shape women's labour supply behaviour, it is significant that within the hired category in larger units in NDMEs, the incidence of part-time women workers is very high. Contrary to the general perception that women are being absorbed in large numbers in hired wage work, they are being hired only on part-time basis. These patterns of contractual arrangements suggest that even within the informal sector, women are only getting a bad deal. She explains that this tendency could be the manifestation of a growing demand for job-specific sweat labour in small manufacturing establishments for which the employers are not willing to provide full-time and/or secure employment, especially since women from poor families are willing to provide their labour on a part-time basis for low and exploitative wages. Part-time work is a form of casual work which is a growing trend. Women's involvement in non-farm employment of a part-time nature may be a distress reaction rather than a healthy sign of growth.

Kundu (2000) warned that an increase in the share of regular/salaried workers among women should not be viewed with enthusiasm as either an indication of the growing capacity of the urban economy to absorb women or a reduction in gender bias. Such employment growth for women has only taken place in sectors of low productivity and low wages. He notes that in several urban sectors, regular female workers were paid the same as male casual workers or even less in the late 80s and believes that the same pattern may have continued into the 90s as well. Kundu suggests that what is going on is probably a "process of organized informalization of the labour market" (Kundu, 1999: 70). Informalization of the workforce that has always been in vogue through such practices as casualization, feminization, job and labour contracting appears to have increased in the recent years. This is not altogether surprising as competition under conditions of liberalization would force employers to seek cheaper workers. Women as a reserve army of labour enter the labour market as bearers of gender to experience these informalization practices in rather different ways from men. While in some industries, they become more regular, in yet others they are likely to become casual. Interesting insights on casualization and feminization of the labour force have been highlighted, some questioning the thesis of feminization, and others warning that increased female employment among regular workers may not be a cause for much rejoicing if those are low productivity and low-wage jobs (Banerjee, 1999).

**Wage Rates for Women**

Table 2.2 indicates the male and female average daily wages for different categories of work. It is clear that in all the categories female wages are lower than male wages. Female wages as proportion of male wages among rural casual workers engaged in other than public works is 63.5%, while the same ratio for those engaged in public works is 75.2%. Clearly it is heartening to note that the public works programme pay women relatively better wages and minimizes gender differentials in wages, but it is still only three-fourths of what men receive. However, it is somewhat surprising that the proportion of female to male casual workers wages in other than public works in the urban areas is only 58.4% and is lower than the same rural ratio. Clearly, the gender differential is more among urban casual daily wages for which the simple economic explanation of supply of female workers being more than the demand thus lowering the wages may actually hold true. It needs however to be marked that there are likely to be regional differences as well.

The ratio of female to male wages among regular employees in rural areas is 59% and is lower than the ratio for rural casual workers. Clearly, the greatest gender disparity in average daily wages is among the regular workers in the rural areas and casual workers in the urban areas. In the urban areas, the ratio of female to male daily wages among regular workers is 75.4%. Clearly, the female regular employees in urban areas and those engaged in public works in rural areas have lower average wage disparity with their male counterparts.

**Table 2.2**

*Average daily wages of casual and regular workers*
*India – 2004–2005*

*(in ₹)*

| *Categories of Workers* | *Male (%)* | *Female (%)* |
|---|---|---|
| Average daily wages rural casual workers engaged in other than public works | 55.03 | 34.94 |
| Average daily wages rural casual workers engaged in public works | 65.33 | 49.19 |
| Average daily wages urban casual workers engaged in other than public works | 75.10 | 43.88 |
| Average wage/salary per day for regular employees – Rural | 144.93 | 85.53 |
| Average wage/salary per day for regular employees – Urban | 203.28 | 153.19 |

*Source:* NSSO Report No 515: *Employment and Unemployment Situation in India*, 2004–2005 (Part I & II), GoI, September 2006.

Deshpande and Deshpande (1999) concluded that the gender-based wage differentials widened among regular wage/salaried rural and urban workers after liberalization. Women were paid less than men both before and after liberalization, but much more so after than before. In all other types of work, the gender-based wage inequality was reduced. Keeping the gender constant, they found that the casual worker's wage formed a higher share of a regular's after liberalization than before. In 2004–2005, the share of casual workers wage to regular workers wages among males was 38% in the rural areas and 37% in the urban areas. Among women, the same ratio was 41% in the rural areas and 28.6% in the urban areas. Across all categories, casual workers fared poorly in average daily wages than the regular workers.

### Women and Domestic Work

We now turn to the section of women, i.e., those not in the labour force that is generally ignored both by the researchers and the policymakers. The NSS classifies those "not in the labour force" into various activities assigned code numbers 91 to 99. These are students, those engaged in domestic duties, rentiers, pensioners, recipients of remittances, those living on alms, infirm or disabled, too young or too old, prostitutes, smugglers, etc., and casual workers not working due to sickness, etc. Women not in the labour force and engaged in domestic duties are assigned activity codes 92 and 93 (92 refers to women engaged in domestic duties only and 93 refers to women engaged in domestic duties and free collection of goods).

Housework (domestic duties) has been of feminist concern although it is a neglected issue in the domain of public policy. The nature of housework that women largely perform varies not only across societies and over time, but also within groups in a society at a point in time. Such variations in the housework that women do are to a large extent determined by the economic status of the household, the socio-demographic characteristics of the household, the prevalent cultural norms on the division of labour in households and above all the characteristics of the economy itself. In poor agrarian economies with a significant component of non-market activities, the range of what constitutes housework is different from those of the advanced market economies. Boundaries of housework and economically gainful work are difficult to draw in such economies where non-market activities predominate. In the contemporary era of neoliberal market ideology and structural adjustment policies, housework has assumed added significance. Structural adjustment policies are based on the assumption that women's labour is flexible. Moreover, it assumes that women have an unlimited capacity for domestic work and that the household is an entity with unitary interests exhibiting homogeneity of behavioural responses among its members. All these assumptions have been questioned in recent feminist thinking. There is an overwhelming consensus that there are limits to the domestic drudgery that women can bear and that women's bargaining position in households has to be strengthened by making resources and income accessible to them.

Women engaged predominantly in domestic duties also perform a set of activities, of which some could be classified as economic and others as beneficial. The implications of such a heavy involvement in domestic activities for their labour market participation are explored. An analysis of women's willingness to accept work in their household premises, the skills they possess and the type of assistance they require suggest differences in the preference patterns of rural and urban women as well as regional differences. The policy implications of this analysis strongly suggest that feminist sensitivity be incorporated in public policies as the poverty alleviation programmes. If women's empowerment is a goal, then strengthening of women's bargaining position within households by making access to resources and income should be explicitly acknowledged as an objective of these policies.

In what follows, we present the latest available data on the nature of women's domestic duties in rural and urban India. It is clear that women engaged predominantly in domestic duties also perform a set of activities, of which some could be classified as economic and others as beneficial. Forty per cent of the rural women and 50% of the urban women in India were usually (principal status) engaged only in domestic duties, while 37% and 18% of the rural and urban women, respectively usually carried out some economic activities in 2004–2005. However, women engaged in domestic duties also perform other activities such as maintenance of the kitchen garden, work in household poultry, dairy, etc., as well as free collection of fish, firewood and other agricultural products for household consumption. Of those in domestic duties, 54% of the rural women and 10% of the urban women in 2004–2005 pursued one or more activities relating to agricultural production including free collection of agricultural products and processing of primary products produced by the households for home consumption. These constitute 16.4% of the rural and 4.6% of the urban women above five years of age in 2004–2005. If one adds these figures to WPR, then the upper bound on WPR in 53.4% for rural women and 22.6% for urban women in 2004–2005.

In a predominantly agrarian economy, restricting "economic activity" to only marketed activities and ignoring non-market activities that are otherwise economically beneficial leads to a significant non-recognition and consequent underestimation of women's work. A sustained campaign at the international level led to the recognition that boundaries of productive work are rather difficult to delineate and that there exists a set of borderline activities that could in fact be considered "economic". Consequently, the UN Revised System of National Accounts has indicated these borderline non-monetary activities such as free collection of primary goods and processing of goods for own consumption as economic activities. Although India does not fully adhere to the UN (Revised SNA, 1993) for the calculation of national income, the NSS surveys on employment and unemployment in the 38th, 43rd, 50th and later rounds listed a set of activities that women engaged predominantly in the household duties perform and which could in fact be considered as "economically productive" work (NSSO, 2006). Thus activities relating to agricultural production such as maintenance of the kitchen garden, work in household poultry, dairy, etc., including free collection of agricultural products for household consumption can be considered as economic work, while processing of primary products produced by the household for household consumption may be considered as economic according to the recommendations of the UN International standard. Other activities for own consumption such as processing of acquired materials including preparation of cow dung cakes and fetching water from outside the household premises were not considered economic but were recognized to be beneficial to households. Women's participation in these numerous activities provides a comprehensive picture of the work done by women who are predominantly engaged in household duties. This breakup of activities clearly indicates that "housework" is not a homogenous category applicable for all women, and that in addition to the core household chores of cooking, cleaning and childcare, women do engage in varieties of activities, some which are clearly "economically productive work" in an expanded definition of that term, and others are beneficial to the households.

### The Nature of Rural Women's Domestic Work

In 2004–2005 about 40% of the rural women were engaged in domestic duties as their principal usual status, while in 1993–1994 it was 38%. Of these, in 2004–2005, 58.8% were engaged in any one of the activities such as kitchen garden, poultry, dairy, free collection of fish and firewood, i.e., activities clearly recognized as "economic". This figure rises to 61.1% when processing of primary products produced by the household for household consumption is taken into account. They were also engaged in other activities beneficial to the households. In 2004–2005, 46% of the rural women engaged in domestic duties prepared cow dung cakes that are an important source of fuel in the rural households, 44.5% fetched water from outside the household premises and nearly 1.2% fetched water from outside the villages and 27.6% were engaged in sewing and tailoring for the household.

There are of course wide variations across states in the nature of such activities performed by women as Table 2.3 indicates. On the one hand, Andhra Pradesh records in 2004–2005 the lowest percentage of 30.3% followed closely by Maharashtra (31%), Kerala (40.2%) and Karnataka (41.3%), of women doing domestic duties who are also engaged in maintenance of the kitchen garden, poultry, dairy and free collection of fish, firewood, etc., i.e., activities considered economic. On the other hand, all the North-eastern states, and Himachal Pradesh, Jammu & Kashmir, Jharkhand, Rajasthan, Uttaranchal and West Bengal show over 70% of women engaged in such activities. Also, most of the states except Assam, Orissa, Punjab and West Bengal record a decrease in the percentage of women engaged in maintenance of the kitchen garden, poultry, etc., over the period 1993–1994 to 2004–2005. One of the reasons for this wide difference between the two sets of states is that in all three states where low percentages are recorded, there is not sufficient encouragement for undertaking works such as maintenance of the kitchen gardens, poultry and dairy. But these are also considered as the more developed states where women probably do not need to engage in these activities to supplement household income. However, such large differences between the states are not observed in the case of percentage of women engaged in any activity that is economic or beneficial.

**Table 2.3**

*Percentage distribution of women usually engaged in domestic duties and also participating in other activities in selected states – 2004–2005 and 1993–1994*

| *States* | *Engaged in kitchen garden, poultry, dairy, free collection of fish, firewood, etc.* | *Engaged in maintenance, free collection and processing of own produce for household consumption* | *Engaged in any activity either economic or beneficial to the household* |
|---|---|---|---|
| Andhra Pradesh | 30.3 (42.7) | 32.2 (44.2) | 69.6 (79.8) |
| Assam | 86.7 (80.1) | 88.7 (83.8) | 94.5 (91.2) |
| Bihar | 57.0 (60.9) | 63.3 (67.9) | 86.8 (89.0) |
| Gujarat | 59.8 (61.5) | 60.0 (61.9) | 75.7 (81.0) |
| Haryana | 66.1 (83.4) | 66.4 (83.5) | 87.3 (96.8) |
| Himachal Pradesh | 82.8 (83.8) | 83.8 (83.8) | 94.4 (94.6) |
| Karnataka | 41.3 (46.1) | 43.7 (48.5) | 79.5 (87.6) |
| Kerala | 40.2 (53.6) | 41.0 (54.7) | 62.4 (75.0) |
| Madhya Pradesh | 69.2 (70.0) | 70.5 (73.1) | 04.0 (93.7) |
| Maharashtra | 31.0 (43.3) | 31.6 (43.7) | 69.8 (89.60) |
| Orissa | 66.5 (63.4) | 69.9 (70.4) | 91.9 (99.1) |
| Punjab | 59.0 (51.6) | 59.2 (51.7) | 81.0 |
| Rajasthan | 71.0 (74.8) | 71.1 (75.3) | 86.9 (92.0) |

*Cont'd...*

*Cont'd...*

| | | | |
|---|---|---|---|
| Tamil Nadu | 41.8 (53.4) | 43.3 (58.1) | 82.9 (91.0) |
| Uttar Pradesh | 51.9 (55.3) | 54.2 (59.9) | 82.3 (90.0) |
| West Bengal | 76.5 (74.4) | 78.8 (76.2) | 93.0 (94.6) |
| All-India | 58.8 (61.0) | 61.1 (64.4) | 84.4 (89.2) |

*Note:* Figures in the bracket indicate percentages for 1993–1994.

*Source:* Compiled from *Sarvekshana*, Vol XXI, No. 2, 73rd Issue, October-December 1997 and NSSO Report No. 518: *Participation of Women in Specified Activities along with Domestic Duties*, 2004–2005.

There is also some arbitrariness in the classification of borderline activities that are "economic" and those that are not economic but beneficial to the household. For instance, while free collection of firewood, etc., is considered economic, preparation of cowdung cakes is considered only beneficial, although both these activities fulfil the household fuel requirements. Table 2.4 presents the percentage of women doing domestic duties and engaged in the free collection of firewood, etc., preparation of cowdung cakes and in the fetching of water from outside the household premises. Here too there are noteworthy differences across states. While only around 23–25% in Andhra Pradesh, Kerala, Punjab and Maharashtra are involved in the collection of firewood. etc., nearly two-thirds are involved in Himachal Pradesh. The proportion of housewives engaged in the preparation of cowdung cakes also varies widely, from an insignificant 0.2% in Kerala to over 60% in Haryana, Madhya Pradesh and nearly so in Uttar Pradesh.

**Table 2.4**

*Percentage of women usually engaged in domestic duties involved in the free collection of firewood, etc., preparation of cowdung cakes and bringing water from outside the household premises in the rural areas of selected states – 2004–2005 and 1993–1994*

| *States* | *Engaged in free collection of firewood, etc.* | *Engaged in preparation of cowdung cakes* | *Engaged in bringing water from outside the household premises* |
|---|---|---|---|
| Andhra Pradesh | 22.5 (26.2) | 5.5 (10.8) | 53.5 (65.7) |
| Assam | 49.1 (32.3) | 20.0 (19.5) | 29.1 (40.0) |

*Cont'd...*

*Cont'd...*

| | | | |
|---|---|---|---|
| Bihar | 35.2 (44.5) | 52.6 (64.0) | 32.8 (57.6) |
| Gujarat | 52.1 (53.0) | 37.6 (51.4) | 45.8 (58.6) |
| Haryana | 45.6 (56.7) | 65.2 (81.9) | 46.4 (77.7) |
| Himachal Pradesh | 63.5 (62.0) | 39.8 (41.9) | 49.4 (70.2) |
| Karnataka | 32.6 (32.8) | 19.0 (29.4) | 63.0 (73.1) |
| Kerala | 22.5 (27.3) | 0.2 (01.5) | 20.0 (24.0) |
| Madhya Pradesh | 53.4 (60.0) | 72.7 (69.9) | 65.3 (77.3) |
| Maharashtra | 25.3 (34.4) | 23.5 (34.4) | 51.5 (60.8) |
| Orissa | 43.8 (39.6) | 36.5 (34.5) | 74.3 (78.6) |
| Punjab | 22.9 (24.7) | 55.5 (65.4) | 6.2 (14.2) |
| Rajasthan | 54.2 (58.2) | 54.3 (68.9) | 63.2 (72.4) |
| Tamil Nadu | 32.0 (40.9) | 6.6 (13.3) | 69.4 (74.7) |
| Uttar Pradesh | 29.5 (29.6) | 59.6 (73.6) | 27.8 (41.8) |
| West Bengal | 58.1 (48.3) | 63.1 (67.4) | 62.1 (71.6) |
| All-India | 39.6 (40.3) | 46.0 (53.7) | 45.7 (58.1) |

*Note:* Figures in the bracket indicate percentages for 1993–1994.

*Source:* Compiled from *Sarvekshana*, Vol. XXI, No. 2, 73rd Issue, October-December 1997 and NSSO Report No. 518: *Participation of Women in Specified Activities along with Domestic Duties*, 2004–2005.

Fetching water from outside the household premises is yet another chore that shows marked variation. It is 74.3% of the women in Orissa, 69% in Tamil Nadu, 65.3% in Madhya Pradesh, around 63% in Rajasthan, Karnataka and West Bengal in 2004–2005. Only 6.2% in Punjab and 20% in Kerala do so. Of all the rural women above 15 years of age who were usually engaged in domestic duties by principal status, 87.8% reported that they were required to spend most of their days in domestic duties, while only 12.2% reported otherwise in 2004–2005. Such a heavy involvement in domestic duties is likely to discourage women from the labour market participation. In what follows, we shall explore how women themselves perceive housework as constraining or not in their labour market participation, and what it suggests by way of employment policies that are sensitive to the needs of this section of women.

### Constraints on Labour Market Participation by Rural Women

In 2004–2005, 51.8% of the rural women above 15 years of age were engaged in domestic duties as their usual principal status and 33% of them were willing to accept work in their household premises. So, one-third of the rural women have expressed willingness to accept work at home. The corresponding figures in 1993–1994 were that 56.2% of the rural women were engaged in domestic duties as their principal usual status and 30.4% indicated their willingness to accept work in their household premises. Given the fact that a little over half of the rural women workers in the country are anyway self-employed, it is not surprising that a third of the rural women have indicated their willingness to work at home. Among the activities, dairying is the most desired, for the returns are considered higher if the venture is successful. 10.1% of those who were willing to accept work in the household premises in 2004–2005 wanted to take up dairy work. Tailoring is the second most desired activity with 9% expressing their preference for it. Here too, there are differences across states as Table 2.5 below shows:

**Table 2.5**

*Percentage distribution of women (age 15 years and above) engaged in domestic duties and willing to accept work in the household premises, as well as those desiring to take up dairy work and tailoring in the selected states – 2004–2005 and 1993–1994*

| *States* | *Willing to accept work in the household premises* | *Desiring to take up dairy work* | *Desiring to take up tailoring* |
|---|---|---|---|
| Andhra Pradesh | 20.9 (26.1) | 4.2 (11.7) | 9.0 (06.1) |
| Assam | 39.6 (33.8) | 4.8 (03.0) | 3.9 (02.3) |
| Bihar | 32.9 (37.1) | 8.3 (09.2) | 9.5 (06.4) |
| Gujarat | 22.4 (27.3) | 11.6 (09.7) | 4.6 (05.6) |
| Haryana | 22.0 (32.4) | 7.8 (14.6) | 8.3 (09.7) |
| Himachal Pradesh | 40.0 (21.9) | 6.7 (07.8) | 15.3 (07.8) |
| Karnataka | 22.8 (25.2) | 4.2 (12.6) | 5.6 (05.8) |
| Kerala | 42.6 (24.8) | 12.1 (06.7) | 9.9 (04.9) |
| Madhya Pradesh | 27.5 (22.3) | 6.4 (07.3) | 9.1 (06.3) |
| Maharashtra | 26.6 (24.9) | 3.6 (04.3) | 9.5 (08.6) |
| Orissa | 38.6 (41.2) | 16.9 (16.3) | 10.8 (07.0) |
| Punjab | 33.6 (30.7) | 18.3 (07.7) | 8.4 (12.2) |
| Rajasthan | 27.8 (18.0) | 13.7 (06.8) | 6.9 (05.4) |
| Tamil Nadu | 24.5 (21.3) | 7.6 (08.7) | 9.8 (05.0) |

*Cont'd...*

*Cont'd...*

| | | | |
|---|---|---|---|
| Uttar Pradesh | 35.9 (21.3) | 14.4 (08.7) | 11.7 (05.0) |
| West Bengal | 39.9 (32.2) | 9.3 (12.0) | 6.9 (03.8) |
| All-India | 33.0 (30.4) | 10.1 (10.6) | 9.0 (06.2) |

*Note:* Figures in the bracket indicate percentages for 1993–1994.

*Source:* Compiled from *Sarvekshana*, Vol. XXI, No. 2, 73rd Issue, October-December 1997 and NSSO Report No. 518: *Participation of Women in Specified Activities along with Domestic Duties*, 2004–2005.

Somewhat surprisingly rural women in Kerala have the highest preference for work in the household at nearly 43% in 2004–2005, a marked increase from 24.8% in 1993–1994 followed by Himachal Pradesh at 40% in 2004–2005 from its 1993–1994 level of 21.9%. Barring these two states, no other state has such a sharp increase, clearly suggesting severe work scarcity in Kerala and Himachal Pradesh. In 1993–1994, the women in Orissa had the highest preference for work in their household premises followed by the women in Bihar. Andhra Pradesh, Bihar, Gujarat, Karnataka and Orissa record a decrease in the percentage between 1993–1994 and 2004–2005, while the other states record an increase in percentage of women willing to accept work in the household premises.

There are wide variations across states regarding the preference for dairy work. In 2004–2005, the rural women in Punjab, Orissa, Kerala, Uttar Pradesh, Rajasthan and Gujarat have a markedly higher preference for dairy work than other states. Such variations are also evident in the case of tailoring, though rural women in Himachal Pradesh, Orissa and Uttar Pradesh have a marked preference for it, while those of Assam and Gujarat do not reveal an enthusiasm for it. It is equally significant to note that the rural women in many states have indicated preferences for other activities. The data suggest that greater efforts should be made in the coverage of various rural development schemes to reach out to those women who are primarily engaged in domestic duties and have indicated a preference for some income-generating activities in their home premises such as dairy and tailoring work. There has also to be more imaginative efforts in identifying a set of unconventional occupations as supplementary activities for such rural women that are specific to particular regions.

Table 2.6 presents state-wise percentage of the rural women of age 15 years and above usually engaged in domestic duties and willing to accept work at the household by type of assistance in 2004–2005 and 1993–1994. Thirty-three per cent of the rural women have expressed willingness to accept work in their household premises. Not surprisingly, the proportion of women in the younger age groups (up to 29 years) who are willing to accept work in the household premises are higher than those in the older age groups (30 years and above). About 71.9% of those willing to accept work wanted only part-time work, but they wanted the work to be regular. This shows that their engagement with domestic duties did not permit them to engage in full-time economic work, although their desire for regularity of part-time work suggests their need to have access to a regular income stream. Here too, there are variations between states. In the states of Andhra Pradesh, Haryana, Himachal Pradesh, Punjab, Madhya Pradesh, Maharashtra, Rajasthan and Tamil Nadu, a greater proportion of women would prefer to have full-time work than the other states.

Women also expressed the type of assistance they required in order to take up work in the household premises. The predominant type of assistance they sought was financial assistance, including initial finance on easy terms to start the work activity, and subsequent working finance facilities. Sixty-two per cent of the rural women engaged primarily in household duties in the country expressed their need for financial assistance in 2004–2005, whereas 77% had done so in 1993–1994; 47.7% wanted initial finance on easy terms and 14.5% wanted working finance assistance; 14.9% of the women sought assistance by way of training and 6.4% wanted assured market. State-wise differences in the type of assistance sought are presented in Table 2.6 below:

**Table 2.6**

*Percentage distribution of rural women of age 15 years and above usually engaged in domestic duties and willing to accept work at the household by type of assistance required in selected states – 2004–2005 and 1993–1994*

| *States* | *Initial finance on easy terms* | *Working finance facilities* | *Assured market* | *Training* |
|---|---|---|---|---|
| Andhra Pradesh | 51.3 (57.8) | 9.4 (29.1) | 5.4 | 22.7 (4.7) |
| Assam | 49.4 (57.6) | 19.6 (12.5) | 8.7 | 3.4 (1.3) |

*Cont'd...*

*Cont'd...*

| | | | | |
|---|---|---|---|---|
| Bihar | 37.4 (50.7) | 13.2 (23.9) | 11.5 | 11.3 (16.4) |
| Gujarat | 68.6 (62.1) | 3.8 (9.5) | 3.8 | 9.0 (9.0) |
| Haryana | 27.3 (61.6) | 30.7 (11.2) | 13.7 | 15.1 (11.1) |
| Himachal Pradesh | 28.8 (53.7) | 13.8 (19.7) | 14.8 | 20.0 (6.6) |
| Karnataka | 39.6 (57.0) | 9.0 (20.9) | 7.9 | 16.2 (7.7) |
| Kerala | 64.9 (54.4) | 6.1 (8.3) | 2.5 | 10.1 (8.6) |
| Madhya Pradesh | 52.0 (51.6) | 12.8 (21.1) | 7.5 | 14.8 (16.3) |
| Maharashtra | 45.7 (68.5) | 11.3 (9.5) | 11.2 | 20.4 (11.7) |
| Orissa | 57.6 (68.1) | 19.3 (7.4) | 2.0 | 16.9 (10.6) |
| Punjab | 53.7 (64.2) | 13.5 (16.1) | 9.2 | 10.3 (4.3) |
| Rajasthan | 55.9 (52.1) | 18.4 (22.6) | 6.7 | 6.9 (10.0) |
| Tamil Nadu | 52.8 (74.5) | 5.4 (3.4) | 5.4 | 5.4 (11.0) |
| Uttar Pradesh | 47.8 (50.0) | 15.5 (32.7) | 4.0 | 18.0 (10.2) |
| West Bengal | 43.6 (59.0) | 14.9 (17.6) | 6.8 | 15.3 (7.5) |
| All-India | 47.7 (56.5) | 14.5 (20.4) | 6.4 | 14.9 (10.4) |

*Note:* Figures in the bracket indicate percentages for 1993–1994.

*Source:* Compiled from *Sarvekshana*, Vol. XXI, No. 2, 73rd Issue, October-December 1997 and NSSO Report No. 518: *Participation of Women in Specified Activities along with Domestic Duties*, 2004–2005.

There are no significant inter-state variations regarding the requirement of initial finance on easy terms, with more than half the women in all states requesting such assistance. Only Gujarat, Kerala, Madhya Pradesh and Rajasthan recorded increase in the percentage of women requiring initial finance from 1993–1994. All the other states indicate a decrease in the percentage of those requiring initial finance from 1993–1994 to 2004–2005, the decrease in Tamil Nadu being quite striking from three-quarters to a half. But there are wide variations across states as regards the requirement of working finance facilities with only an insignificant 3.8% of the women in Gujarat seeking such assistance, while 30% of the women in Haryana wanted such assistance in 2004–2005; 14.9% of the women wanted assistance in training with higher percentage of women in Andhra Pradesh, Tamil Nadu, Maharashtra, Himachal Pradesh indicating the need for training. Easy availability of raw materials or an assured market for products which are generally perceived as problems facing home-based producers were reported as constraints by 3.1% and 6.4% of the rural women in 2004–2005. Women who felt the need for assured market was reportedly higher in Bihar, Haryana, Himachal Pradesh and Maharashtra. Other unspecified assistance which needs to be enquired and taken into account in the framing of policies were reportedly high in the North-eastern states, the hill states of Sikkim, Uttaranchal, Jammu & Kashmir and Himachal Pradesh, and the states of Bihar, Karnataka and West Bengal. What needs to be underlined is that only 3.8% of the women willing to accept work in 2004–2005 stated that they needed no assistance, while about 96% wanted some kind of assistance.

### Nature of Urban Women's Domestic Work

Fifty per cent of the urban women in the country are usually engaged in domestic duties as their principal status in 2004–2005. However, with an expanded notion of economic work that includes maintenance of the kitchen garden, work in household dairy and poultry, free collection of fish, firewood, etc., and processing of own produce for household consumption, 10% of women engaged in domestic duties can be said to be engaged in some kind of economic work.

**Table 2.7**

*Percentage distribution of women usually engaged in domestic duties and also participating in other activities in selected states – 1993–1994 and 2004–2005*

| *States* | *Engaged in kitchen garden, poultry, dairy, free collection of fish, firewood, etc.* | *Engaged in maintenance, free collection and processing of own produce for household consumption* | *Engaged in any activity either economic or beneficial to the household* |
|---|---|---|---|
| Andhra Pradesh | 8.0 (11.8) | 8.3 (12.2) | 48.6 (58.3) |
| Assam | 36.8 (28.1) | 37.5 (29.4) | 84.4 (65.9) |
| Bihar | 18.1 (22.5) | 19.9 (26.5) | 62.2 (68.5) |
| Gujarat | 7.3 (11.2) | 7.5 (11.4) | 35.2 (40.4) |
| Haryana | 12.1 (20.9) | 12.6 (20.9) | 54.4 (85.2) |
| Himachal Pradesh | 15.1 (31.2) | 17.0 (31.2) | 76.3 (74.5) |
| Karnataka | 7.8 (13.8) | 8.2 (14.2) | 46.2 (54.3) |

*Cont'd...*

*Cont'd...*

| | | | |
|---|---|---|---|
| Kerala | 18.8 (31.6) | 20.1 (35.1) | 52.3 (62.4) |
| Madhya Pradesh | 15.4 (15.7) | 15.7 (16.5) | 71.3 (68.8) |
| Maharashtra | 4.1 (5.5) | 4.1 (5.7) | 34.8 (41.8) |
| Orissa | 22.4 (19.7) | 25.0 (22.6) | 70.6 (80.3) |
| Punjab | 6.2 (10.8) | 6.4 (11.0) | 61.1 (64.4) |
| Rajasthan | 17.5 (20.8) | 17.6 (20.9) | 54.8 (63.5) |
| Tamil Nadu | 7.0 (16.1) | 7.6 (20.4) | 57.7 (78.5) |
| Uttar Pradesh | 10.4 (15.8) | 10.7 (16.3) | 56.3 (69.5) |
| West Bengal | 17.5 (21.1) | 17.9 (21.4) | 72.4 (73.4) |
| All-India | 11.1 (15.1) | 11.5 (16.1) | 53.4 (62.5) |

*Note:* Figures in the bracket indicate percentages for 1993–1994.

*Source:* Compiled from *Sarvekshana*, Vol. XXI, No. 2, 73rd Issue, October-December 1997 and NSSO Report No. 518: *Participation of Women in Specified Activities along with Domestic Duties*, 2004–2005.

If we consider any activity that is "economic" in the expanded notion of the term or merely beneficial to the household, we note that 53.4% of the women engaged in domestic activities do perform such activities. Table 2.7 shows the disparities between states in the urban housewives' involvement in economic activities in 2004–2005 and 1993–1994. While 37.5% of the urban women in Assam, 25% in Orissa and 20.0% in Kerala were engaged in economic work in 2004–2005, only about 6.4% do so in Punjab and 4.1% in Maharashtra. If we consider activities that are economic and beneficial, there are once again wide differences between states. While 85% of the urban housewives in Assam, 76% in Himachal Pradesh and 72% in West Bengal engage in such activities, only 35% in Gujarat and Maharashtra do so.

The activities that urban housewives predominantly engage in are tailoring as more than a quarter of the women are engaged in it and fetching water wherein one-fifth of women are involved. Tutoring of own children ranks third at 12.6% in 2004–2005, unlike in the case of rural women whose involvement in tutoring was not significant. Similarly, free collection of firewood and preparation of cowdung cakes recorded a high participation of the rural housewives at 40% and 54%, respectively, but these two activities for urban women are in comparison quite marginal with only 6% of the urban housewives engaged in them. Clearly, the activity patterns of rural and urban women engaged predominantly in domestic duties are markedly different.

**Table 2.8**

*Percentage of women usually engaged in domestic duties involved in the free collection of firewood, etc., preparation of cowdung cakes, tutoring of own children, bringing water from outside the household premises and engaged in tailoring in the urban areas of selected states – 1993–1994 and 2004–2005*

| *States* | *Engaged in free collection of firewood, etc.* | *Engaged in the preparation of cowdung cakes* | *Engaged in tutoring own children* | *Engaged in bringing water from outside the household premises* | *Engaged in sewing, tailoring, etc.* |
|---|---|---|---|---|---|
| Andhra Pradesh | 5.3 (5.1) | 0.6 (2.4) | 10.1 (6.5) | 29.4 (44.6) | 7.6 (7.2) |
| Assam | 11.9 (3.6) | 7.9 (2.9) | 29.2 (18.8) | 15.3 (15.2) | 64.4 (39.7) |
| Bihar | 10.9 (13.0) | 14.6 (18.6) | 17.7 (12.8) | 11.7 (29.0) | 39.2 (35.4) |
| Gujarat | 6.7 (7.0) | 3.1 (7.2) | 11.5 (9.1) | 9.4 (20.0) | 11.9 (7.1) |
| Haryana | 7.8 (10.5) | 9.7 (22.4) | 13.5 (17.6) | 10.0 (24.5) | 42.0 (64.1) |
| Himachal Pradesh | 5.0 (15.6) | 4.1 (13.6) | 40.8 (26.3) | 18.9 (22.9) | 56.5 (50.4) |
| Karnataka | 4.6 (5.6) | 1.9 (5.6) | 11.1 (12.1) | 26.7 (36.0) | 7.9 (9.6) |
| Kerala | 6.7 (10.1) | 0.2 (5.0) | 12.3 (8.6) | 13.1 (18.5) | 6.8 (6.8) |
| Madhya Pradesh | 9.2 (9.0) | 14.3 (13.7) | 15.1 (14.0) | 28.6 (41.0) | 35.0 (27.2) |
| Maharashtra | 2.5 (2.7) | 4.1 (2.7) | 11.9 (10.0) | 17.6 (23.4) | 9.2 (13.7) |
| Orissa | 12.6 (8.8) | 8.5 (7.5) | 11.8 (9.5) | 43.0 (50.2) | 13.5 (18.3) |
| Punjab | 1.9 (3.8) | 6.5 (12.2) | 14.3 (15.3) | 1.4 (3.9) | 52.6 (53.5) |
| Rajasthan | 12.0 (13.2) | 11.2 (15.9) | 8.7 (10.4) | 16.4 (21.9) | 32.4 (35.2) |
| Tamil Nadu | 3.7 (7.1) | 0.8 (4.0) | 10.9 (12.2) | 34.1 (47.3) | 6.9 (8.3) |
| Uttar Pradesh | 5.4 (6.0) | 9.2 (16.5) | 12.8 (15.5) | 11.3 (16.9) | 37.1 (47.9) |
| West Bengal | 8.3 (10.8) | 10.9 (15.3) | 15.9 (16.5) | 32.4 (41.4) | 53.6 (39.1) |
| All-India | 6.1 (7.0) | 6.0 (9.2) | 12.6 (12.4) | 20.1 (29.6) | 25.1 (25.8) |

*Note:* Figures in the bracket indicate percentages for 1993–1994.

*Source:* Compiled from *Sarvekshana*, Vol. XXI, No. 2, 73rd Issue, October-December 1997 and NSSO Report No. 518: *Participation of Women in Specified Activities Along with Domestic Duties*, 2004–2005.

Further, there are differences across states as well, as Table 2.8 indicates. While 43% of the women in Orissa fetch water, only 1.4% do so in Punjab. Even in tailoring, such differences between states exist. While a little less than 7% of the urban women in Kerala and Tamil Nadu are engaged in tailoring, about 64% in Assam, 56% in Himachal Pradesh and about 53% in Punjab and West Bengal engage in that activity. Tutoring of children which in general is the third most popular activity does not reveal such wide differences between states, although fewer women in Andhra Pradesh and Tamil Nadu engage in that.

A slightly higher proportion of urban women than rural women seemed more committed to domestic duties in terms of time involvement. About 89% of the urban women engaged in domestic duties reported that they were required to spend most of their days in domestic duties, while only 88% of the rural women did so. Not surprisingly, women in the age group of 30–44 years revealed greater commitment to domestic duties in both rural and urban areas. In what ways urban women engaged predominantly in domestic duties perceive such involvement as constraining to their participation in the labour market, at least by way of self-employment in their household premises is examined below.

## Constraints on Labour Market Participation for Urban Women

Table 2.9 presents the proportion of women aged 15 years and above engaged in domestic duties and willing to accept work in the household premises, and those desiring to take up tailoring and other work in 1993–1994 and 2004–2005. Sixty-three per cent of the urban women above the age of 15 years were engaged in domestic duties in 2004–2005 – a reduction by 2% over the 1993–1994 figure. Nearly 27% of them were willing to accept work in their household premises. There are differences across states in women's willingness to accept work. Urban women engaged primarily in domestic duties in Tamil Nadu, Karnataka and Andhra Pradesh have markedly lower preference to take up such work, while urban women in Assam, Bihar, Himachal Pradesh, Kerala, Madhya Pradesh, Rajasthan, Uttar Pradesh and West Bengal rank high in their willingness to accept work in their household premises. This is true for all urban women as well as those in the currently married status of women engaged in domestic duties. It is a well-known fact that women in southern India have culturally far greater freedom in working outside their homes. Thus, the lower proportion of those willing to accept work in their household premises could as well be due to the fact that those willing to work do reveal themselves as "unemployed" and thus are part of the labour force, and those outside the labour force on account of domestic duties are committed to a greater extent to domestic work for various reasons and are not therefore cases of "concealed or camouflaged unemployment". Kerala's percentage increase of 10% in the urban women's willingness to accept work in the household premises is likely to be on account of what appears a severe job scarcity in that state in the recent years.

**Table 2.9**

*Percentage distribution of women (age 15 years and above) engaged in domestic duties and willing to accept work in the household premises, as well as those desiring to take up tailoring and other work in the selected states – 1993–1994 and 2004–2005 (urban)*

| *States* | *Willing to accept work in the household premises* | *Desiring to take up tailoring* | *Willing to take up other unspecified work* |
|---|---|---|---|
| Andhra Pradesh | 16.4 (24.8) | 7.7 (13.1) | 5.6 (5.4) |
| Assam | 37.2 (32.1) | 7.4 (7.8) | 11.4 (11.8) |
| Bihar | 34.3 (34.9) | 15.2 (10.6) | 10.2 (5.0) |
| Gujarat | 25.4 (28.4) | 11.6 (14.2) | 9.3 (8.0) |
| Haryana | 20.1 (27.1) | 9.9 (15.9) | 6.5 (3.1) |
| Himachal Pradesh | 53.9 (34.0) | 27.4 (14.4) | 16.8 (7.4) |
| Karnataka | 22.4 (20.1) | 11.6 (8.6) | 7.4 (5.4) |
| Kerala | 33.5 (23.7) | 9.0 (6.9) | 8.6 (6.4) |
| Madhya Pradesh | 36.8 (30.9) | 15.1 (15.5) | 8.3 (6.3) |
| Maharashtra | 22.8 (26.8) | 8.6 (14.4) | 7.0 (7.5) |
| Orissa | 29.8 (32.0) | 12.3 (9.8) | 7.2 (12.3) |
| Punjab | 21.8 (32.1) | 10.3 (16.8) | 3.8 (6.8) |
| Rajasthan | 33.6 (26.4) | 19.4 (13.2) | 7.0 (4.4) |
| Tamil Nadu | 19.8 (19.5) | 8.3 (6.7) | 6.6 (6.9) |
| Uttar Pradesh | 36.5 (29.9) | 17.9 (11.8) | 7.5 (3.5) |
| West Bengal | 33.7 (28.0) | 12.8 (8.9) | 12.9 (9.6) |
| All-India | 27.3 (26.6) | 11.8 (11.5) | 7.9 (6.4) |

*Note:* Figures in the bracket indicate percentages for 1993–1994.

*Source:* Compiled from *Sarvekshana*, Vol. XXI, No. 2, 73rd Issue, October-December 1997 and NSSO Report No. 518: *Participation of Women in Specified Activities along with Domestic Duties*, 2004–2005.

On account of their commitment to domestic duties and the various other activities, both economic and beneficial that these women engage in, 68% of the women who expressed willingness to accept work preferred only part-time work, although they wanted such work to be regular rather than irregular. A greater proportion of the urban women willing to accept work in Haryana, Punjab, Tamil Nadu and Andhra Pradesh preferred full-time work to part-time work.

Tailoring was the most preferred activity, with 11.8% out of the 27% expressing a preference for it. Unspecified other activities ranked second with 7.9% expressing their preference. These preferences are in general valid for all states despite the fact that urban women in the northern states have a higher preference for tailoring than women in the southern states. There is thus a marked difference in the revealed preferences of rural and urban women. Dairy work which was most sought by rural women was not very popular with the urban women. Once again, greater imaginative efforts are needed to identify a set of activities that presently constitute the unspecified category of "others" and that are acceptable to women, as urban women have expressed a preference for these over the conventional activities.

Nearly 58.1% of those willing to accept work claimed that they possessed the required skills for the work in 2004–2005. A greater proportion claimed to possess the skills required among those willing to accept dairy work, poultry, manufacture of wood and cane products, spinning and weaving, and tailoring. In general, more women in the younger age groups, i.e., those in the 15–19 years and 20–24 years, did not possess the skills that were required, although they were willing to accept work. Clearly, this is the age group of urban women who need to be targeted for skill acquisition programmes. Table 2.10 below shows the type of assistance that women required:

**Table 2.10**

*Percentage distribution of urban women of age 15 years and above usually engaged in domestic duties and willing to accept work at the household by type of assistance required in selected states – 1993–1994 and 2004–2005*

| *States* | *Initial finance on easy terms* | *Working finance facilities* | *Training* | *Assured market* |
|---|---|---|---|---|
| Andhra Pradesh | 38.2 (67.9) | 15.0 (13.6) | 23.2 (8.6) | 9.6 |
| Assam | 46.6 (34.9) | 9.5 (16.0) | 10.4 (4.0) | 5.3 |

*Cont'd...*

*Cont'd...*

| | | | | |
|---|---|---|---|---|
| Bihar | 36.5 (44.1) | 11.3 (28.8) | 18.3 (10.1) | 10.0 |
| Gujarat | 40.3 (52.6) | 13.6 (6.5) | 14.1 (20.1) | 11.4 |
| Haryana | 27.1 (37.7) | 16.2 (9.6) | 19.7 (12.3) | 15.9 |
| Himachal Pradesh | 43.5 (40.1) | 1.4 (20.3) | 16.0(6.3) | 13.9 |
| Karnataka | 25.9 (40.3) | 14.2 (23.9) | 23.6 (13.6) | 16.8 |
| Kerala | 61.4 (57.6) | 7.4 (10.8) | 13.6 (8.8) | 3.1 |
| Madhya Pradesh | 30.5 (50.0) | 12.0 (13.9) | 17.7 (23.4) | 13.9 |
| Maharashtra | 31.4 (46.4) | 11.7 (9.0) | 17.7 (18.7) | 13.8 |
| Orissa | 49.9 (55.0) | 18.3 (8.8) | 21.1 (12.9) | 4.0 |
| Punjab | 26.8 (45.8) | 20.1 (17.4) | 21.4 (11.2) | 13.9 |
| Rajasthan | 45.6 (47.7) | 10.3 (11.7) | 7.3 (12.3) | 6.3 |
| Tamil Nadu | 42.8 (62.6) | 8.4 (5.3) | 18.7 (10.6) | 8.0 |
| Uttar Pradesh | 39.7 (52.3) | 18.1 (22.6) | 13.7 (12.2) | 7.4 |
| West Bengal | 25.4 (46.2) | 17.9 (16.0) | 20.1 (12.3) | 15.4 |
| All-India | 35.3 (50.0) | 13.7 (14.9) | 17.0 (13.8) | 10.5 |

*Note:* Figures in the bracket indicate percentages for 1993–1994.

*Source:* Compiled from *Sarvekshana*, Vol. XXI, No. 2, 73rd Issue, October-December 1997 and NSSO Report No. 518: *Participation of Women in Specified Activities along with Domestic Duties*, 2004–2005.

Clearly, initial finance on easy terms, i.e., start-up capital was required by a little over one-third of the urban women willing to accept work. More women from Assam, Kerala, Himachal Pradesh, Orissa, Rajasthan and Tamil Nadu especially have indicated initial finance as a requirement, while more women from Andhra Pradesh, Gujarat, Haryana, Punjab, Orissa, Uttar Pradesh and West Bengal have requested for working finance facilities. Training ranked second with more women especially from the states of Andhra Pradesh, Karnataka, Orissa, Punjab and West Bengal requesting that they be imparted training for the various activities. Other types of unspecified assistance figured highly in the many states. The nature of assistance in these cases needs to be probed for the framing of appropriate policies. Like the rural women, the urban women also did not perceive the availability of raw materials as a constraint but wanted an assured market for the products. In the country, as a whole, only 5.5% of the urban women willing to accept work stated that they required no assistance.

Analysis of women's willingness to accept work in their household premises, the skills they possess and the type of assistance they require suggest differences in the preference patterns of rural and urban women as well as regional differences. The policy implication of this analysis is to strengthen women's bargaining position within the households by making access to resources and income through various public policies.

**Youth Unemployment**

Here we explore aspects of youth unemployment, focussing especially on the gender issues of the problem, relating to measurement as well as policies. Statistics of unemployment for women in the younger age groups are likely to be understated as women do not reveal that they are unemployed, on account of their predominant engagement with domestic duties. Both the patriarchal ideologies that govern women's participation in domestic duties and the labour market, as well as the frames used for the statistical measurement of unemployment, play a role in understating unemployment among younger women.

The NSS survey data on employment and unemployment for 2004–2005 and 1993–1994 bring into sharp focus the incidence of youth unemployment in rural and urban India. From Table 2.11 below, it is clear that the CDS unemployment rate in 2004–2005 was quite high in all categories with urban rates higher than the rural ones. While the male rate is highest in the 15–19 years age group, the female rate is highest in 20–24 years age group. Male unemployment rates fall significantly in the 25–29 years age group, but remain quite high for females in both rural and urban India. Urban female unemployment rates are quite high and highest is in the 20–24 years age group at 27.3%.

**Table 2.11**

*Current daily status unemployment rate among the youth (15–29 years) in India – 2004–2005*

| *Age* | *15–19 years (in %)* | *20–24 years (in %)* | *25–29 years (in %)* |
|---|---|---|---|
| Rural Male | 15.0 | 12.9 | 8.8 |
| Rural Female | 12.6 | 14.9 | 10.7 |
| Urban Male | 18.4 | 15.8 | 9.5 |
| Urban Female | 16.4 | 27.3 | 18.1 |

*Source:* NSSO Report No. 515: *Employment and Unemployment Situation in India, 2004–2005* (Part I & II), GoI, September 2006.

## Issues of Unemployment

It is by now well known that there are different estimates of unemployment that enables us to understand various facets of unemployment, such as chronic unemployment which is of a long-term nature, as well as unemployment that is both seasonal and intermittent. In an economy where the primary sector, i.e., agriculture and the allied sectors still absorb the majority of the workforce, both seasonal and intermittent unemployment become important dimensions to be understood, quantified and explained in order to orient employment policies in the economy to tackle this facet of unemployment along with policy measures to reduce chronic unemployment in the economy. Both chronic and intermittent unemployment can be reduced by growth and occupational diversification of employment in the economy. For the formulation of employment policies, we need to understand which sections of the population are most affected by unemployment. While rural unemployment would call for policies that promote greater occupational diversification and growth of non-farm employment opportunities in rural areas, urban unemployment would call for measures to increase employment opportunities in the organized manufacturing sector and the service sectors as well as measures to absorb the residual urban job aspirants in the informal sectors at socially acceptable levels of income, productivity and employment conditions.

Equally, if unemployment affects those in the younger age groups, then employment policies will have to focus on generating employment that would absorb the youth, provide training and facilitate skill acquisition that would enable their absorption and increase both their retention in the educational sector for longer years as well as impart education that would make them more employable in the market. Such policies that focus on the absorption of youth in a growing labour market are different from the policies that would be needed to absorb the older persons who have been displaced from the shrinking sectors of the economy and who need to be retrained to be absorbed elsewhere.

In case of women, in developing economies, the problem of employment and unemployment acquire other nuances as the "discouraged worker effect" operates in the case of women in such a way that women withdraw from the labour force itself when they are unemployed for a long time. And when they withdraw from the labour force, they are not idle either. As noted earlier, in subsistence economies women who withdraw from the labour force do engage themselves in activities that supplement the income of the poor households even if the activity itself does not generate cash income by way of wages or produce sale. The products of such activities are indeed crucial to the survival strategies of the poor households. Women often combine these activities with their domestic activities. This means that women do not reveal as men do that they are in fact unemployed and seeking work. The measurement of unemployment has to account for this phenomenon.

**Revealed Preference for Unemployment and Measurement Issue**

Measurement of unemployment presupposes congruence between the objective state of "being unemployed" as well as the subjective cognizance of the person concerned of "being unemployed". The category of unemployment is derivative, dependent on the category of employment. In general, economists define employment as being engaged in economically productive work which generally captures all marketed work and some, but not all, non-market activities. As "unemployment" is a category of the market economy, there are many situations in economies where non-market activities are still resilient, wherein this category fails at least partially in its representational function. In all these instances, there is no congruence between the objective state and the subjective perception. That is why unemployment is never measured in itself but is measured always in conjunction with employment in the national data collection systems. It is hoped that if employment is measured in as inclusive a manner as possible, then to some extent the divergence between the objective state and subjective perception is obviated. But this is only partially true.

The problem at hand is something like this. The category "unemployed" ought to have more or less people than it actually does, which is why it does not perform its representational function fully. When it has more than what is supposed to be there, it is the case that many who are employed in some subsidiary status (as full workers are always likely to be counted) are not counted as workers and are reported in this category as unemployed. For this group, a more inclusive enumeration of workers will suffice. There is however the other scenario that it has fewer reported in the category than what is supposed to be there. Then the question is: where have these people been included? The reverse situation of those unemployed being classified as employed never occurs for long-duration measures like "usual status", for by the inclusive definition of workers, they would be in the employed category although it is likely to happen for short-duration measures of unemployment such as the "CDS" measure. There is no reason to suppose that a person unemployed over a long duration is likely to be classified in the employment category. Then the obvious category where the potentially unemployed could have been tucked away are the activity categories outside the labour force which act as containers to hold the potentially unemployed.

It is necessary to understand how, in fact, this possibility can arise. This is more an instance of misidentification than misclassification. Even when the measurement frame uses as objective a criterion as "time spent" on the various activities to appropriately classify persons, persons do get wrongly classified on account of misidentification. Women who are potentially unemployed disclose their main activity as domestic duties, and hence go out of the labour force while measuring unemployment, but otherwise express a willingness to accept work at home. While workers employed in the household enterprises get classified as workers, there is no corresponding measurement category to identify those available for work and seeking work in their home itself, especially since they spend most of their time on domestic duties.

The NSSO framework, as is by now well known, has a number of activity categories for those outside the labour force. Of these, the activity categories domestic duties (code 92) and domestic duties plus free collection of products (code 93) serve as containers to hold the potentially unemployed. Other categories such as students, rentiers, pensioners, sick and disabled are only likely to accommodate those who ought to be there rather than act as containers to hold the potentially unemployed. The prevailing social norms relating to domestic duties, however, make these two domestic activity categories, hold only the potentially unemployed among women rather than men. Hence, the estimates of unemployed in the female population in respective age groups are understated especially in the younger age groups.

Economists and policymakers need to be sensitive to the fact that, apart from varieties of unemployment such as chronic, seasonal, intermittent, disguised, cyclical and so on, there is a category of "concealed and camouflaged unemployment" rendered possible both by the statistical frames of reference and the ideologies and practices of patriarchy and domesticity, both acting in conjunction to produce this category of "concealed or camouflaged unemployment". The statistical analysis of NSSO data on employment and unemployment from the 61st and 50th round surveys for the years 2004–2005 and 1993–1994 respectively shows that this is especially true for women in younger age groups in rural and urban India.

**Age-wise Distribution of Unemployed**

Tables 2.12 and 2.13 reveal some remarkable features of the usual status or the long duration/chronic unemployment in the various age categories.

**Table 2.12**

*Age-wise distribution of unemployed by usual status – rural India – 2004–2005 and 1993–1994*

| *Category* | *10–14 years* | *15–19 years* | *20–24 years* | *25–29 years* | *30–34 years* | *15–24 years* | *Total* |
|---|---|---|---|---|---|---|---|
| Total - Male | 2.9<br>(1.9) | 33.4<br>(24.8) | 36.7<br>(44.1) | 14.2<br>(21.2) | 5.7<br>(5.0) | 70.1<br>(68.9) | 100<br>(100) |
| Total - Female | 1.8<br>(2.5) | 18.1<br>(23.4) | 33<br>(41.9) | 20.1<br>(18.1) | 12<br>(1.6) | 51.1<br>(65.3) | 100<br>(100) |

*Note:* Figures in the brackets are for 1993–1994.

*Source:* NSSO, *Sarvekshana*, Vol. 22, No. 4, 79th Issue, April-June 1999 and NSSO Report No. 515: *Employment and Unemployment Situation in India 2004–2005* (Part I & II), GOI, September 2006.

**Table 2.13**

*Age-wise distribution of unemployed by usual status – urban India– 2004–2005 and 1993–1994*

| *Category* | *10–14 years* | *15–19 years* | *20–24 years* | *25–29 years* | *30–34 years* | *15–24 years* | *Total* |
|---|---|---|---|---|---|---|---|
| Total – Male | 2.3<br>(1.5) | 22.5<br>(23.7) | 39.6<br>(41.5) | 19.6<br>(22.1) | 6.6<br>(6.6) | 62.1<br>(65.2) | 100<br>(100) |
| Total – Female | 1.2<br>(0.9) | 12.3<br>(17.8) | 39.7<br>(46.6) | 22.5<br>(21.6) | 12<br>(8.5) | 52<br>(64.4) | 100<br>(100) |

*Note:* Figures in the brackets are for 1993–1994.

*Source:* NSSO, *Sarvekshana*, Vol. 22, No. 4, 79th Issue, April-June 1999 and NSSO Report No. 515: *Employment and Unemployment Situation in India 2004–2005* (Part I & II), GOI, September 2006.

It can be noted from Tables 2.12 and 2.13 that the greater proportion of the unemployed in rural and urban India are in the age group of 15–24 years. For easier exposition, this age category of unemployment can be termed "youth unemployment" and the unemployment in the 10–14 years as "early teen unemployment" and the 25–29 years as the "young adult unemployment". The proportion of unemployed in the 25–29 years, i.e., the "young adult unemployment" is nearly a fifth of all the unemployed except among rural males. While there is no significant difference in the proportions of youth unemployment in general between rural and urban India, it is still higher among rural males. Female youth unemployment, like that of the male, is the most significant component of unemployment and is around 50% of all the female unemployment in rural and urban India. Hence, any policy to tackle unemployment has to be primarily targeted at "youth" and "young adult" unemployment.

**Activity-wise Distribution of Persons**

The unemployment data, as noted earlier, does not capture all those who are potentially unemployed since there is a tendency to withdraw from the labour force. Hence, the distribution of population across all activities will provide a better understanding as there are certain activities that act as containers to hold those potentially unemployed but do not reveal it. As the primary focus here is on youth unemployment, the activity-wise distribution of persons is analysed only for persons in the 15–19 years and 20–24 years age groups as these constitute the category of youth.

Tables 2.14 and 2.15 provide the distribution of persons in the two age groups for various principal activities in rural and urban areas.

**Table 2.14**

*Distribution of all persons across activities in youth age groups – rural (usual principal activity only) – 2004–2005 and 1993–1994*

| *Usual Activity* | *Males age 15–19 years (in %)* | *Females age 15–19 years (in %)* | *Males age 20–24 years (in %)* | *Females age 20–24 years (in %)* | *Females age 25–29 years (in %)* |
|---|---|---|---|---|---|
| Self-employed | 21.3<br>(28.5) | 11.7<br>(12.8) | 42.7<br>(46.0) | 15.3<br>(15.0) | 19.4<br>(15.9) |
| Regular wage work | 3.3<br>(2.6) | 0.9<br>(0.7) | 7.9<br>(6.5) | 1.6<br>(1.4) | 2.1<br>(1.7) |

*Cont'd...*

*Cont'd...*

| | | | | | |
|---|---|---|---|---|---|
| Casual work | 20.7<br>(21.3) | 9.7<br>(12.9) | 31.4<br>(29.9) | 11.4<br>(15.4) | 15.1<br>(17.9) |
| Unemployed | 3.9<br>(2.6) | 1.6<br>(0.9) | 5.4<br>(5.9) | 2.0<br>(1.5) | 2.0<br>(0.7) |
| Education | 47.1<br>(41.3) | 33.0<br>(20.0) | 10.8<br>(9.9) | 4.1<br>(2.0) | 0.3<br>(0.2) |
| Domestic duties | 0.4<br>(0.4) | 22.4<br>(27.3) | 0.3<br>(0.4) | 34<br>(32.1) | 28.3<br>(29.7) |
| Domestic plus collection | 0.4<br>(0.4) | 19<br>(23.3) | 0.3<br>(0.2) | 29.6<br>(31.8) | 31.9<br>(33.5) |
| Total | 100 | 100 | 100 | 100 | 100 |

*Note:* Figures in the brackets are for 1993–1994.

*Source:* NSSO, *Sarvekshana*, Vol. 22, No. 4, 79th Issues, April-June 1999 and NSSO Report No. 515: *Employment and Unemployment Situation in India 2004–2005* (Part I & II), GOI, September 2006.

Table 2.14 indicates that rural males in the 15–19 years age group are primarily in self-employment and casual work; these two activities account for 41% of the rural males in that age group. While 47% were still in education attending schools and colleges, 3.9% were reportedly unemployed in 2004–2005. In the 20–24 years age group, there is a significant shift in activity distribution. Though not a cohort analysis, the distribution does suggest that there is a significant decrease in the proportion in education, this decrease being absorbed predominantly by work in self-employment activities and to a lesser extent by the casual and regular work. The percentage of unemployed also increases. What is significant to note is that the two activities "domestic duties" and "domestic duties plus collection" show marginal decrease between the two age groups. This, however, is not the case with females. In the 15–19 years age group, persons in activities outside the labour force are over 70% as compared to 48% for men, and the proportion of females in work activities and unemployment are correspondingly lower. In the 20–24 years age group for rural females, the percentage in education drops significantly as compared to the 15–19 years age group and this decrease is primarily absorbed in the two activities denoting domestic duties and domestic duties plus collection.

**Table 2.15**

*Distribution of all persons across activities in youth age groups – urban (usual principal activity only) – 2004–2005 and 1993–1994*

| *Usual activity* | *Males age 15–19 years (in %)* | *Females age 15–19 years (in %)* | *Males age 20–24 years (in %)* | *Females age 20–24 years (in %)* | *Females age 25–29 years (in %)* |
|---|---|---|---|---|---|
| Self-employment | 11.4<br>(13.2) | 4.1<br>(3.7) | 25.4<br>(29.4) | 5.8<br>(4.6) | 7.2<br>(5.7) |
| Regular wage work | 11.2<br>(9.7) | 3.2<br>(2.3) | 26.8<br>(21.5) | 7.5<br>(5.3) | 8.8<br>(7.0) |
| Casual work | 8.8<br>(10.8) | 1.9<br>(3.4) | 14.0<br>(14.5) | 2.2<br>(3.8) | 2.6<br>(4.8) |
| Unemployed | 5.1<br>(5.2) | 1.7<br>(1.9) | 9.5<br>(10.6) | 5.4<br>(5.2) | 3.5<br>(2.6) |
| Education | 60.2<br>(57.3) | 57.7<br>(49.6) | 22.6<br>(21.6) | 15.6<br>(12.6) | 1.0<br>(0.8) |
| Domestic duties | 0.4<br>(0.4) | 23.6<br>(29.4) | 0.2<br>(0.5) | 48.3<br>(53.1) | 56.9<br>(59.7) |
| Domestic plus collection | 0.1<br>(0.2) | 6.2<br>(7.8) | 0.1<br>(0.2) | 14.4<br>(14.4) | 19.3<br>(18.8) |
| Total | 100 | 100 | 100 | 100 | 100 |

*Note:* Figures in the brackets are for 1993–1994.

*Source:* NSSO, *Sarvekshana*, Vol. 22, No. 4, 79th Issue, April-June 1999 and NSSO Report No. 515: *Employment and Unemployment Situation in India 2004–2005* (Part I & II), GOI, September 2006.

A glance at Table 2.15 suggests that the same patterns are prevalent for the urban population as well, with the variations being on account of both the absorption in work activities, especially in regular work and the greater unemployment rates recorded for males. The pattern of activity distribution for urban females remained nearly the same as for rural females.

### Implications of Activity Pattern

Let us reflect on what this pattern suggests for both the measurement of unemployment and policy orientation. Clearly, there is reason to believe that female youth unemployment is underestimated, especially as the category of "youth" encompasses the two age groups 15–19 and 20–24. The shift in the activity distribution between these two age groups indicates the possibility of females who are potentially unemployed to be classified into either of the two domestic duties categories. An explanation for this likely phenomenon is in order here. Hitherto, analyses of women's employment and unemployment have highlighted the fact that women tend to withdraw from the labour force after a period of unsuccessful search for employment and, hence, it was believed that estimates of unemployment did not reveal the true extent of unemployment in the case of women. In the case of female "youth", an alternative explanation is needed, for the period of job search, if at all there was one is likely to have been very short, not justifying withdrawal from the labour force.

It appears that 20–24 years is a turning point when women who have completed their education join the ranks of those outside the labour force. Even in the 15–19 years, the two domestic categories account for 41% of the rural women and 30% of the urban women in that age group. Clearly, then, domestic duties appear as the norm, and what is happening is that the women who complete their education seem more inclined to fit the norm. Many of these women do get married and the rest hope to shortly. Thus, it is not altogether speculative when we say that most women in the "youth" age groups are governed by the patriarchal norm of the male breadwinner in the family and of their position as a dependent spouse.

Individual behaviour that conforms to social norms can arise both out of social compulsions and individual volition. Often, socially imposed ideology of dependence becomes unsustainable in the face of economic and psychological constraints imposed by the dependence ideology. It is, therefore, not surprising that 41.8% of the rural women and 38% of the urban women in the 20–24 years age group, engaged in activities in either of the two domestic duties categories have expressed willingness to accept work in the household premises. In fact, as Table 2.16 indicates, the willingness to accept work at home is higher in the age groups of 15–29 years for both the rural and urban women. The proportion of women willing to accept work is even higher for those women engaged in domestic duties as principal activity and also involved in work as subsidiary activity. Especially among urban women of that category, 70% have expressed willingness to accept work.

**Table 2.16**

*Willingness to accept work in household premises among women engaged in domestic duties by various age groups – 2004–2005 and 1993–1994*

| *Women in domestic duties (codes 92 and 93)* | *15–19 years (in %)* | *20–24 years (in %)* | *25–29 years (in %)* | *All ages (in %)* |
|---|---|---|---|---|
| Rural without subsidiary work | 41.0 (36.6) | 41.8 (38.8) | 40.8 (37.4) | 30.2 (28.7) |
| Rural with subsidiary work | 50.9 (41.1) | 48.7 (41.2) | 48.6 (41.3) | 41.5 (35.7) |
| Urban without subsidiary work | 41.7 (38.3) | 38 (34.7) | 36 (32.8) | 25.1 (25.3) |
| Urban with subsidiary work | 62.5 (54.8) | 70.2 (53.9) | 70.9 (51.2) | 61.2 (44.0) |

*Note:* Figures in the brackets are for 1993–1994.

*Source:* NSSO, *Sarvekshana*, Vol. 21, No. 2, 73rd Issue, October-December, 1997 and NSSO Report No. 515: *Employment and Unemployment Situation in India 2004–2005* (Part I & II), GOI, September 2006.

Such expressed willingness to accept work raises issues on the measurement of unemployment at both the subjective and objective levels. At the subjective level, it is of interest to note that women respondents do not subjectively transpose their state of "willingness" into one of "being available and/or seeking work" for, then, they would have been considered as unemployed and in the labour force. Rather by foregrounding their engagement in domestic duties as primary, they have unwittingly fitted themselves into the socially expected patriarchal norm. Neither are the women to be completely blamed for it, for the objective frame of measurement itself often encourages such preference revelations.

At the objective level of measurement, it seems pertinent to argue the case for the inclusion of such women who have expressed "willingness to accept work" in the category of unemployed. Just as much as the boundaries of productive work are difficult to define, the boundaries of unemployment are equally fuzzy. On the face of it, it is difficult to understand why "those available or seeking work" are classified as unemployed, while those "willing to accept work at home" are not. That it has been possible to keep those "willing to accept work" as outside the labour force only because of the "time-spent criterion" used for classifying persons by activity categories is quite obvious, and the argument here is not to question or contest that criterion.

There is no doubt that the "time-spent criterion" is an objective and measurable criterion that overrides subjective perceptions, but we ought to have a clearer understanding of the social-psychological dynamics at the household level and how they influence women's lives. It is generally recognized, at least by most women, that domestic duties are usually so flexible and stretchable that they could be made to fill up the day. Especially when younger women are fitting into a patriarchal social norm of domesticity, it cannot be expected that they would either self-consciously reveal that they were "available or seeking work" by the time-spent criterion or indeed actually even spend lengths of time seeking work. Fulfilling the norm of domesticity does, in fact, demand that women actually appear to be spending more time on domestic duties. There is, therefore, a valid claim that those women engaged in domestic duties and who have expressed willingness to work at home be actually considered as unemployed.

Table 2.17 provides revised percentage of persons in unemployment if "willingness to accept work" is considered as unemployed. It can be noted from Table 2.17 that the proportion of unemployment in the female population after considering willingness to work in the respective age groups is markedly higher than before such adjustment. At least from the point of view of formulating policies to tackle unemployment, the adjusted unemployment figures have to be considered more seriously. Unadjusted unemployment rate among females is much lower than the one adjusted taking "willingness to work" into account.

**Table 2.17**

*Percentage of rural and urban women in unemployment before and after adjusting for "willingness to accept work" usual activity principal only – 2004–2005*

| *Rural* | *15–19 years (in %)* | *20–24 years (in %)* | *25–29 years (in %)* |
|---|---|---|---|
| Unemployed – unadjusted | 6.7 | 9.3 | 5.2 |
| Percentage of (92 and 93) willing to work | 42.9 | 43.1 | 42.7 |
| Unemployed adjusted – addition of those willing to accept work | 46.50 | 51.63 | 43.02 |

*Cont'd...*

*Cont'd...*

| *Urban* | | | |
|---|---|---|---|
| Unemployed – unadjusted | 15.6 | 25.8 | 15.8 |
| Percentage of (92 and 93) willing to work | 43.4 | 40.6 | 37.8 |
| Unemployed adjusted – addition of those willing to accept work | 53.09 | 66.57 | 63.46 |

*Note:* 'Unemployed adjusted' is a calculated figure.

*Source:* NSSO Report No. 515: *Employment and Unemployment Situation in India 2004–2005* (Part I & II), GoI, September 2006 and NSSO Report No. 518: *Participation of Women in Specified Activities along with Domestic Duties, 2004–2005.*

## Policy Implications

### *Gender Sensitivity in Youth Unemployment Policy*

Policy measures to tackle youth unemployment need to be sensitive to the gender dimensions of the problem, as also the regional differences and the differences between various social groups. Clearly, this analysis has indicated that the significant shift in activity distribution from the 15–19 years age group to the 20–24 years age group need to be addressed primarily by way of increasing the proportion in educational activity through a longer period of retention in education for both men and women in rural and urban areas. Retention for a longer period in educational activity will be possible only when the gains from such retention are made appealing to the youth. A mass vocational training programme with scope for earning while learning in the new and modern sectors of employment such as information technology, marketing and sales, small industries services, insurance and financial services promoted on a widespread basis with state and industry participation will have the desired effect. Such a vocational training programme should be made available for both men and women and be accessible to the youth at different levels of completion of their formal education such as school, junior college, degree college and post-graduate levels. The near stagnancy of the organized sector employment and the non-diversification of rural employment which have been the structural malaise of the Indian economy can be alleviated through such a mass vocational programme geared to the growing sectors of the economy.

The analysis of the gender dimensions of youth unemployment has suggested that there exists a significant number of female youth in the domestic activities categories who have expressed their willingness to accept work if work was provided in their homes, and it has been argued that they be considered as unemployed as well. Not only have these women expressed their willingness to work but have also revealed their preferences for the kinds of work that they would like to be engaged in. An analysis of their work preferences revealed that the rural women preferred activities such as dairy work and tailoring, while the urban women desired tailoring. Preference for these kinds of work is no doubt shaped by the currently prevailing social norms of "men's work" and "women's work", as well as the prevailing developmental schemes which the respondents would like to access. Younger women especially who expressed willingness to work wanted part-time rather than full-time work, and younger urban women willing to work wanted assistance in skill acquisition.

Developmental schemes that provide access to cash income for such women willing to work in homes through a range of conventional and non-conventional work activities linked with the growing sectors of the economy is necessary to tackle female youth unemployment in the rural and urban areas. Expansion in the scale and coverage of microcredit for women with such credit schemes linked to a range of developmental inputs and accessed through peer group formation is indeed very vital to harness youth power for development as well.

These suggestions for policies are in the nature of both increasing and diversifying the opportunities for employment. However, the analysis of the gender issues has also revealed the likelihood of younger women attempting to fit into a patriarchal model that consequently does not enable transposing their subjective condition of "willingness to accept work at home" into "available or seeking work". Especially if their preference is to work at home, putting themselves as "available or seeking work" is rendered even more difficult as "available or seeking work" is generally associated with work outside the homes. It is therefore suggested that some administrative practice be evolved that enables young women over time to resist being fitted into a patriarchal model of role expectations which would enable them to transpose their "willingness" which is a subjectively passive condition of unemployment, into a subjectively more active condition of unemployment such as "available or seeking work". In fact, such a transposition would also over time change their preference for work at home to one of work outside their homes. Their reason for preferring work at home on account of involvement in domestic duties appears less convincing as there are also many others who work outside their homes and still combine it with domestic duties.

***Domestic Duties and Access to Income***

Clearly, the implications of the above analysis is that both rural and urban women engaged predominantly in domestic duties also engage in other work, some of it is clearly economic and some beneficial to the household. But they do not have access to a regular stream of cash income. Their willingness to take up work in their household is as much an indication of their desire to have access to cash income. Merely complaining about the lack of visibility of women's work and giving statistics about their involvement in domestic duties, or theoretical debates on valuation of women's non-marketed work in estimates of GDP are not sufficient for the empowerment of women in practice. What is needed is to make access to cash income possible for them. Many feminist studies across the world have highlighted the importance of access to resources and income to strengthen women's bargaining position in the households (Dwyer and Bruce, 1988). Patriarchal dominance in households can only be countered by strengthening women's bargaining position (Sen, 1990; Agarwal, 1997; Katz, 1997).

It is of utmost importance to incorporate gender sensitivity into many of the public policies and poverty alleviation programmes. It needs to be noted that women engaged in domestic status in their usual principal status but are engaged in gainful work in their subsidiary status, although comparatively fewer in number, are probably the most desperate category of women. Their involvement in other activities such as maintenance of the kitchen garden, dairy, poultry and all other beneficial activities in both the rural and urban areas are significantly higher than those women engaged in domestic duties in their principal status and without work as subsidiary status are. The data for this group are not provided here, but are available in the NSS reports. This is an indication that these women are in desperate need of resources and income, and probably also the most over-worked group of women. If in spite of that they have expressed a willingness to take up work, their needs ought to be given priority in policy formulation.

Such policies that seek to make available a regular stream of cash income to women engaged predominantly in domestic duties should also be extended to cover women engaged in subsistence occupations. The NSS 46th (1990–1991) round data on small trading units indicated that there are 41 lakhs women workers in small trades in the country, of whom 33 lakhs are in rural areas (*Sarvekshana*, Vol. XXI, No. 1, 72nd Issue, July-September, 1997). About 40% of them (about 13 lakhs) are engaged in gathering of uncultivated materials and firewood for small retail trades. These are subsistence occupations that entail long hours of work and no capital whatsoever.

It is absolutely necessary to formulate development policies that are sensitive to the differing requirements of different sections of women – young and old, rural and urban, married and unmarried, educated and illiterate and so on. Also, there are regional differences regarding a variety of women's preferences that need to be taken into account.

Even if housework is not perceived as an activity that enhances women's status and self-esteem by women themselves and by modern society in general, for the many millions of women involved, it is a daily compulsory round of drudgery. Moreover, it is a well-known sociological fact that in the patriarchal societies governed by norms of custom and tradition, there is a tendency for women to withdraw from paid outside work as household income increases. The norms of patriarchy dictate that men protect the honour of women and provide for the support of women. This undermines women's bargaining power within the household. It does seem necessary that the unrealistic Western feminist ideal of an earlier phase of the feminist movement in the West, viz., the wages for housework movement, be made into a realistic agenda of providing access to a regular stream of cash income to housewives in a developing country like ours.

### *Registration of "Willing" Women*

One administrative measure that could be taken up is quarterly or half-yearly registration of such women willing to accept work at home on a voluntary basis with the village panchayats and town municipalities or even in the post offices at no cost to the women through the passbook method. Schemes of financial assistance for such women, to take up their preferred activities, should be linked with the frequency and regularity of registration – something akin to employment exchange registration but, here, primarily for home-based workers. Periodic registration by the women themselves voluntarily will obviously change their own perceptions of themselves as those who are "available or seeking work". This will bring them within the fold of the labour force.

With such a registration scheme in vogue, it is possible to conceive of innovative transmutations in the existing policies of weaker section – lending or microcredit schemes. For instance, any group of eight or 10 women possessing passbooks with continuous registration can voluntarily form a peer group and approach any bank for microcredit and serve as mutual guarantors. Microcredit schemes through peer group formation have been generally recognized as successful and even the central government has encouraged it with the formation of the "Rashtriya Mahila Kosh". It is a widely known fact that women everywhere, both rural and urban, often join and manage informal credit groups themselves, such as the chit funds. This policy of registration and making access to microcredit possible through a simple process will expand the scale of microcredit for women in the country. It will help young women to free themselves from the patriarchal role expectations that constrain them.

## Note

1. Versions of this chapter analysing earlier rounds of NSS data have been published. See Kalpagam, U. (1999) 'Women, Work and Domestic Duties: Income Planning for Housewives', *The Indian Journal of Labour Economics*, pp. 567–580, Vol. 42, No. 4. Also see Kalpagam, U. (2000) 'Gender Dimensions of Youth Unemployment in India', *The Indian Journal of Labour Economics*, Vol. 43, No. 4, pp. 673–682.

# 3

# Globalization, Liberalization and Women Workers in the Informal Sector[1]

Globalization of the economy has affected the women workers in the informal sector in the country in rather contradictory ways. Liberalization of the economy, distinctly since the early 90s and with tendencies since the mid-80s, is a distinct break from the earlier development strategy of mixed economy and public sector, import-substitution industrialization and so on. Specifically, the new development strategy seeks to make the allocative processes of the markets more efficient and this is sought to be achieved through a greater integration with the global markets through export promotion, foreign direct investments in the economy, as well as through reducing controls, fiscal deficits, subsidies, divestment of public sector units, liberalization of financial markets, power sector reforms, increase in infrastructure investments among others. These policies constituting the reforms packages are to bring about a structural adjustment in the economy. Structural adjustment policies will impact on the labour market as well, just as they are likely to impact on commodity and factor markets. The new development strategy does acknowledge that in the transition period, the unequal burdens of the structural adjustment on different sections of the population need to be counterbalanced through appropriate "safety net" mechanisms. Although a little late in its realization, the new development strategy also acknowledges that weak players on the market require their capabilities to be enhanced in order to increase their entitlements and the state has to play a proactive role in the social sector and human development.

The impact of the new development strategy on women workers in both the rural and urban informal sectors of the economy is explored in this chapter. Drawing empirical evidence from a wide range of micro studies, it examines the recent changes in the working conditions of women workers in various industries and occupations. Factors such as increased agrarian impoverishment risks on account of both the market forces as well as natural causes, increase in rural-urban migration and urban development impact on the informal sector as well as the women workers in that sector, feminization of poverty against the general trend of a decrease in poverty merits inquiry, as well as how the spheres of production and reproduction operate in ways that are constraining rather than enabling for women workers in the informal sector.

Research on the impact of economic reforms on women's employment suggests that although women are getting more jobs, they are by and large employed in low-skilled jobs, usually non-unionized, and experience adverse working conditions such as low wages and long working hours (Dev, 2000a). Macro level data on employment reveal only the trends in the economy. It is necessary to complement the macro trends with micro level evidence to appreciate fully the impact of the far reaching changes ushered in by these processes. Dev (2000a) also notes that the impact of liberalization on employment and labour incomes depends on whether one is viewing it at the macro level or micro level. This is because integration with the global markets proceeds at an uneven pace across industries and regions, and liberalization signifying a shift in policy regimes comprises of a set of policy instruments that are both general to the economy and particular with respect to industries and commodities. Also, due to the domination of the informal sector in the employment share, one may not find an increase in unemployment rates at the macro level, but micro level experiences could tell a different story (Dev, 2000a).

The advent of globalization in India has seen an increasing informalization of employment, including home-based, contract and casual labour. Coupled with this is the complete absence of any wide spread system of social security in this sector. The unorganized sector accounts for 96% of the women workers. Women are concentrated in the lower end of the spectrum, their work is insecure, low paid, irregular and often unrecognized. They balance between children, home and work, and their income is not commensurate with their work (Jhabwala and Sinha, 2002). If we examine the impact of globalization on employment and income of women workers, some distinct trends are visible: First is the loss of existing employment without creation of new employment. Second, employment changes occur due to mechanization and new technology. Third, employment changes take place due to informalization and fourth, there is creation of new employment opportunities. In what follows, selective micro level evidence of the impact of globalization and liberalization on women workers in the economy is examined.

**The Effects on Women Workers**

Liberalization emphasizes export growth among others in the economy. This augurs well for women's employment in those export industries in which female employment intensity is high. Equally, it also subjects those export industries without an adequate domestic market to the vagaries of international competition. In the crafts sector for example, employment has grown at a fast pace. This sector now directly links a big traditional rural economy with the far distant metropolitan and global markets, providing visibility to a large number of artisans through their work. The sector witnessed a dramatic increase in the number of crafts persons: from 48.25 lakhs persons during 1991–1992 to 81.05 lakhs in 1997–1998 (Jhabwala and Sinha, 2002: 2039).

In the manufacture of certain export commodities, such as garments and electronics, women's employment has generally been high. Many of the manufacturing units in these industries have been in the informal sector under some kind of subcontracting relations, either process subcontracting or product subcontracting, with either larger units or with merchant exporters themselves. Numerous studies of these industries have shown that there is a great deal left to be desired in terms of the nature of work and working conditions (Kalpagam, 1994). Manufacturing units of these export commodities that are in the formal sector also resort to the informalization processes thus rendering some workers, especially women, as informal labour in the formal sector. Such conditions also prevail in units located in export processing zones (EPZs). Vanamala (2001) has through a case study of an engineering unit shown that informalization and feminization are prevalent in the formal sector non-exporting industries as well.

In export processing zones around the globe, women workers are generally preferred over men. A number of factors have been cited for this preference, such as the relative docility of women workers and the fact that women are "nimble fingered". In a study of the Noida Export Processing Zone (NEPZ), it was found that women constitute a substantial section of the workforce and the general working conditions are far from satisfactory (Rajalakshmi, 1999). Established in 1985, it employs 17,000 workers in its 143 units of whom 4,000 are women workers. The proportion of women workers had increased between 1994 and 1996. In 1997–1998, the export earnings of NEPZ was ₹ 2,938.60 million, and more than two-thirds of the export earnings were from the women intensive industries namely electronics, garments and gem and jewellery units. But many women workers did not receive even the minimum wages and often received lower amounts than what they had signed for. Many other statutory benefits too were denied to them. Further by granting the units in NEPZ the status of "public utility", it has made it difficult for workers to resort to strikes without going through the process of conciliation. Union activity is discouraged, and the fear of job loss is so strong that women apparently refuse to talk about the working conditions (Rajalakshmi, 1999). Though these women are employed in registered NEPZ units, their conditions of work are not very different from those in the informal sector. Soni-Sinha (2006) analysed the gendering of the labour process in the hand-made jewellery units located in NEPZ as well as those in Delhi. The hand-made jewellery units in NEPZ did not employ women but migrant male workers from Medinipur in West Bengal. She noted that different discursive practices are deployed in the exclusion of women and these discourses help to construct women as housewives and men as breadwinners. She also found that the male artisans and employees in the NEPZ units worked in unhygienic and unsafe conditions with most of them residing in the workshops on account of difficulty in finding rented accommodation. Mazumdar (2007) also noted the long and uncertain hours of work were coupled with low piece rate wages. Nor is NEPZ the exception; many studies indicate that the Santacruz Electronics Export Processing Zone (SEEPZ) in Mumbai is also noteworthy for its poor working conditions.

Indian products are displaced by imports leading to loss of jobs. Thousands of women silk spinners and twisters of Bihar have totally lost their employment due to the import of "China-Kores" silk yarn. Weavers and consumers prefer this yarn as it is somewhat cheaper and also has a shine. Similar displacement has come with the entry of large fishing vessels into Indian waters. These vessels take away the fish that used to be collected by Indian fishing vessels, thereby destroying the employment of fishermen and women fish sorters, dryers, vendors and net-makers. In Gujarat, women gum collectors who were picking from the *Prosposis julifera* (Baval) trees lost their employment due to the import of cheaper gum from Sudan. In almost all cities of India, the rag pickers lost some of their employment due to import of waste paper from developed countries (Jhabwala and Sinha, 2002: 2037) Liberalization has also resulted in massive imports of consumer electronics items from East-Asian countries, especially China, that are competitively priced with domestically manufactured or assembled products. Such competition often results in price-cutting strategies by domestic firms, with the costs of it being transferred on the vulnerable labour groups such as women workers. This results in further informalization and worsening of working conditions in formal and informal production units.

Liberalization of agriculture has many facets. Some of them are the promotion of agro-products exports, reduction of fertilizer and power subsidies to the agricultural sector, rolling back of state interventions in food grains market such as price support and procurement policies, pricing of irrigation services, liberalized imports of agricultural and food products, and increased penetration of agriculture by multinational seed and biotechnology firms. Liberalization of agriculture is part of the WTO agreement to which the Indian government is a signatory and the objective is to make the Indian farmers globally competitive. By April 2001, trade barriers on 825 farm items were lifted in the country. The WTO agreement on agriculture is already affecting the farmers adversely. There is surplus stockpile of food grains co-existing with hunger and starvation. We have already noted that in large parts of the country, women are being pushed back into agriculture on account of lack of employment opportunities in the rural non-farm sector and the bulging of the urban informal sector. Simultaneously, farming households are rendered more vulnerable undermining the livelihood security of both women and men. Another aspect of the impact of globalization and liberalization of the rural sector is the conversion of rural into data for the new patent regime, thus undermining indigenous and traditional knowledge. Women of indigenous communities were not only involved in field labour but also in conservation practices. Sharpe and Spivak (2003) note, "the virtualization of the rural and its transformation into data within finance capital involves and does indeed obliterate women's practices" (p. 612).

Also, the liberalized imports of food products under the WTO agreement are bound to affect domestic farmers severely. Cheaper imports of edible oils, skimmed milk powder and commodities such as coconut, apples and grapes have made the domestic farmers feel the impact in the shape of depressed prices and low demand. With the lifting of quantitative restrictions from April 2001, the Indian market is flooded with cheap imports thus throwing out small and marginal farmers from agriculture. Needless to say, a majority of women cultivators are small and marginal farmers in the country. Political concern in the country is veering around the suggestion of seeking a "livelihood security box" in the AOA (Agreement on Agriculture) of WTO much like the "green box" protection given to the USA.

Equally, the emphasis on non-traditional agro exports such as oilseeds and soybeans has resulted in a reduction of acreage under inferior cereals in central and western India, which are now taken over by these export crops, thus affecting the food security and nutritional requirements of the poorer classes (Patnaik, 1996). In many parts, inferior cereals were considered women's crops, as they were engaged in their cultivation and were predominantly subsistence rather than commercial crops. In parts of south India, paddy land has been given over to shrimp farming for exports, only to be abandoned with the decline in shrimp productivity and the land is now unfit for paddy cultivation. The paradox of endemic hunger in regions of commercial cropping is in fact a shocking reality (Menon, 2000). Moreover, risks associated with commercial crops for export has made the farmers more vulnerable to impoverishment and destitution with unfavourable weather conditions. Farmers take more loans for growing commercial crops such as cotton or groundnut in anticipation of higher profits with higher productivity than under subsistence cropping, and impoverishment risks attendant with the failure has in recent years led to a spate of suicides by farmers in Andhra Pradesh and Karnataka. Such debt burdens on agricultural households impact on women as well. Women, whose farmer husbands commit suicides have the responsibility of running their homes, doing cultivation work and repaying the debt.

The fishing industry is yet another instance where liberalization is undermining the livelihood security of the traditional fisher folk. The waters of the Indian Ocean have been given over to more than 25,000 vessels from South Korea, Japan, Thailand, Taiwan, Russia, the USA and the European Community to promote industrial fisheries and aquaculture, thus destroying the environment and livelihood options of millions of traditional fisher folk (Rajalakshmi, 1997). Women's roles in traditional fishing communities such as unloading from boats, helping in net-making and local retailing are now seriously undermined. In the

Chilka lake, the largest brackish water lake spread over three coastal districts of Orissa – Puri, Khurda and Ganjam, traditional fisher folks are asserting their rights over the prawn fishers who are engaged in "culture fishery" for a booming prawn export market rather than "catch fishing", thus destroying the marine life of the lake. About 2 lakhs people in the 145 villages around the lagoon have for several years resisted the encroachment of the "prawn mafia" which have wrested control of the traditional fishing grounds in order to cultivate prawns. Being squeezed out of their area of operation, traditional fisher folk experienced a dwindling of their catch. For most fisher people who depend on the lake for their livelihood, poverty has been stalking them (*Frontline*, 2000). The fisheries sector of Kerala too is confronting the same problem between the traditional fisher folk and those in the mechanized sector engaged in large-scale export business. The increasing marginalization of the traditional fisher folk and the depletion of resources caused by induced imbalance in the marine ecosystem have prompted the State Planning Board's Taskforce on Livelihood Security of Fishing Communities to put forward a radical reform measure. The acquarian reform measure like its agrarian reform predecessor seeks to confer on the traditional fisher folk the exclusive legal right to own fishing craft and gear, and the statutory right for first sale of their produce. Such a radical reform would make illegal the operation of a large number of mechanized and motorized craft and the business activities of a number of traders who are not from the fishing community. Persons who undertake such activities will be given the option of phasing out their fishing units in three years or accepting compensation. The boats thus acquired will be allotted to *bona fide* fisher folk or used to create a village level sea safety and resource management fleet or may even be sunk to create artificial reefs or trawler barriers. The traditional fisher folk in Kerala resorted to agitation to demand grass-roots level reforms in the fisheries sector (Krishnakumar, 1999).

Livelihood security has assumed increasing importance. This is not to suggest that only sectors and industries that are integrated with global markets impose such vulnerabilities on those dependent on these industries. A large number of other occupations and livelihoods are also imposing insecurities on the people owing to lack of rights and statutory protection. For instance, denotification of protected areas is undermining the livelihood security of many tribals who were dependent on forests, flora and fauna in these protected areas as it now throws open these areas to other settlers who often engage in business activities such as quarrying and mining in the peripheries of these protected areas, or open the way for hydel projects and road construction that hardly benefit the tribals anyway (Kothari, 1999). Similarly, quarry workers in many parts of the country are in perpetual debt bondage to quarry owners and contractors since the workers do not hold the lease themselves for quarrying. An innovative scheme to empower women quarry workers was tried out a few years ago in Pudukkottai district of Tamil Nadu where lease rights for quarries were given to groups of women under the Development of Women and Children in Rural Areas (DWRCA) scheme. But once the lease rights expired, the administration yielded to the quarry lobbies and the situation has reverted to the old situation despite the interventions of a union on behalf of the women workers. Women who had started to send their children to school as a consequence of greater control over household earnings were later forced to withdraw the children from schools as their incomes had fallen (Sivaraman, 1999).

Measures to promote competition include unhindered imports so as to create a level-playing field for domestic manufacturers. The Exim policy announced in March 2000 removed quantitative restrictions on imports with respect to 714 items. While the Indian consumers' interests were to be protected both by the range of choice in commodities available and in terms of prices, as imported goods were to be cheaper and would thereby also force down domestic prices, the small producers' interests were not taken into account. As many as 229 items of the list of 714 on the "freed" list were agricultural commodities and 37 were textile products. Commodities such as fish and fishery products, tea, coffee, milk, spices, vegetables and rubber products figured prominently on the list of items that could be imported freely. The policy threatened the livelihood of millions of primary commodity producers. Sridhar (2000) has noted that many of these producers cultivate small landholdings or operate tiny business units and their asset base is poor. For instance, women run a substantial proportion of the milk-producing units; and a large section of the milk producers consists of those with small livestock holdings. In case of the fisheries, women bore the indirect impact of the reduction in the incomes of fish-workers households as fishery imports meant to undercut the high profit margins of the middlemen were transmitted to some extent as lower shore prices as well.

There was formerly a reserved list for small-scale industries by which as many as 812 items could only be produced by them, now only very few items are on the reserved list. More and more of the small-scale industries have to compete with the products from the international market, and there exists an anomalous situation where these products are not allowed to be produced by the large domestic companies but foreign competition is permitted (Mahalingam, 2000). In general, small manufacturing enterprises, especially the Own-Account Manufacturing Enterprises (OAMEs) are female intensive. So, it can be expected that forcing small enterprises to face international competition will affect female employment as many of the enterprises find it difficult to survive. The toy industry is one such where the domestic market is flooded with cheap imports from China. Toy-making is a traditional cottage industry in many parts of the country and employs predominantly female family labour. Now the traditional toy-makers are suffering on account of lack of demand, and many traditional skills in the making of particular toys that women especially possessed are on the wane.

Many other household industries are also facing similar problems as they undergo restructuring to face the competition in the international market. The handloom industry is the biggest employer after agriculture with an estimated 10 million workers employed directly and indirectly, of whom four million are employed directly by the industry. It provides employment to a very large number of women, of whom a significant proportion is family labour. The handloom industry faced severe problems induced by the policy changes (Krishnakumar, 2000). Liberalization emphasized export growth, which resulted in large-scale export of cotton, yarn and dyes, and lowered their availability and increased their prices in the domestic market. The mushrooming of unregistered power looms and the economic crisis in 1997 in South-East Asia, a major export market for handlooms, sent the industry spiralling into a recession. In many parts of Tamil Nadu, a major region of handloom production in the country, the looms were lying idle, thus affecting weaving households in both the cooperative and non-cooperative sectors. Indiscriminate reduction of subsidies to weavers in Andhra Pradesh threatened the livelihood of weavers and compelled a few to commit suicide (Hirway, 1996). With the Multi-Fiber Agreement being phased out, the industry had to face global competition. But without an adequate domestic market, it was exposed to the vagaries of international competition, and the livelihoods of weaving households, largely in the informal sector were put in jeopardy.

The silk industry feared imports of silk yarn, which was justified on account of yarn shortage. Although the government claimed that only the import of raw silk of Grade 2A and above was to be allowed, which quality of yarn was not used in the traditional silk sarees, there were protests from the government of Karnataka and the organization of mulberry farmers and reelers. Mulberry cultivation is undertaken predominantly by small and marginal farmers in Karnataka, and significant numbers of women are engaged both in mulberry cultivation as well as rearing of silk worms. Large numbers of women are also employed as reelers and twisters, as also in the production of hand-spun yarn in cottage-based industries. It was feared that these women would be pushed out of their jobs. Silk productivity in India is lower as compared to China and needs to be increased (Menon, 1999). Imports of cheap yarn from China also rendered havoc to the industry in Varanasi.

Even the Mill sector of the textile industry was pushed into a recession in Coimbatore on account of liberalization policies. The industry expanded its capacity such that excess capacity plagued the industry. Many mills closed down and retrenched the workers, and others functioned below capacity. To take advantage of the lower labour costs in the rural and interior parts of the neighbouring districts of Coimbatore, small spinning factories mushroomed in what were once cattle sheds or coconut groves. Many retrenched workers from the Coimbatore mills began to be employed in these units at wages that were only a third of the wages they received in the Coimbatore mills. Although women constitute only a small proportion of the mill sector workforce, they too were affected (Sridhar, 1999).

How the dislocating effects of globalization can lead to reconfigurations of gender roles and gender power relations has been highlighted in Bremen and Patel (2004) in their study on the closure of textile mills in Ahmedabad city. The workload of women became more burdensome and their main task as household manager has been split up into many roles, some of which were fulfilled simultaneously. Describing the inclusion of women and children in the labour process due to the process of liberalization they say that more than any other criterion the enormous drop in income as a consequence of mills closure illustrates the degree to which the quality of life of the former workers deteriorated. After the closure, the weavers earn their living in small enterprises and do the same work, but for much lower pay with work uncertainty. Most ex-mill workers, who earned a daily wage between ₹ 90 and 100 at the time of closure (at eight hours a day, six days a week, this amounted to between to ₹ 2,000 and ₹ 2,500 per month) now earn less than half of that, while a sizeable minority has to make do with less than a third of what they earned before. The fall in income has forced other members of the household to work. The stigmatization of Dalits also made it difficult for their wives to find paid work. Muslim women were not permitted to work outside the home, while the higher Hindu castes such as Patel were restricted by similar taboos. The wages brought home by the man of the house was sufficient to allow these customs to be observed or imposed, but after the closure of mills there was no longer the financial freedom for such sensitivities. Home-working allowed Muslim and some Hindu women to take an active part in earning income without having to break the social code for appropriate social behaviour. But in many cases, women and children were also forced to work outside the house. While many women from OBC could be found selling vegetables in the markets and streets, their Dalit sisters became domestic servants or moved around as scrap collectors, scavengers and rag pickers. Wife of one mill worker started scrap collecting since he lost his mill job in 1994, for which she left home daily at 4 a.m. Many houses have been converted into workshops, in what used to be living space machines have been installed, which are operated early morning until late at night by men, women and also children. The balance of power in the household has drastically changed since the men lost their mill jobs and most women had to join in the search for additional income.

Yet another industry that employs a significant number of women and that was poised for growth under liberalization is the food-processing industry, which suffered on account of imports of processed food. Gujarat where a number of women were employed in food processing has suffered the most (Hirway, 1996). The industry witnessed automation taking place in the field of pickle-making, and dry salty eatables killing the jobs of millions of women who were engaged in home-based and cooperative production for their livelihood.

A study of women and work in the cashew industry in Kerala reveals that with the development of a strong trade union movement there, a powerful state sector emerged that took care of the welfare of the cashew workers in the organized sector. It is during this period that the minimum wage legislation was implemented, but with the integration of India into the global market and the policies of liberalization the nature of development has limited the scope of employment. Today, it is an open system where, with the informalization of the sector there is putting out of work to small units where wages are meagre and the rights of workers are unprotected to make the export-oriented sector more competitive in the globalized economic environment. The case is quite similar to other industries such as garments and the fish-processing sector where too the same dismal conditions of work prevail (Lundberg, 2001).

In some industries, the growth in exports and/or an increase in domestic demand have increased women's home-based employment. Knorringa (1999) has shown that in the Agra footwear industry that has always been characterized by instability, there was a shift in demand from dress shoes to casuals. This caused a tremendous increase in women's employment in the 90s, although the industry as a whole was faced with the threat of unemployment and underemployment. Certain operations became labour intensive in the shift in demand. Upper-making which is a labour-intensive task began to be farmed out to women who worked from their home, and there are reportedly some 6000–10,000 women engaged in this. In the case of small workshops, upper artisans bring home the work which is then done by their female relatives as unpaid family workers.

If the illustrations that have so far been provided all indicate the negative consequences of globalization and liberalization, it becomes relevant to ask why then it has been suggested as growth inducing in the first place. The idea of trade-propelled growth has been with us at least since the time of Ricardo. The historical experience of imperialism and colonialism has proved how trading relations between unequal partners can be detrimental to the weaker ones. The current phase of globalization induces optimism about its growth potential for developing countries on account of the rapid technological changes that have taken place, the shift from mass-production techniques to fragmented-production techniques that allows for spatial division of labour beyond the single factory, making off-shore production and on-shore assembly possible, the rise of Information Technology (IT) industry globally and the rapid increase in service sector employment in most economies. Critics of the globalization process, on the other hand, are pessimistic about its favourable impact on large developing economies. Not only have the terms of trade been always adverse to developing economies, vis-à-vis the developed market economies, but the unequal global power now manifested in numerous global institutions such as WTO, IMF and World Bank only reinforces their unfavourable position in the world economy. The structural malaise of surplus labour in large developing economies like India means that the globalization process makes the labour force more and more vulnerable. China has however emerged as a global power with its vast and cheap labour force.

It is generally believed in policymaking circles that globalization by linking the urban centres to the global economy will give a boost to urban growth. Critics of globalization accept the premise of urban growth although they view it as a consequence of agrarian destabilization on account of the new trade policy and consequent rural-urban migration. The critics hold the view that employment generated as a consequence of urban growth would only be the growth of low productivity employment and poverty with negative effects on the quality of urban life (Kundu, 2000). Kundu (2000) has shown that in the state of Gujarat there is a dramatic rise in the share of female employment in communication and other services. These constitute the residual service sector which is absorbing a large share of the incremental female workforce and has very low productivity. His analysis cautions us about making generalizations on urban growth and employment structures, for there are rather complex dynamics at the regional level. Citing from a SEWA survey, Mahadevia (1998) notes that between 1992 and 1995, wages in most of the trades in Ahmedabad were more than 50% below the minimum wages, confirming that supply-induced growth of employment for women especially, is not a conducive kind of employment.

Globalization is governed by norms of flexibility both with regard to labour use as well as in a wide range of other strategies. Breman (1999) has noted that the current trends of contractualization, enforced migration and casualization all facilitate the flexibilization of labour. Systemic biases in employment, with respect to factors such as caste, gender, education and skill are likely to be reinforced under an unregulated labour regime with pervasive flexible contracts. In the context of flexibility, the prospects of women's employment in the formal sector are rather unfavourable. There does exist contrary evidence on flexibility and feminization as Banerjee (1999) has noted. In some of the multinational pharmaceutical firms in the Mumbai/Thane belt, over time women workers have been displaced on account of subcontracting or farming out, and the relentless search for cheap labour under globalization typifies certain sections of the workforce such as women, migrants and children as "cheap labour". How a new industry that emerged in the era of globalization in South India is using gender ideologies as a mediating force in labour relations is analysed by Kapadia (1999) for the case of the synthetic gem-cutting industry. This industry study clearly shows that while analysing the impact of any policy on women, it is necessary to deconstruct the category "women" as they are not a homogenous group. Caste, age and education differences between women engender differential impacts on them.

At the upper end of the informal sector requiring both education and skills, the emerging IT sector has provided numerous opportunities for women through outsourcing and delocalization of work with numerous other contrary effects. A global team explored the potential employment opportunities which telework could create for women in India (Mitter, 2000). Telework refers to a specific mode of distant working, where employees or freelancers offer their services using telematics, on a site that is geographically separated from the main office. Telework offers women, at least potentially, the scope to combine family with career (Mitter and Sen, 2000). Home-based teleworking is still very small even in a dynamic centre like Mumbai, although in some individual companies the home-based workers have increased 10–fold since 1990. In the software sector, women do not generally provide services in the field of software but are engaged in e-publishing and back office processing, activities considered less complex and needing less monitoring (ibid.). More women in the digital economy are employed in online information processing work such as medical transcriptions or data entry. In Mumbai, while young women work in offices of foreign airline companies in the export processing zones, older women, with young children, opt for and receive home-based telework. Women receive a very large proportion of remote processing jobs (ibid.). However, these new types of jobs can be accessible only to the fairly well off and educated sections of the society. Even jobs that are at the lowest rung of the telework hierarchy may not be available to the poorer sections.

Employment in the IT industry and IT-enabled services sector are not all in the formal sector, although estimates of the size of the IT informal sector are difficult to obtain. It is believed that the IT informal sector has grown in the recent years largely due to outsourcing, teleworking, STD kiosks, share brokering, etc., using the new information technology (Unni and Rani, 2000). The productivity in these activities is generally high even though they are in the informal sector, which is likely to play a positive role in reducing poverty and income disparities. Unni and Rani (2000) noted that IT has brought about a change in the nature of work. According to them, there is no longer a guarantee of lifetime employment but lifetime employability. The IT industry offers the new security of *employability security*.

There is an intensified stratification among women workers with some very visible women earning high wages in executive positions or in jobs in the beauty and glamorous sectors or in high tech offices, and the others are the underpaid, overworked, poor women who lack any job security or legal protection. There are therefore fears of "increasing polarisation within society and within the workforce" (Gothoskar, 2000).

**Neoliberal Urbanism, Women and Migration**

Given the fact that cities and urban centres are the sites of neoliberal restructuring projects, proponents of neoliberalism place much hope on the urban-led growth. Whereas in the earlier phase of development thought, both the urban bias of development and uneven development were viewed negatively, in the contemporary period there is much hope on uneven urban development as a growth promoting strategy, through neoliberalism catapulting growth everywhere. Urban restructuring projects are going on at a frenzied pace all over the country rapidly transforming the urban landscapes. The Indian state through its liberalization and reform processes seeks to create market-friendly urban sites conducive for the motives and aspirations of global capital and of those harnessed to the circuits of global capital as surplus extractors. In cities, new kinds of office and residential spaces have come up dotted with swanky shopping malls, high-rise building, multiplexes, metros, flyovers, bill boards and neon-lights that it all seems as though Indian cities are hoping to become a New York or a Shanghai. Neoliberal urbanism is sustained by cheap migrant labour.

According to the 2001 Census, the total population of India was 1.02 billion, of which 307 million (30%) were reported migrants by place of birth, this proportion is slightly more than what was reported in the 1991 Census (27.4%). While rural to rural migration within the country is 53.3%, migration to urban areas account for nearly 35% of all the migration, of which rural to urban migration is 20.5% and urban to urban migration is 14.3%. Nearly 60% of the urban male migrants and 59% of the urban female migrants had migrated from the rural areas.

Migration rate defined as the percentage of migrants in the urban population was 25.9% among the urban males and 45.6% among the urban females. While 55.7% of the urban male migrants migrated for employment-related reasons, only 2.7% of the urban female migrants did so for employment reasons as marriage-related migration is the more dominant one among females. It appears that migration strategy for women to access the opportunities of neoliberal urbanism are far less than that of men as indicated in Table 3.1.

NSSO 64th round data (2007–2008) present the urban female migrants activity before migration and after migration by usual principal activity. Tables 3.1 and 3.2 below present the data.

**Table 3.1**

*Distribution (per 1,000) of urban female migrants by their usual principal activity status before and after migration for different categories of migrants during 2007–2008 – All India*

| *Usual principal activity status* | *Female* | |
|---|---|---|
| | *Before migration* | *After migration* |
| Self-employed | 31 | 53 |
| Regular employees | 19 | 59 |
| Casual labour | 31 | 31 |
| Worker | 81 | 142 |
| Unemployed | 7 | 5 |
| Not in labour force | 910 | 853 |
| All | 1000 | 1000 |

*Source:* GoI, NSS Report No. 533: *Migration in India 2007–2008*, June 2010.

Table 3.1 shows the distribution of migrants by activity categories before and after migration. It is clear that after migration there is an increase in the proportion of those in self-employment and as regular employees as also an increase in work participation.

Table 3.2 below presents the after migration status for each status category before migration.

**Table 3.2**

*Distribution of migrants by usual principal activity category after migration for each usual activity before migration All India urban female 2007–2008*

| *After Migration →* | | *Self-employed* | | *Regular wage salaried* | | *Casual labour* | | *Total employed* | | *Not in labour force* | | |
|---|---|---|---|---|---|---|---|---|---|---|---|---|
| *Status Before Migration ↓* | *Industry* | *Agri (01–05)* | *Non-agri (10–99)* | *Agri (01–05)* | *Non-agri (10–99)* | *Agri (01–05)* | *Non-agri (10–99)* | *Agri (01–05)* | *Non-agri (10–99)* | *Unem-ployed* | *Not in labour force* | *Total* |
| Self-employed | Agri | 10.3 | 9.2 | 0.0 | 6.7 | 2.6 | 3.7 | 13.0 | 19.7 | 0.0 | 67.3 | 100 |
| Self-employed | Non-agri | 0.0 | 51.3 | 0.0 | 8.1 | 0.2 | 2.1 | 0.2 | 61.6 | 0.0 | 38.3 | 100 |
| Self-employed | All (incln.r.) | 6.1 | 26.4 | 0.0 | 7.3 | 1.6 | 3.1 | 7.8 | 36.7 | 0.0 | 55.5 | 100 |
| Regular wage salaried | Agri | 3.4 | 0.0 | 1.7 | 0.0 | 0.0 | 0.0 | 5.1 | 0.0 | 0.0 | 94.9 | 100 |
| Regular wage salaried | Non-agri | 0.4 | 4.0 | 0.0 | 68.1 | 0.0 | 0.8 | 0.4 | 72.9 | 1.4 | 25.3 | 100 |
| Regular wage salaried | All (incln.r.) | 0.4 | 4.0 | 0.0 | 67.6 | 0.0 | 0.7 | 0.4 | 72.3 | 1.4 | 25.9 | 100 |
| Casual labour | Agri | 3.1 | 8.5 | 0.6 | 11.6 | 17.3 | 13.6 | 20.9 | 33.7 | 0.3 | 45.0 | 100 |
| Casual labour | Non-agri | 0.9 | 4.4 | 0.0 | 10.2 | 0.2 | 51.0 | 1.1 | 65.6 | 0.6 | 32.8 | 100 |
| Casual labour | All (incln.r.) | 2.8 | 7.9 | 0.5 | 11.6 | 14.8 | 18.7 | 18.1 | 38.2 | 0.4 | 43.3 | 100 |
| Total employed | Agr | 6.0 | 8.7 | 0.4 | 9.6 | 11.3 | 9.6 | 17.7 | 28.0 | 0.2 | 54.1 | 100 |
| Total employed | Non-agri | 0.3 | 20.7 | 0.0 | 40.0 | 0.1 | 7.3 | 0.4 | 68.0 | 0.8 | 30.8 | 100 |
| Total employed | All (incln.r.) | 3.5 | 14.0 | 0.2 | 23.0 | 6.4 | 8.6 | 10.1 | 45.6 | 0.5 | 43.8 | 100 |
| Not in lab force | All | 0.8 | 3.4 | 0.0 | 4.2 | 0.6 | 1.4 | 1.4 | 8.9 | 0.3 | 89.3 | 100 |

*Source:* GOI, NSS Report No. 533: *Migration in India 2007–2008*, June 2010.

In the case of urban females, it is evident that 43.4% moved out of the labour force after migration perhaps on account of difficulty in getting jobs. This is especially true of females engaged in agriculture prior to migration as 67% of those self-employed in agriculture, 95% who worked as regular wage employees in agriculture and 45% of the female casual workers in agriculture moved out of the labour force after migration, which indicates that women agricultural workers find it difficult to obtain urban employment after migration. Of those self-employed in non-agriculture prior to migration, 51.3% continued to remain self-employed after migration, 8% became regular wage workers and 2% obtained casual employment. Of those engaged as regular wage/salaried workers prior to migration, 68% continued to remain as regular wage/salaried workers and 4% became self-employed and a negligible percentage worked as casual labour. Twenty-four per cent remained outside the labour force indicating their non-preference for casual labour in the absence of regular wage employment. Of those engaged as casual labour in non-agriculture before migration, 51% continued to remain so after migration, 10% obtained regular wage employment and 4.4% became self-employed. Women engaged as casual labour in agriculture before migration had some occupational and status mobility as 13.6% got jobs as casual labour in non-agriculture, 11.6% got regular wage employment, 8.5% became self-employed in non-agriculture and only 17% remained as casual labour in agriculture with 45% opting out of the labour force. The overall scenario for women is that the urban employment opportunities after migration are limited and many move out of the labour force. There is also very limited status mobility and the majority of them continue to remain in their former status as self-employed, regular wage and casual labour. Clearly, their low levels of literacy, skills, their multiple roles and sexual division of labour appear to have constrained and limited women's opportunities in the labour market through migration.

While women migrants to urban areas for purposes of employment can be stratified by age, education, marital status, class and occupational background, and each of these factors determine both the success of the migration strategy and the work they are able to secure, it is evident that a large number of young migrant women work in the factories coming up in the EPZs and the newly industrializing towns. Research has revealed the poor working and living conditions of women workers in garment, electronics, food processing and fish canning factories, and has also highlighted that young single women are subjected to eve-teasing and sexual harassment as well. Despite these, most young women factory workers find it a liberating experience to move into towns and cities from rural areas and lead an independent life, more often financially supporting their families including their sibling's education and marriage. Wolf has noted that it is important to understand how women's identities are affected by shifts in work, and by the meaning of labour, wages, consumption and modernization. She notes, "it is possible to capture the significance of change by asking individuals about their understanding of it from various angles and in several ways. This then can be linked with a broader discussion of material conditions, belief systems, and ideologies. The iterative comparison of the two levels of analysis offers the best path to comprehend how social transformation may shift the meaning that people assign to work, femininity, masculinity, marriage, consumption and the like" (Fernandez-Kelly and Wolf, 2001: 1245). Such kinds of studies are now emerging of women factory workers in India. Warrier (2010) has examined changing women's identities in the context of migrant workers in the fish-processing factories and how globalization has brought in new forms of work and survival strategies.

Poor women migrants to urban areas are drawn into low-paid domestic service as well. Recent trends show that all big cities have become centres to recruit poor women as domestic workers. The lack of education and skill limits their choices of employment when they come to the big cities, and they become easy victims of exploitation. The non-availability of jobs in rural or tribal areas facilitate continuous supply of women workers to cities, a major reason of this being a sharp increase of middle class women in employment. The National Commission for Women attempted to address some of these concerns through a Domestic Workers (Registration, Social Security and Welfare) Bill, 2008, the fate of which is yet to be decided. The proposal seeks to establish a compulsory registration procedure for all domestic workers, including part-time and full-time workers, the setting up of a Domestic Workers Welfare Fund, the registration of placement agencies, the regulation of working conditions, and the imposition of fines and imprisonment for violation of the provisions of the bill. The recent efforts of the ILO to introduce a Convention on Domestic Work will strengthen the ongoing efforts in bringing a national legislation into force.

**Lifestyle Changes and Employment**

The widening inter-regional differences in growth and the regional differences in human development suggest that there may be varying impact of the globalization process on growth centres and non-growth centres. Methodologically, most studies on globalization effects on workers have used the all too familiar classifications of regular, casual and self-employed which as administrative categories help in policy design and debates. But these often club together too many diverse and heterogeneous elements. Sectoral studies such as export-oriented units or IT industry serve a role in highlighting the problems of workers in these industries. The overwhelmingly negative analysis of globalization effects in terms of livelihood insecurities masks the simultaneous processes of rejuvenation in certain regions and the immense lifestyle changes that have occurred. Studies that consider the changes in the "form of life" are likely to cover a wider range of occupations that has emerged as a consequence of globalization.

A labour market analysis that does not differentiate between sets of traditional jobs, non-traditional jobs and new jobs as a result of globalization will fail to understand the linkages and dynamics between these. If in policy circles starting from the ILO the concern is for "decent work", then we ought to stress on the possibilities and potentialities of generating "decent work" as a result of globalization, especially if the possibilities of "decent work" in traditional and non-traditional jobs have eluded us for long. Understanding the varied nuances of vulnerabilities, insecurities and discrimination in the changed context requires us to take cognizance of lifestyle changes not just at one end of the spectrum in terms of destruction of traditional livelihoods but the changes at the opposite end as well. Whether "decent" jobs are generated in the process of lifestyle changes is still a moot question but new perceptions, expectations, norms and vulnerabilities are engendered as a consequence, which even if it affects only a section of the population do have wider ramifications.

The uneven impact of globalization across regions means that changes in the "form of life" are only evident in regions of high growth, while in the backward regions of low economic growth there has been only minimal employment growth as a consequence of globalization. By juxtaposing ethnographic evidence from two such regions, the city of Chennai in Tamil Nadu which is in a region of high growth with significant expansion of new jobs and the region of Uttar Pradesh, Allahabad, with low growth and general backwardness the vulnerabilities, insecurities and discrimination in the different labouring worlds under globalization become evident.

Significant lifestyle changes have taken place in recent years in Chennai city. All over the city, apartment complexes, new shopping arcades, malls, restaurants and eat-outs have come up apart from the Export Processing Zones and the IT parks. These changes have generated new jobs as well as new aspirations and expectations. These have also impacted on the old jobs.

Kuppamma, a long time resident of a slum in Mylapore observed, "these days, boys don't seem to do well in studies like the girls. There are lots of jobs and all the jobs now available are only for girls. A salesgirl in Suriya Sweets gets ₹ 2,000 a month". This perception of jobs being available for young girls, those of high school and above, is quite widespread in Chennai. But they do not question as to why one does not encounter older women as sales girls in these new kinds of shops that call themselves as "Departmental Stores". Is it a myopic exuberance on everybody's part and are these young girls going to be retained by these shops as they grow older? Is there some insecurity that is still not very perceptible? Or is it the expectation that once they get married they will either withdraw from the labour market or seek some other job? Even among these sales girls, there are differences in their vulnerabilities and mobility. A proud father said that he sent all his four daughters to the USA for higher studies and the youngest one was a sales girl in a Pizza shop in Adyar corner before she went to Syracuse for media studies. For most salesgirls, such opportunities are not common. But surely the well groomed youngsters working in some of the shops in *Spencers Shopping* Mall do not belong to the same class as those in smaller department stores such as *Subiksh* or in the numerous Xerox shops that dot the streets of Chennai. These are clearly the young high school pass girls of nearby slum families whose mothers are mostly domestic servants. As new sales jobs come up, they reinforce gender-based division of labour. While young girls are hired as counter and sales girls, they rarely work as waitresses in restaurants. A few restaurants have started hiring young girls at the counter or in the parcel section but not as table waiters. But women work at food vending on the road sides especially when meals are cooked and served for autorickshaw drivers and so on.

Sowriamma, a former construction *chithaal* (helper) cannot do the construction work anymore as her husband in one of his violent bouts caused injury to her neck and shoulder. Now she has no income and laments "to get five rupees I have to suffer five beatings". But with much hopefulness she declared that her daughter was studying "plus two, Commerce group". Being illiterate herself, she does not understand the word "commerce" and is merely repeating what her daughter has told her. She is hopeful that her daughter will get a job as a sales girl for ₹ 2,000 a month, or even something better, and that to her and those of her class is a significant intergenerational progress. Intergenerational mobility to higher income and higher status jobs, especially for women and girls is prevalent in Chennai, a region of high growth on account of globalization. A domestic servant's daughter or a construction worker's daughter can and do move up with school education.

However, in the life cycle of any single worker, the chances of upward mobility both for high status or high income jobs are not that encouraging, except when grown up children with better jobs begin to support their parents or force them to withdraw from work. Although these days it is quite difficult to find young girls offering for work as domestic servants in many localities of Chennai, the ones who are already in it can now increase their incomes only by working for more number of households. Receiving an average wage of ₹ 700–800 per month from each household, most domestic servants work on an average in three-four houses and net in a salary of ₹ 2,000–2,500 per month.

How has construction workers' lives changed in the city of Chennai that has been experiencing a boom in construction activity? Whereas earlier construction workers were associated with a particular *maistry* (the chief construction worker), now the greater and more flexible demand for the number of workers has led to the emergence of local construction labour markets. In various city spots, construction workers assemble from 7.30 in the morning and hang out there till 10 a.m., for any *maistry* to come and offer them work for the day. So workers, both men and women, face uncertainty everyday as to whether they will get a job for the day or not. I approached a group that seemed both colourful and cheerful one morning, thinking they were on an excursion trip to some temple when they told me they were waiting for the day's work! With all the road digging and paving going on, one would expect that construction workers contracted by government departments get a better deal. But that is far from the case. Women construction workers engaged in road work, just let their children hang around for the whole day with no facility of creche or pre-school class. It was indeed a poignant moment when a child of three years came and asked me for a pen (probably he wanted a colour sketch pen) to sit and scribble to while away the whole day there. But more shocking was the case of a construction worker hired by a private contractor who tied up her child like a dog so as to prevent him from running onto the streets and meeting with an accident. When I told her I will complain to the police for child abuse, she looked bewildered for she thought she had done the best thing under the circumstances.

Studies on discrimination generally do not consider discrimination among women themselves. Here is an example where it is even difficult to classify whether discrimination has been eased or has been strengthened! Caste-based discrimination in terms of division of labour has existed in Chennai for long. Scheduled caste women, known in Tamil as "Parayal or Paratchi" never worked as domestic servants because the higher castes will not employ them. So invariably, "Naicker" caste and other OBC castes dominated as domestic servants in the city. Some of the scheduled caste women joined the municipal corporation as sweepers, for they had traditionally been involved in roles as scavengers. Today, with a multinational firm having bagged the contract for sweeping and garbage collection, one can see young girls/women and young men in smart uniforms doing the street cleaning. And these are not scheduled castes (some may be), but the association of scheduled caste with municipal sweeper job has now vanished. All of a sudden the stigma of "paratchi" associated with "sweeper" women seems to have been erased. So have the jobs of toilet cleaning in bungalows and homes of middle class done by the scheduled caste women disappeared in the last decade as bungalows got pulled down to give way to apartments. Many domestic servants of Naicker and OBC castes who earlier refused to clean toilets now do so in the apartments where toilets and baths are attached. But the scheduled caste women have not yet managed to enter the homes of upper castes as domestic servants. Some in the cleaning jobs work as "ayahs" in hospitals, nursing homes and schools, and the younger girls seek factory employment. Many rag pickers in the city are from the scheduled castes as well.

Factory employment is both in export units and non-exporting units, though the former units employ more young women in certain industries such as garments and electronics. Whereas more than 20 years ago young women seemed to prefer factory employment despite all odds, today the preference is clearly for work as sales girl. Young girls of lower castes, lower education and recent migrants move into factory work in export units and the others for jobs as sales girls. Women who joined nearly 20 years ago in some export units still continue to work in those units. But such prolonged work does impact on the health of the worker as the case of 41–year-old Vasuki working in an export garment unit, who often goes to work without taking any food. One day she fainted at work and was rushed to the ESI hospital. She had severe hip and thigh pain, and despite nine injections was still lying bedridden after nearly a week. From what her aged mother Radhamma described to me of her daughter's condition, it appears that Vasuki will not be able to take up the tailoring work even after she gets well. All of a sudden, Radhamma's seemingly secure old age has been shattered.

Many of the city's elderly are very vulnerable lacking as they do any means of income or old age security. Parents of NRI children can by paying a sum of ₹ 10 lakhs move their aged parents into a well-provided Senior Citizen's home along the East Coast road, but the elderly of the poor and lower middle class seem to bear the brunt. Suddenly homes for orphaned elderly have sprung up and I saw a small home in Thiruvanmiyur converted into one such with folding beds laid out right from the front gate, being over crowded with their meagre belongings bundled by their side. But Selvi's mother came up with an altogether different alternative. When she could no longer work in the paper factory where she was doing odds and ends, she set up a roadside temple of Mariamman both as a calling from God and as a vocation. Practising as a "folk astrologer" in the temple, she makes a living on the temple earnings after first providing for all the temple needs.

There is a lot of euphoria over IT sector development in Chennai fuelled further by the mass production of IT graduates. Young girls of all caste backgrounds are encouraged to go for IT, and Bachelor's and Master's degrees in Computer Applications (BCA/MCA degrees). Many have expressed surprise at the fact that women are now in such large numbers in Engineering colleges, whereas a few years ago they were still few in number. Parents of young girls even send their daughters to Bangalore or Pune if employment offers come up and seem to cherish the fact that they are employed in such MNC/American company. Many however have their eyes set on jobs in foreign countries and for women with IT qualification, a marriage to a similarly qualified IT professional with the chance of going abroad is a much sought after goal. But processing jobs in medical transcription, back office or call centres can be less attractive in reality on account of long and odd hours, and jobs being essentially on contract basis have a built-in bias against permanency. Youth unemployment in Chennai would have been worse off without the IT boon, and for young educated women the market has certainly aided in their liberation in terms of education and employment even as it seems to have reinforced the role of marriage. High technical education and high income for women has not made them choose other lifestyle alternatives to marriages.

However, it is not the reinforcement of marriage ideal that has been worrying many, but the widespread dowry demands that have become onerous for many middle- and low-income families of most non-Brahmin castes. Among Brahmins, dowry has recently transformed into "decent marriage", with "decent" being subjectively defined by the concerned families' socio-economic status. While many agree that the rise in dowry demand is in many ways linked to the changes in the "form of life" associated with globalization, few except the women's organizations are willing to resist it. Marriage halls too have seen upgradation in recent years along with shopping malls and that has jacked up their rental charges as well. But marriages have recently spawned new business ventures for there are shops with boards that say "Marriage contracts undertaken" where they undertake everything related to marriage like putting *pandals* and preparing "*seer murukku*".

An encouraging development is the emergence of a number of private employment agencies that match up the demand for particular kinds of household workers such as cooks, patient attendants, drivers, ayahs, baby sitters, etc., according to the specification from a registered list of such workers for a commission. Some of these are exclusively for women and are women-managed organizations. These help especially the recently arrived migrants in their job search. The difficulty of finding appropriate jobs and appropriate workers even under conditions of optimistic growth and buoyancy cannot be overstated.

It is often stated that there is ease of entry into informal sector jobs, but the reality is far from it. Not only do skill and education act as barriers but some informal sector jobs need much more than a good reference. The nature of entry barriers in all informal sector jobs and the implications of that for labour market participation of all household members, especially of women need greater probing. There is optimism among some that globalization has increased informal sector employment, which are now more regular and more so for women. But this needs to be cautiously assessed against the background of all hidden costs and burdens.

Lifestyle changes have been accompanied by technological changes in non-IT sectors as well. Earlier when cars were fewer, there were many car mechanic workshops. Now with more cars on the roads, most of these workshops have vanished because the fabrication technology of automobiles has apparently changed. New kinds of technicians are needed, such as air conditioners and elevators maintenance technicians, but these are all predominantly male jobs.

Perhaps the one sector that has generated a considerable number of jobs in Chennai is the health sector. The medical topography of Chennai has dramatically changed in the recent years with numerous small and big private hospitals, clinics, charitable dispensaries and varieties of diagnostic testing facilities and laboratories. Women and young girls find employment in the health sector as doctors, nurses, ayahs, para-medical staff such as physiotherapist, secretarial staff, and a few as lab technicians and as technicians in ultra-sound scan and echocompucardiography, but the bulk of the technicians jobs in other diagnostic facilities are still male jobs.

What is truly ironic is despite all the healthcare facilities, most informal sector workers are not covered under any health insurance. This has placed the sick and elderly under difficulties and has made poor workers very vulnerable. Over the years, healthcare has become costlier not just on account of medicines but the range of diagnostic tests that the doctors require these days. The poor and low-income women could somehow manage treatment for short and simple sicknesses, but what is truly burdensome are the surgeries as even the bumped rates in government hospitals are prohibitively high. While the poor are facing such burdens on the health front, the rich are seeking large sums as risk cover by taking out insurance policies with high premiums.

Thus, the effects of globalization in a centre of relative prosperity and "not so virulent patriarchy" have allowed women to access new opportunities. But new insecurities and vulnerabilities have compounded with the older ones, while new demands, expectations and vulnerabilities as a consequence have arisen on account of widespread lifestyle changes with feelings of relative deprivation becoming stronger. Today, even children of low-income families ask for "Midi, Jeans and T-shirts" from their parents as birthday gifts, and those parents who find it difficult to buy them experience a sense of relative deprivation.

Chennai's sense of well-being and hopefulness is not found in a region of relative backwardness, Allahabad city in the state of Uttar Pradesh. Lifestyle changes ushered in by globalization in other urban centres such as residential complexes, new shopping malls are only slowly catching up and therefore there is much less of construction activity, development of property markets or the development of health infrastructures, IT sector, etc. It is doubtful even if the effects of globalization become stronger in this region in terms of lifestyle changes, whether the women would be able to access the opportunities, it being a region of "strong patriarchy". Women in this region still live under a kind of *purdah*, such that unlike Chennai, one does not see women moving around much in public spaces, engaged in economic activities in independent capacity and so on. The Human Development Index (HDI) and Gender Disparity Index (GDI) for this region are low relative to Tamil Nadu. Unless the patriarchal grip is released, it is unlikely that women can access the benefits of globalization. It can only be surmised that under such a context women will experience greater vulnerabilities. The hypothesis that is suggested here is that the uneven impact of globalization across regions needs to be complemented with the understanding of the uneven chances of women accessing its benefits, which is dependent among other factors, on the social conditions of patriarchy in the region as well.

Recently, an article in *Hindustan Times* (January 9, 2011) did a similar comparison of Bolangir in Orissa, one of the poorest districts in the country and Nellore in Andhra Pradesh, the richest and fastest growing. It reported that new entrepreneurial opportunities in Nellore such as sale of mobile phones made some people wealthy in a matter of a decade, even as the construction of a new port at Krishnapatnam caused traditional fisher folk to lose out on fishing activity and were compelled to become truck cleaners for trucks carrying iron ore to the new port. In both regions, women and girls had fewer employment opportunities. More of local comparative studies could give more insights on local opportunities and impacts for women as a consequence of globalization.

**Wages and Incomes in the Informal Sector**

So far we have analysed the micro evidence of the effects of globalization and liberalization on women workers in the informal sector. Although a small percentage is in the high growth and high productivity IT sector, the bulk of the informal sector women workers are in low-paying, unskilled and semi-skilled jobs with little or no possibility of mobility and with little or no welfare benefits. Globalization has been accompanied by informalization and fragmentation of employment resulting in falling real wages, erosion of labour rights, increased hazards and environmental degradation, longer hours of work, increasing quotas, growing poverty and unemployment. The human and social costs include the destruction of families and erosion of the social fabric.

In general, women receive lower wages than men. This is true across all occupations from agricultural labourers to informal sector and factory sectors workers. This difference in wage rates cannot be fully explained as owing to differences in education and skill level. Sex discrimination on the labour market does take place. While education tends to lower the wage gap, the gap remains high even after controlling for education. Kingdon (1999) shows that only 22% of the male-female differences in wages were due to education; 78% of the wage gap was due to higher returns on education in the case of men than of women. Chadha (1999) has noted that the male-female wage differential is widest at the level of illiterate workers and gets totally obliterated at higher educational levels. Further, the male-female wage differentials appear to have widened after liberalization (Deshpande and Deshpande, 1999). In 1987–1988, education narrowed the gender-based wage gap, but after liberalization, it did so only after the woman had completed her secondary education.

According to Unni (1999), the real agricultural wage rates for both adult women and men have been stagnating in the 90s, after a period of increase in the 80s spurred largely by the diversification of workforce into the non-agricultural sector. The real wage rates of the rural non-agricultural sectors tended to decline in the 90s. Unni (1999) notes that stagnating real wages in the agricultural sector as a whole implies less favourable conditions of employment for women agricultural workers in the recent years. The All-India ratio of male wage earnings to female wage earnings in agriculture declined in the 80s, and thereafter it ceased to decline and stagnated in most states till 1996. In some states such as Bihar, Maharashtra, Tamil Nadu, Andhra Pradesh and Karnataka, there was a relatively faster rise of male wage rates in 1993–1994, thus widening the male-female earnings gap. Women in agriculture received low wages, often below the prescribed minimum.

For rural women in agriculture to overcome the discrimination they face on the labour market, Chadha (1999) has underlined the importance of acquiring education and skills. Educational attainment according to him is a highly facilitating support for a shift from agriculture to non-agriculture. Emphasizing that the future job market would be highly education and skill-intensive, the vast majority of illiterate women workers in rural India would have a much more difficult job market situation to face.

Jhabvala (1999) has noted that the low wages in the informal sector leads to high levels of poverty, in terms of calorie intake, healthcare and education – as reflected in the human development index. She attributes the existence of low wages in the informal sector to the functioning of labour markets and how they are affected by both market and non-market forces. These non-market factors in rural areas refer to the state of economic and social relations between employers and workers. Workers are often under some tied kinds of arrangements with employers either on account of debt bondage, caste ties, customary use of village or private lands for fodder or because of the system of *jajmani* relations. In all these instances of tied arrangement, the employer has the power to determine and push down the wages. These non-market conditions have an even more constraining effect on women as it severely restricts their mobility and prevents them from taking up remunerative jobs. Much of the informal sector jobs are supply-induced employment, which also accounts for the low wages. Often the labour supply to this sector in the rural areas and in urban areas through migration increases on account of lack of access to water or destruction of forest resources on which their livelihoods depended.

Not only do women workers in the informal sector face low wages and discrimination, but they also have to combine multiple tasks such as domestic work, childcare as well as multiple jobs even in the informal sector. There has been very little alleviation of domestic drudgery both in rural and urban areas for low-income women; if at all the burdens have increased with problems of water, sanitation, fuel needs, public distribution schemes, homestead land and housing, urban transportation, medical services, etc. A study, comparing women's activity patterns in four states – Gujarat, Meghalaya, Mizoram and Kerala – reported that nearly 22% of the women's time in a day was spent in household activities, either indoor or outdoor, and leisure accounted for 9–10%, during which time anyway women were engaged in community activities (Sriram and Ganapathy, 1997). Moreover, the conditions of work in numerous occupations are very poor and often hazardous. Women informal sector workers too in some regions are compelled to labour nomadism. Women and working girls run the risk of sexual abuse by employers and contractors; often the male members of their families make discreet inquiries before a woman accepts job at a particular workplace (Breman, 1996). Bonded Kol tribals working in the Shankargarh quarries are so afraid of the contractors that they even lock up the women in their homes for fear of contractors' sexual oppression on them (Roy, 2000). In the era of globalization in the 90s, there was a growing suspicion that violence against women in all spheres has markedly increased.

Trends in poverty, according to Dev (2000b), present conflicting results, but the general impression gaining ground is that both rural and urban poverty rates have declined in the 90s, although the rate of decline may not have been as high as it was in the 80s. Patnaik (2007) has strongly argued that the NSS estimates of the rural poor for 1999–2000 and 2004–2005 are severely underestimated, and that neoliberalism's deflationary expenditure policy by treating the agricultural sector as a "soft" target has let capital formation in the sector to stagnate in real terms. Also, inequalities in consumption distribution have increased in both rural and urban areas (Dev, 2000b). Non-income indicators such as education, health and nutrition present rather mixed evidence. The share of government expenditure for primary education and health has in recent years declined. Oommen (2000) analysed the 50th round NSSO data on food consumption and has shown that nutritional levels have fallen below the prescribed standards both with respect to calories and protein consumption. This will have implications for maternal and child nutrition and will increase morbidity and mortality. Panchamukhi (2000) has presented disturbing data of a decline in the percentage of deaths by type of medical attention received before death, suggesting that medical attention for the needy is on the decline. It is clear that women workers in the informal sector suffer multiple vulnerabilities. It is necessary both to identify them across occupations and regions, and address these issues in various policy formulations so as to provide them and their families a decent living.

Trade unions in India have raised concerns over globalization as women faced threats of voluntary retirement schemes and transfers to difficult places, job freeze and downsizing and outsourcing, and the implementation of new economic policies put their job security in grave peril. Women are under pressure to leave their jobs. Women are also being pushed to unhealthy work conditions, devoid of unions and denial of minimum social security in the Export Promotion Zones and Special Economic Zones. The instances of sexual harassment at work place are also growing. The atrocities on women are growing in the post globalization era as more of consumerist culture is promoting denigration. Growth of consumerism in the process of globalization has literally shadowed the laws to curb dowry and dowry-related violence. Another impact of globalization is displacements, migrations and extreme poverty situations in absence of livelihood; the scenario has pushed many a women of destitute families into flesh trade.

An ILO report entitled "Global Employment Trends" noted that particularly hard hit have been women and youth, who often have jobs that are vulnerable to economic shocks. The report noted that unemployed workers pushed into informal sector jobs in search of work faced even more uncertainty due to the sector's almost total lack of unemployment or social security coverage. The ILO has placed women as the largest discriminated group at workplace. Women constitute the single largest group discriminated against at the workplace with low wages, adverse working conditions, low rate of employment and greater insecurity. The rate of unemployment is higher among women compared to men. Discrimination can occur at every stage, from recruitment to education and remuneration, occupational segregation and at the time of lay-off. Women tend to be employed in a narrower range of occupations than men, and are more likely to work part-time or short-term; they also face greater barriers to promotions and career advancement. Even though export-led industrial development has opened many occupations to women, inequalities remain in terms of pay, hierarchy and promotion. Occupation segregation also persists in new areas of work related to information and communication technologies. Government policy can play a major role in either exacerbating these insecurities and ill-effects or secure and support the rights and livelihoods of all their citizens, including women workers.

## Conclusion

Many feel that today globalization is not an option but an indisputable fact of life and that the forces of globalization should be harnessed to benefit human welfare and to limit some of its undoubtedly adverse effects (Bardhan, 2001). By and large, the responses from the women's movements have been either a total rejection, or a cautious assessment and selective appropriation, or an ideologically backed internationalism that appears at times contrary to their own empirical analysis. Hensman

(2004) sees in all anti-globalization the ugly side of nationalism, even as she herself has been a pioneer on studies on flexibilization, subcontracting and the insecurities of informal sector employment for women. She would also disapprove of the conflation of globalization with economic policies and insists that it is a phase of capitalism that must be understood as evolving in all its complexity. Krishnaraj (2003) notes that feminists' responses to actual and possible effects of economic reforms on women's position, and the rising violence in the society has been more in the form of a generalized anxiety rather than clear analysis and understanding of the nature of polity and changes therein; the nature of economic reforms and how they have been carried out; policy shifts in many areas and their impact on different sections of women. In a later chapter, we will explore the possibilities of evolving multiple securities and securing gender needs of women informal sector workers.

## Note

1. This is partly a revised and expanded version of the paper published in Amitabh Kundu and Alakh Sharma (eds): *Informal Sector: Perspectives and Policies*, New Delhi: Manohar Publications, 2001. It also draws from another paper by U. Kalpagam and Binod Narayan "Vulnerabilities, Insecurities and Discrimination of Women Workers" published in *Man & Development*, Vol. XXVIII, No. 3, pp. 23–44, September 2006.

# 4

# ICT and Women in the Informal Sector*

A distinguishing feature of the globalization process is the space-time compression made possible through the worldwide spread of information and communication technologies. This has made possible even remote corners of the world to be connected with one another. Seemingly isolated villages of India can now transact with the world at large. Globalization and ICT studies are now cognizing the implications of such a transformation that is underway. ICT is seen as enabling developing countries to "leap frog" on the development trajectory.

This chapter attempts an assessment of the ICT needs of poor women in the informal sector, many of whom are self-employed micro-entrepreneurs and the impact of these technologies on their livelihood and well-being, by differentiating these technologies as computers, internet and cellphones. In so doing, it shifts the focus from the more common supply-driven approach to the much needed demand-driven analysis and highlights the urban-rural and gender digital divide in terms of access, usage and impact.

There has been considerable interest on the gender impact of ICT and the ways in which it could empower women (Anand, 2002; Huyer and Carr, 2002; Faulkner and Lie, 2007). Studies have inquired into issues of access, training and skills acquisition, the kinds of employment these technologies have generated, the nature of such work and gender issues related to it like wage disparities and labour market discrimination (Hafkin, 2002; Mitter, 2004; Antony and Gayathri, 2008). These studies deal with educated women possessing high literacy skills (Kelkar

* A version of this was presented jointly with R. Asha and S. Nandini, Programme Cordinators of WWF (I) at the International Seminar on *ICT4D and Microenterprises* at IIT, New Delhi in March 2010.

et al., 2002; Umrani and Ghadially, 2003). There are very few studies on how ICTs impact poor women (Gurumurthy, 2006).

Studies on the use of ICT by women entrepreneurs, some adopting an enterprise perspective and others within the gender and livelihood perspectives (Heeks et al., 2004; Buskens and Webb, 2009) have examined how microcredit and ICT could be used to promote women entrepreneurship, have sought to analyse the entrepreneurial traits among women that motivate them to adopt ICTs, and of the ways women's businesses could be promoted through e-commerce (Sharma, 2003; Ndubisi and Kahraman, 2005). These studies too are concerned with educated women entrepreneurs who are not the low-end entrepreneurs of the informal sector of the developing countries. Recent studies on the use of mobile phones by low-income African women have assessed women's communication needs, their quest for business self-sufficiency and the ways ICT could promote women's rights through network formation (Bantebya-Kyomuhendo, 2009; Abraham, 2009; Comfort and Dada, 2009; Sane and Traore, 2009). Studies on women entrepreneurship and ICT adoption in the Indian context are only now emerging.

The ICT for rural poverty reduction has received considerable attention (Arunachalam, 2002; Cecehini and Scott, 2003; Madon, 2004; Kumar and Best, 2006a; Singh, 2006; Urquhart and Kah, 2007; Saith, 2008; Tewari, 2008). Case studies have highlighted the successful initiatives in areas of rural healthcare, dairy cooperatives, revenue records and land deeds, rural postal system, extension training, rural telecentres, e-choupals and others such as the Warana experiment in India and the *Grameen Phone* of Bangladesh (Bhatnagar, 2000; Bhatnagar and Schware, 2000; Keniston, 2002; Kumar and Best, 2006b, Best and Kumar, 2008). In these studies too, the gender concerns have been highlighted only with regard to the training needs of women development workers and does not concern with the mass of rural women.

## Theoretical Framework and Methodology

The classical literature on women and technology concerned itself with changes in the labour process with the introduction of machinery under capitalist production and the ways in which women workers were incorporated in the new labour process or were as a consequence deskilled and/or rendered redundant (Kalpagam, 1994). The literature on technology has so far failed to distinguish clearly between technologies that change the labour process and consequently the labour-use pattern and the technologies that do not change the labour process but nevertheless bring about increased productive efficiency, profitability and other social benefits.

Within ICT too, it has been remarked by Heeks et al. (2004) that its application could be classified as "intensive" use such as computerized machinery used in production process and "extensive" use such as computers being used for administrative tasks such as maintaining firm records, etc. Women's access and usage of ICT are more likely to be in its "extensive" applications. Aminuzzaman et al., (2003) in their study on Village Phone Scheme in Bangladesh have distinguished technologies that have a ripple-effect and those that have segmentation impact. The latter effect technologies are those that segment the society into the modernized and the non-modernized sections contributing to uneven development, while ripple-effect technologies have an all round effect. It is also clear from their analysis that the ripple effects of technologies extend beyond the economic impacts to include other social effects as well, and they found the mobile phone to create such ripple effects in the Bangladesh rural society. Of the older ICT technologies, we could consider the transistor radio to have had ripple effects on the Indian society. Although not a communication technology, it was an information technology that was accessed by the poorer classes and which contribution to the evolution of a popular democratic culture at large can never be overstated.

With the emergence of the internet that allows for quick information transfers in a borderless virtual world, anthropologists and sociologists have been examining the potential of a networked society (Castells, 2006). Communication technologies like cell phones do not change the labour process but enable access to information that is likely to enhance productivity and profitability by lowering transaction costs. They also help to promote network growth in the society and increase the density of social interactions thereby reducing isolation, improving trust and the formation of social capital.

Alampay (2005) has suggested that Sen's "capabilities" approach could be used to assess the impact of ICTs as the adoption of ICT leads to expansion of capabilities of people, increases their choices and helps to choose the lives they want to live. Through ICTs their capabilities are expanded as people now gain more freedom that enhances their functioning as well, if matched with a set of entitlements. Drawing from Sen's conceptual repertoire of "capabilities", "choice", "freedom", "functioning" and "entitlements", Alampy (ibid.) argues that with universal access to ICT, people in diverse circumstances determined by age, gender, class, education, location, etc., will access ICT to improve their capabilities.

It is these theoretical issues that informed this research that attempted to study the impact of ICT adoption by poor women in the informal sector as part of the overall discourse of ICT4D. Foley (2004) suggests that there are four stages in studying the effect of ICT, namely awareness, access, skills and training, and the impact. It was felt that the factors and effects of ICT adoption at the level of the organization adopting a transformative strategy of women's empowerment, as in the case of the microcredit lending of Working Women's Forum (India) and those at the level of individual adopters of ICT are different, but when combined cause significant empowering effects on poor women.*

A random survey based on 100 urban and 100 rural women members of WWF (I) was conducted in July-August 2009. A questionnaire in the vernacular was canvassed to collect the data from members of four branches in three southern states of Tamil Nadu, Karnataka and Andhra Pradesh (Chennai, Adiramapattinam, Bidar and Narsapur). The rural sample aggregated respondents from three states and hence does not capture likely regional and cultural variations. The data collected relate to the impact of cell phone, computers and internet on the clients' own business, impacts on their household and in their personal well-being. Special emphasis was placed on inviting respondents to speak about the changes that had occurred over the period of time. Several discussions were also held to supplement the quantitative survey with qualitative data to offer insights into causes and consequences of problems as well as effectiveness of ICT. Each member was interviewed individually at their residences.

In what follows, we discuss the access and usage of ICT by poor urban and rural women and its effects on their livelihood and well-being.

## ICT and Women in the Informal Sector

Working Women's Forum (India) is a microcredit women's NGO that has been working for the empowerment of poor women in the informal sector for the last 30 years in the three southern states of Tamil Nadu, Karnataka and Andhra Pradesh, and has over the years touched the lives of over a million women. In order to promote women's solidarity and empowerment, credit is given to groups of women with the group leader

* Project Report *ICT and Informal Sector Development: Working Women's Forum (India) reaches out to poor women*, Working Women's Forum (India), Chennai, October, 2009.

acting as a grassroots leader. This has promoted solidarity among women who as a collective take up numerous issues affecting their lives and work, which strengthen their bargaining and decision-making power in their occupations and in their households as well (Chen, 1983; Arunachalam and Landwehr, 2003).

All the 200 women respondents of Working Women's Forum (India) are involved in low-paying informal sector work. The survey sought to examine the extent to which each of these ICTs (cell phone, computer, internet and e-mail) is being used by these women and the benefits gained on the livelihood and employment fronts, family and social matters, and access to public and community services, as such effects were considered to be empowering women. Empowerment is here understood to be both economic and social empowerment that includes access and control over resources, greater decision-making powers and less dependency on others. When women perceived benefits of ICT and claimed that it had been advantageous to them, then it was taken as an indicator that these technologies empower them.

All the 200 respondents are involved in informal sector work and have availed micro-loans for business from WWF (I). No loans have been given by WWF (I) to purchase mobile phones but many possess the mobile phone. The profile of the respondents according to age, occupation, literacy, education, language fluency and membership in the forum is presented in Table 4.1. Around three-fourths of the respondents in general were in the age group of 26–45 years, the economically active age group. Slightly less than one-third of the rural women were illiterate while only 13% of the urban women were illiterate. All else had varying levels of education ranging from primary schooling till college graduation, although nearly a half in the rural and urban areas had education only up to secondary level of 6th-10th standard. Seventy-four per cent of the urban women and 61% of the rural women reported that they could read fluently in their local language, while only 54% of the urban women and 60% of the rural women said that they could write fluently in their local language.

Occupation-wise, in urban areas, the women were predominantly engaged as service specialists (37%) such as tailoring, grinding, washerwomen, lace and coir making, housemaid, saleswomen, or engaged in micro-business (29%) such as cut-piece and sari sales, petty shop, vending snacks such as idly (rice cakes), etc., or as hawkers/vendors (13%) of flowers, fruits, vegetables. Among the rural women, a little over half (52%) were service specialists and only 5% were engaged in agriculture.

The survey sample consisted mostly of those whose membership in the organization is less than five years. Sixty-one per cent of the urban women and 67% of the rural women have received micro-loans from WWF (I) in the last five years. It is the general practice to give a second loan only after they have repaid the first loan. So, it can be surmised that the respondents represent a group that is considered more stable and of those who have proved their worth and it implies that they are seriously engaged in their micro-business. Such a proven group helps to better understand the links between microcredit, ICT including mobile phone and income enhancement. Timely and low cost microcredit helps these micro-entrepreneurs in their business, for they need not depend on usurious moneylenders for their working capital requirements. Carrying on their business transactions partly through the aid of the ICT and mobile phone is likely to enable better access to market information, suppliers and clientele, and efficiency in dealing with microcredit transactions as well.

**Table 4.1**

*Characteristics of respondents*

| *Features* | *Urban (Chennai) (%)* | *Rural (%)* |
|---|---|---|
| Age 26–45 years | 78 | 75 |
| **Literacy and Education** | | |
| Illiterate | 13 | 30 |
| Primary (1–5) | 13 | 12 |
| Secondary (5–10) | 49 | 50 |
| Senior Secondary (11–12) | 19 | 5 |
| Degree | 6 | 3 |
| Total | 100 | 100 |
| **Occupations** | | |
| Hawkers/vendors | 13 | 7 |
| Manufacturers/producers | 9 | 4 |
| Micro-business | 29 | 6 |
| Dairy products | 5 | 9 |
| Service specialist | 37 | 52 |
| Handicraft | 2 | 4 |
| Wage Workers | 3 | 4 |

*Cont'd...*

*Cont'd...*

| | | |
|---|---|---|
| Agriculture | 0 | 5 |
| Fish sellers | 2 | 9 |
| Total | 100 | 100 |
| **Membership in the Forum** | | |
| 1–5 years | 57 | 67 |
| 6–10 years | 33 | 18 |
| 11–15 years | 6 | 10 |
| 16–20 years | 3 | 3 |
| Above 20 years | 1 | 2 |
| Total | 100 | 100 |

*Source:* Survey data WWF(I), 2009.

## Mobile Phone Possession and Use

A significant proportion (76%) of the urban and 48% of the rural women possess mobile phones. Also, 86% spouses in the urban areas and 66% spouses in the rural areas possess mobile phone, clearly indicating that in three-fourths of the urban households and nearly half of the rural households of WWF (I) members there is more than one mobile phone in the household. Other family members such as children also sometimes possess mobile phones. Twenty-five per cent of the urban and 15% of the rural respondents' sons possess mobile phones. However, in the case of daughters, only 14% in the urban and 4% in the rural areas possess mobile phones. Clearly, there is some gender discrimination in mobile phone possession between sons and daughters. Only among 5% of the urban respondents both brother and sister have mobile phones. Whereas earlier, possession of landline phone at home was a marker of class status, the ubiquitous mobile phone seems to have lost its status as a class marker. None of the respondents who possessed mobile phones have had landline phones in their homes before; so clearly these are possessing phones for the first time, although they have used landline phones for communication through the paid PCO/STD booths either frequently or infrequently.

While mobile phone penetration has been quite rapid, still a little over half the rural respondents and nearly a quarter of the urban respondents do not possess a mobile phone. If "information poverty" can be indexed by the non-possession of mobile phone, there is clearly "information poverty" that needs to be overcome.

Forty-seven per cent of the urban and 21% of the rural respondents use the mobile phones frequently, and 29% of the urban and 27% of the rural respondents use the mobile phones infrequently. It was left to the subjective assessment of the respondent to decide whether their use was frequent or infrequent and no attempt was made to measure it and quantify it on a scale. However, most of the respondents claimed that they only attend the calls and sometimes give "missed" calls. In the case of "missed" calls, the caller just dials the number and quickly disconnects the call such that the call is recorded on the receiver's mobile but no conversation takes place. There is usually some prior understanding between the two parties over the message to be conveyed; in some instances the receiver may call back. The respondents claimed that they give "missed" calls because there is not enough prepaid balance in their mobile accounts to make a long duration call.

Seventy-five per cent of the urban and 84% of the rural respondents who possess mobile phones claimed that the other family members who possess the mobile phone allow them to use it. Although fewer rural women possess the mobile phone, their access to mobile phones possessed by others in the household is not restricted. In urban areas, more women face restriction on sharing the mobile phone, perhaps because the frequency of usage by women in urban areas was likely to be high thus escalating the cost.

The cost of mobile phone is the initial lump-sum investment that users need to spend which women informal sector workers may find burdensome, especially as retailers generally do not offer the facility of payment by instalments. Forty-one per cent of the urban and 23% of the rural respondents purchased a mobile phone from their own earnings. Table 4.2 shows the cost of the mobile phone owned by the members. It needs to be noted that 22% of the urban women and 16% of the rural women bought mobile phone costing between ₹ 1,501–2,000 ($32–$42), while only 7% of the urban and 2% of the rural women bought mobile phones costing below ₹ 1,500 ($32), although less costly ones are available on the market. Twelve per cent of the urban women and 5% of the rural women could afford higher priced ones. From the price of mobile phone, it is evident that these are the ones with basic features and with no add-ons such as camera, FM radio and internet as with these features the cost of the mobile phone would be more. Clearly, these women are using the mobile phone only for making calls for their communication needs in business and social life. The other features are not serving their needs, come with additional cost that they find difficult to afford and perhaps features they cannot operate.

**Table 4.2**

*Cost of mobile phone*

| *Price range (in ₹)* | *Urban (%)* | *Rural (%)* |
|---|---|---|
| 1000–1500 | 7 | 2 |
| 1501–2000 | 22 | 16 |
| 2001–3000 | 9 | 3 |
| Above 3000 | 3 | 2 |
| Those who bought from their income | 41 | 23 |

*Source:* Survey data WWF(I), 2009.

Thirty-five per cent of the urban women and 25% of the rural women who possessed mobile phones did not buy it from their own income, but were financially assisted by a family member in the purchase of the phone. With low income earnings, these women have other priorities in their expenditures relating to family's and children's needs. Sometimes the mobile phone is given as a gift from their spouse or children who perceive their communication needs. Table 4.3 indicates the person from whom they received assistance. Twenty-four per cent of the urban women and 10% of the rural women received assistance from their husband.

**Table 4.3**

*Assistance in purchase of mobile phone*

| *Family member who bought it for them* | *Urban (%)* | *Rural (%)* |
|---|---|---|
| Husband | 24 | 10 |
| Brother | 3 | 6 |
| Brother-in-law | 0 | 2 |
| Sister-in-law | 0 | 1 |
| Father | 3 | 1 |
| Mother | 3 | 1 |
| Son | 1 | 2 |
| Daughter-in-law | 1 | 0 |
| Sister | 0 | 2 |
| Those assisted by family members to obtain mobile phone | 35 | 25 |

*Source:* Survey data WWF(I), 2009.

In general, it can be seen that male assistance, from husband, brother, brother-in-law, father and son, has been crucial for these women to acquire the mobile phone. Thus, a simple lesson on bridging gender divide in mobile phone access for informal sector women is male cooperation. Such cooperation is likely if men also recognize the need for women to possess mobile phone. The necessity of communication between family members as urban lives become fast-paced with family members travelling long distances and work hours at different times are important factors for men to cognize women's mobile phone needs. One respondent observed that "the mobile phone is useful. I call up my husband to know where he is and what is he doing. Sometimes I also ask my husband to pick up the children from the school"; another respondent noted "when one is stuck in heavy traffic one can call up and inform home". Many have been quick to realize the efficacy of better communication and have sought to acquire more than one mobile phone in the household so that family members can communicate with each other.

Recharging the mobile phone is a recurring expenditure and the use of mobile phone in terms of calls dialled and duration of talk time depends on the recharge costs as perceived by the users. Table 4.4 indicates that 52.6% of the urban respondents incur monthly recharge expense in the range of ₹ 201–300 (US $ 4–6) which is the highest range and strikingly no rural respondent incurs expense of that amount. Clearly, the ability of rural mobile phone users to bear recharge costs is quite limited compared to the urban respondents. About 70.8% of the rural respondents incur recharge expense of up to ₹ 100 per month and 22.9% of the rural women incur only less than ₹ 50 per month as compared to 2.6% urban women.

**Table 4.4**

*Monthly expenses on recharge*

| *Monthly expense on recharge (in ₹)* | *Urban (%)* | *Rural (%)* |
|---|---|---|
| Below 50 | 2.6 | 22.9 |
| 50–100 | 31.6 | 47.9 |
| 101–200 | 13.1 | 29.2 |
| 201–300 | 52.6 | 0 |
| Total | 100 | 100 |

*Source:* Survey data WWF (I), 2009.

Table 4.5 indicates the frequency of recharge. Sixty-six per cent of the urban women recharge their mobile phone weekly, while only 25% of the rural women do so. Fifty-two per cent of the rural women recharge their mobile phone fortnightly. This is because urban women use their mobile phone more often for their business purposes. Rural women often have their markets and clients in their villages, and use the mobile phone less for business purposes. The weekly and fortnightly recharge when matched with the monthly expenses of recharge indicates that each time they recharge it only for small sums of money under the pre-paid scheme.

**Table 4.5**
*Frequency of recharge*

| *Frequency of recharge* | *Urban (%)* | *Rural (%)* |
|---|---|---|
| Twice in a month | 18.4 | 52.1 |
| Once in a month | 5.3 | 18.6 |
| Weekly once | 65.8 | 25.0 |
| Three months | 9.2 | 4.2 |
| Yearly once | 1.3 | 0 |
| Total | 100 | 100 |

*Source:* Survey data WWF (I), 2009.

Although the cost of mobile phone usage may be one of the lowest in the world, it is still important to explore ways of reducing the cost of mobile phone usage to the low-income groups. Some initiatives in technology and design towards this end that provide features such as call duration warnings, etc., are being thought of with some success (Deepak and Bhamidipaty, 2007).

### *Purpose of Using Mobile Phone*

The survey sought to probe the use of mobile phone for various purposes relating to occupation, family-related matters, social interaction and to access services. The responses indicated the following.

#### *Occupation and Livelihood*

Nearly 70% of the urban women who possess mobile phones use it frequently for occupation-related purposes, whereas only 27% of the rural women do so. Fifty per cent of the rural women who possess mobile phones use it infrequently for the occupational/business purpose and 23% of the rural women never use it for occupation-related purposes. This is not surprising as it is expected that urban women would use mobile phones more frequently for their businesses both because such activities are more varied and also requires information from and coordination with suppliers and clientele spread across the city, whereas in the rural areas both markets and clients are located close by for many small businesses.

*Family-related Communication*

In all, 65.8% of the urban and 64.5% of the rural women who possess mobile phone use it frequently to communicate with their family, while 34.2% of the urban and 35.4% of the rural respondents use it infrequently. There is not much difference between rural and urban areas and the use of mobile phone, for family-related communication is significant for both groups of women.

*Social Interaction with Relatives and Friends*

A total of 77.6% of the urban and 35.4% of the rural women possessing mobile phones communicate with relatives and friends through it frequently, while 22.4% of the urban and 64.6% of the rural women communicate infrequently. Clearly, urban women use it more for social interaction than rural women. Social networks in a city are more spread out than in a village that probably accounts for frequent social calls, while frequent social calls outside of the village area may be unaffordable for rural women and within village social calls are mostly considered unnecessary.

*To Access Other Services*

About Majority of the respondents claimed that they have not accessed other services. 31.6% of the urban and 22.9% of the rural women possessing mobile phones claimed that they use it infrequently and most of them have availed the service for having consultation with doctors regarding their problems and fixing up an appointment. Only one member said that she had called up the police when there was disturbance in her area.

Table 4.6 indicates the services accessed through mobile phone. Forty-eight per cent of the urban women and 22% of the rural women have used it to find out about matters relating to microcredit of WWF (I) and many use for communication with family and friends and for business-related purposes.

**Table 4.6**

*Important services accessed through mobile phone*

| *Services Accessed* | *Urban* | *Rural* |
|---|---|---|
| Enquiry about loan dates | 48 | 22 |
| Business purpose | 53 | 24 |
| Communication – husband/son/daughter/relatives/friends | 75 | 36 |
| Enquiry about house | 3 | 0 |
| Job enquiry | 4 | 0 |
| Enquiry about ration card | 7 | 0 |
| Communication with school correspondent | 1 | 0 |
| Gas booking | 17 | 14 |
| Exam results (12th) | 5 | 4 |
| Enquiry about power supply | 6 | 0 |
| Booking tickets, hire auto rickshaw | 15 | 0 |
| To enquire about insurance details of a dead member | 1 | 1 |
| Communication with parents for birthday | 3 | 1 |
| Business communication with friends | 2 | 0 |
| Pass information about loan dates to the group members | 1 | 0 |
| Enquiry about teacher training | 1 | 0 |
| To listen to music/alarm/torch/store number | 11 | 1 |

*Source:* Survey data WWF (I), 2009 (data refer to the number of respondents out of a total of 100 respondents in each group who claimed to have accessed the service).

In a study on mobile phone use among micro-entrepreneurs in Rwanda, Donner (2005) distinguishes its impact as "amplified" contacts as in the case of friends and "enabled" new contacts in business. He shows that the early possessors of mobile phone largely had it for business purposes and late possessors for amplifying social contacts and that over time there has been migration from business use to personal use and also shows how there has been a change in social and business networks. Such complex distinctions of mobile phone use in different time phases is difficult to undertake in the Indian context where mobile phone penetration is taking place rapidly, but as most of these women are first time possessors of a phone, it can be concluded that Donner's finding of mobile phones amplifying social contacts and enabling new contacts in business is equally valid here.

When inquired as to whether enterprising women were trying to set up an informal business of mobile phone service to earn some income, it was surprising that no one had done so. This is striking when viewed in comparison to the *Grameen Phone* success in Bangladesh. This could be on account of better coverage of telecom network in rural India than in Bangladesh. Most of them however claimed that they do give their mobile phones to neighbours and friends at times of emergency, but that they do not charge them.

**Perceived Benefits on Livelihood Matters**

When asked whether mobile phone has benefitted in livelihood and employment matters, 41% of the urban and 28% of the rural respondents claimed that it has been so. Twenty-nine per cent of the urban and 12% of the rural respondents used the mobile phone to access information on raw materials and prices, and 30% of the urban and 19% of the rural respondents said the mobile phone has improved the communication with the customers. Most are self-employed women and did not come under the purview of any employer/contractors. Some noted that now-a-days a few companies are conducting job interviews through phones, and hence it was both useful and desirable to have access to mobile phone. Even if they were initially inhibited in doing phone interviews, they felt the more one talks, the communication skills become better.

Across the spectrum of informal sector occupations, women reported that the use of the cell phone has helped them in business through information, orders, customer clientele and so on.

Mobile phone helps to boost business growth. A woman running a petty shop (called *kirana*) observed that customers call on the mobile asking for certain products to be delivered at their door steps. As most couples are working in the city of Chennai these days, they do not have time to come to the shop directly. This helps them deliver the products at their door step. She noted that the mobile phone not only helps in retaining customers but also helps in business growth. Most of the shopkeepers claimed some boost in their income when they have access to mobile phone, although the study did not attempt to quantify it. Another woman who is a tailor claimed similar advantages of possessing mobile phone. She observed that her customers call and enquire whether the clothes have been stitched and if it is very urgent they tell that it be finished soon, and make enquiries about the time of delivery of clothes. Another tailor observed that she was able to take more orders on phone and deliver it at the correct time. A cloth seller claimed that she placed her orders for the clothes (saris, cut pieces) a month before over the mobile phone and later collected them whenever she required. Also, markets in many rural areas open once a week and the vendors had earlier to travel long distance to obtain information on supply, demand and prices. In this way, time is not wasted and travel is made convenient and transaction costs are reduced for petty business as well as for customers.

Mobile phones help inquire details regarding product availability and access information on prices, quantities, supply and crowds at the wholesale markets from where vendors get their procurement. It helps to earn more in the business when they are connected with the market. Surprisingly, even fisherwomen found the mobile phone very useful for the fish business. They could inquire details regarding the availability of various fish and their prices in the bigger markets from where they procure. When the fish required is not available they do not go for purchase. This reduces travelling cost and time. Customers willing to buy fish also call to place their orders and with this the supply chain has now improved. Others such as flower vendors and vegetable vendors claimed similar advantages of accessing information on prices, quantities, supply and crowds at the wholesale markets from where they get their procurement. Fruit vendors claimed that they no longer rely on local traders for the price on fresh produce but can deal directly with the wholesalers of few towns even farther away. Instead of the vendors seeking customers as they usually did, they are now able to get orders over the phone, sometimes even a day in advance. They all claim that being connected with the market helps them earn more in their business.

Some of these women are home-based workers doing their businesses from home. These workers too found mobile phones facilitating their conduct of business. A beautician noted that at the time of wedding and other functions clients call her up when they require her service for bridal make up. She does a booking according to convenient dates and time slots available, sometimes even refusing a potential client when circumstances necessitate it. Another woman earning income through hiring out costume-jewellery said that her customers placed their orders on the mobile phone for the availability of artificial jewellery sets for functions such as marriage. A washerwoman (*dhobi)* observed that her customers call her up to collect the clothes at the particular time for washing and ironing. Sometimes they call up to tell that the clothes have to be delivered urgently. Similarly, housemaids claimed that their employers call up in case of urgency; sometimes they too call them up to inform them that they may not come to work and even give the employers their mobile number to contact in case of emergency. Saleswomen who do door-to-door sales opined that mobile phones allow them to communicate with the clients or any person who intend to meet at anytime, to confirm, to clarify or alter the location and time of meetings.

Women engaged in different informal sector occupations are using mobile phones to promote their livelihood. They feel empowered with the use of mobile phones in diverse areas such as management of daily routines, access to information, communication and contact.

**Mobile Phone and Family**

The survey sought to understand from the women of their perceived benefits of mobile phones in family-related matters such as better communication with family members, parental/marital homes and relatives, and enabling functional efficiency in their different roles and what the negative effects of its use were such as promoting suspicion and disharmony in the family. Fifty per cent of the urban and 36% of the rural respondents claimed that it has benefited them in the family matters, whereas 26% of the urban and 12% of the rural respondents claimed that it has also been a disadvantage as it arouses suspicion. More urban women said that their husband's suspicion is aroused when they receive any calls on their mobile and equally so when their husbands talk to someone on the phone. Similarly, more urban women said they suspect their sons too when they talk to someone on the mobile. Nearly an equal proportion (a little more than one-fifth) of urban and rural women said that suspicion arises when their daughters speak over the mobile.

The advantages in family matters reported by the respondents were the following. Some claimed that using mobile phone has made them very comfortable in family communication as they are able to know any situation immediately. They can be contacted directly with no intermediary person and therefore communication does not get distorted. They claimed that earlier when daughters got married the information about her well-being was not known as she resided in her marital home, but now with the mobile phone they can talk to her even at mid-night. Also earlier when relatives came visiting, their position and place during travel was not known but with the mobile phone one can know exactly how long it would take for them to reach home. Women said that they could get to know the details of the far-off relatives and also about the fights/arguments among them when they occur. As friends/relatives can always reach you, they claimed that it is a great tool to connect with people thereby providing a kind of security knowing we can watch or can be watched over by the people close to our heart.

Women also claimed that it enhanced functional efficiency in their varied roles as wives, mothers and workers. Wives felt that when husband have to do overtime work and would take time to return home, the information can be passed using mobile phone thus lessening their worry. One woman said that she calls up her husband to know where he is and what is he doing and sometimes also asks him to pick up the children from school. Women, whose husbands work abroad as skilled or semi-skilled workers in the Middle East, found the mobile phone very useful as they could now discuss all the family matters on the mobile phone and keep in touch about their well-being.

Women claimed that they used mobile phones to hold private conversations with their parents and siblings far away from the family. Calls made to children relieve them from feelings of anxiety and reassure them that their children are safe. Similarly, mobile phone also helps their sons/daughters relieve feelings of loneliness.

As the mobile phone can be carried anywhere, many respondents felt that it was useful in times of any emergency as one can call whomever one might need to call. For instance, if a lady is being harassed one can contact the police immediately and inform them. When there is a power cut in the area one can use the mobile phone to contact the electricity board. When one is stuck in heavy traffic one can call up and inform the concerned people. Mobile phone is essential for quick response and has definitely made women safer from danger. The sick and elderly too are benefited.

Equally sometimes using mobile phone can also cause disturbance and distress among the family members. While communicating on the phone the mother-in-law and/or husband feels that the woman is sending out a wrong message to others and wants to know to whom one is talking and thus arguments ensue. Mothers felt that college/school students enjoy talking to wrong calls and speak with unknown person for longer time and do not concentrate on their studies. Sometimes the husband and wife are proven to suspicions and anger. If husband talks to another person in a low voice, the wife (mis)understands that her husband is talking to another lady and equally the husband also feel so. Social manners have also become more rude as they noted that now-a-days most of the people are always communicating over the phone and do not bother about others while they are talking to someone. The moment their phone rings, the people with whom they are with cease to exist. Also, if one is not responding to the call, people think they are doing it intentionally. Most of the children/younger persons are completely disinterested in family time; instead they are preoccupied on messaging or constantly talking with others, or playing games or listening to music on their mobile phone that they do not understand the real purpose of phone and waste time in unnecessary interaction, they claimed.

**Advantages Perceived by Rural Women**

Rural women also find mobile phones advantageous on the livelihood front, in family matters, accessing development services and in community involvement. Markets in many rural areas open once a week. The vendors travel long distance to the potential sales market to obtain information on supply, demand and prices, but with the help of mobile phone they can get the information easily.

Fisherwomen use mobile phones frequently. As fisherwomen travel long distance to buy dry fish, cell phones are useful to know the availability of the fish. It also helps them to keep in touch with their family when the fishermen go for fishing and stay away for longer period. Wage workers working as agricultural labourers stay away at least 15 days for work. Earlier they had no information about and communication with their family and children. But now-a-days communication is made easy. Earlier people had to travel to eat fast food/breakfast in hotels, whereas now-a-days people place their orders by mobile phone.

Mobile phone they claimed, improved communication between women and family members. One woman said she was able to hear the voice of her son and grandchildren within a second though they live at long distance. Another said she feels very secure/confident with the use of mobile phone when she goes to town to meet her relatives as she calls up home to inform her family members/husband about her. She is not afraid to travel long distance. Yet another even claimed she fixed her daughter's marriage through mobile phone. She did not travel to search for the groom. She arranged her daughter's marriage with low cost. It was also pointed out that it is easy to contact doctors, as some women do not express their problems to doctor face-to-face, but feel comfortable to express freely over the phone.

Although fewer rural women possess mobile phones than their urban counterparts, they do realize its usefulness. The advantages indicated by these women are similar to what rural women have reported in the African contexts as well (Bakesha et al., 2009; Comfort and Dada, 2009; Sane and Traore, 2009), namely access to information, increased autonomy in work and overcoming rural isolation. Elijah and Ogunlade (2006) also found mobile phones more popular than internet among rural women in Nigeria.

### Importance of Mobile Connectivity

Seventy-six per cent urban and 48% rural respondents claimed that mobile connectivity is important for women and cited reasons that are presented in Table 4.7. Most of the respondents also reported that they do not use the SMS feature on their mobile phones.

**Table 4.7**

*Reasons for the importance of mobile connectivity to women*

| *Reasons specified* | *Urban* | *Rural* |
|---|---|---|
| To call vehicles while bringing the products | 2 | 0 |
| If they have any problem they can solve it by using their mobiles | 1 | 1 |
| To get information/communication – when the family members will reach home | 1 | 6 |
| To get information regarding business | 3 | 3 |
| Exchange of information/communication | 2 | 20 |
| To get orders | 1 | 4 |
| To get clear information | 19 | 0 |
| Maintain contacts with clients through phone | 28 | 0 |
| To place an order | 1 | 5 |
| To stay in touch | 0 | 2 |
| Times of emergency | 0 | 7 |
| To purchase and sell one's products | 18 | 0 |
| Total | 76 | 48 |

*Source:* Survey data WWF (I), 2009 (data refer to the number of respondents who possessed mobile phones and who cited the reason specified).

Table 4.7 clearly indicates that women micro-entrepreneurs in urban areas find mobile connectivity useful and important for their business activities much more than rural women, perhaps on account of the differences in the nature of occupations rural women carry on. Mobile phones may in fact be slowly transforming the way in which informal sector business is being carried on, a move away from face-to-face communication to technology mediated communication over the mobile. Donner (2007) explores how such transformation has impacted on customer acquisition among SMEs in Hyderabad. For women in the informal sector handling multiple roles and responsibilities, mobile phones have facilitated their work in many ways thus easing the juggling of roles and responsibilities.

Most respondents felt that mobile connectivity should be expanded and stated that they would be happy to receive mobile phones if they are supplied free of cost to the Below Poverty Level (BPL) households. It is evident from media publicity that certain state governments such as Tamil Nadu have initiated measures such as free distribution of gas connection and colour television to BPL households. They could also consider supply of mobile phones on demand for BPL households free of cost, and if possible could be made a nation-wide scheme. Increasingly, many welfare and social security schemes, including NREGA, require the poor to open bank accounts so that payments could be channeled through banks. The possession of a mobile phone would improve such service delivery as the banks could provide over the phone information on payment dates, etc. E-governance can be better promoted through mobile phones. Thirty-six per cent urban respondents and 63% rural respondents said that they prefer the distribution of cell phone through the government and 64% urban and 37% rural respondents prefer it be given through the NGOs.

### Computer Awareness and Skills

Most of the members have heard of computers but have not operated it. Eighty-seven per cent of the urban respondents and 63% of the rural respondents said they have heard of computers and 58% of the urban and 23% of the rural members claimed that their children could operate computers. Clearly, rural areas lag behind urban areas in awareness and knowledge of computers. But what is noteworthy and disappointing is the low enthusiasm for attending computer training programme as only 41% of the urban members and 21% of the rural members said that they would be happy to participate in such training programme that is organized for them.

Tewari (2008) has warned that much of the discourse of "ICT for Development" has been a supply-driven rather than a demand-driven discourse. The low enthusiasm for computer training especially from rural women is that they do not perceive or envisage any benefits for themselves perhaps on account of low literacy, skill level and their occupations. Donner (2006) in his study of ICT usage among urban microenterprises in Bangalore also found low use of computers by low income micro-entrepreneurs. But the fact that 87% of the urban members and 69% of the rural members said that they will allow their children to participate in the computer course indicates that they perceive computer skills as a gateway to mobility and to better paying jobs if in fact one possessed the requisite education, which is why they would like their children to attend such training and acquire the computer skills. It is easy to agree with Pal (2008) who persuasively argues that an "aspirational" discourse of ICTD permeates the Indian social environment, which makes parents perceive it as a possible gateway of mobility for their children.

**Internet/E-mail**

Children are the main conduits of computer knowledge for the parents, especially in urban areas. Twenty-one per cent urban respondents and 4% rural respondents claimed they know about internet/e-mail through their children, 7% urban and 2% rural respondents came to know it through television, and 9% urban and 4% rural members had heard of it through others, i.e., through husbands, relatives and friends.

The respondents have not surfed the internet nor do they have an e-mail account. This is because most are poor informal sector workers with low levels of literacy. Neither their occupation nor their low literacy levels permit them to surf the internet for information. They most likely have no idea of what information is available on the net in the first place and secondly, they also think that information that would be useful for their livelihoods such as vending vegetables and snacks would not be available on the net and whatever is available is not of use to them. This again confirms the findings of Donner (2006) of the low use of the internet among urban microenterprise owners, although his sample was largely of men, unlike in this study. However, 44% urban members and 12% rural members wanted to know about it and 37% urban and 10% rural members expressed interest to attend the training programme on internet if offered, and a similar percentage would like to avail the internet service free of cost. Sharpe and Spivak (2003: 613) also noted that the bottom layers of the rural poor have no access to the internet. They do not know what the internet is. They observe, "… and to access the Internet without infrastructural accompaniments does not lead to a just society" (p. 613).

Once again, the low level of interest expressed by rural women indicate that it is necessary to focus more on demand-driven or need-based approaches to encouraging ICT for rural development. Best and Maier (2007) in their study of users and non-users of internet kiosks in a few villages in Tamil Nadu reported that they did not find any evidence that internet use explained any variation around gender empowerment contradicting the widespread assumption that ICT promote gender empowerment. Given the fact that the women in this study are already in the process of being empowered through the microcredit reach and strategy of WWF (I), the low interest in internet especially by rural women confirm the conclusion of Best and Maier (2007). Convergence of technologies such as mobile internet may not be of much use for this population segment with low resource base and low literacy level.

### ICT and WWF (I)

Working Women's Forum (India) has 16 bank branches in the areas it serves. The unique features of this programme are that all work, including the banking operations are done by poor women often only with a secondary or high school education. In order to promote women's solidarity and empowerment, credit is given to groups of women with the group leader acting as a grassroots leader. Initially, the banking operations were undertaken manually when it was initiated in the year 1978. The transaction of business proceeded as per the co-operative rules/regulations. As a result, different records were maintained such as tracking of loan issued, calculating loan outstanding for a member, tracing a member's loan repayment history for granting further loan, membership details, etc. The manual work not only became tedious but also it consumed a lot of time. The work got delayed, processing of loan took a longer period of time, the staff was not able to visit areas frequently, and it took time to respond to members queries. Hence, the need for computerization of the banking operations was felt.

When it was decided to computerize the banking operations, the generally used software packages for banking operations proved inadequate as the loan is disbursed not individually as banks usually do, but through the group system. A separate programme had to be created. It was at this time that Citigroup (the multinational American bank) entered into partnership with WWF (I) in 1998 and initially helped to proceed with the computerization of the banking services. As more details had to be incorporated, a consultant created a special software package where all data required for the bank could be saved/maintained.

The bank had to face tremendous challenges and hurdles in the process of its computerization work. The Citibank officials trained the co-operative banking staff at the WWF (I) headquarters in Chennai when they entered into partnership with them. When the staff was entering the 30,000 members' data into the systems, there was a technical error and all the data were corrupted. The banking staff faced the herculean task of entering the data again into the system. Another software was created in the year 2000 where all the details of the borrowers/clients had to be entered in the system. The system could not take the entire data, as a result the data-feeding work was difficult to handle and for nearly two years the co-operative bank staff had to manage both computer and manual records till the system accepted the programme and facilitated the smooth entry of essential data without any mistake.

When the process of computerization was initiated in the headquarters, the staff from various branches was trained in computer skills to equip them in handling the banking transactions. Later, the trained staff visited the other branches to train the staff there. As staff members are either illiterate or semi-literate, they are trained in a software designed especially for them that is simple and user friendly. This enables them to learn/handle the system in a matter of days regardless of the educational level or computer training.

The staff was trained from the basic such as registration of bill, loan disbursement, collection repayment, ageing charts, default list, etc. When the staff trained at computers handles the system independently, there are also chances that the staff sometimes makes mistakes while typing. Under such circumstances both manuals and print-outs are taken and checked again. They are again retrained in computers. Thus, the success in computerizing the banking operations with a set of not highly educated women has been achieved only slowly.

The computerization of banking services helps in accessing information easily regarding the borrowers. It helps to get members details and default list within minutes. This facilitates the banking staff to keep track of the members and follow up their status. It also improves customer (client) service and has promoted greater confidence among the clients. This has facilitated the reach of microcredit to a greater extent.

Computerization also enabled the integration of banking services where various reports such as the default list, ageing chart and other lists could be generated under various categories such as area organizer, group leader, area/locality, occupation, calendar month and loan amount for better monitoring and greater efficiency. Earlier, prior to computerization, all these records were maintained manually. The banking staff had to spend time in looking for these records. Now, all the reports can be taken out almost immediately and the work load has been reduced. As a result, the staff has now more time to attend to either the default members or in enrolling new members. As the members demands/needs/grievances regarding lending, repayment, savings, insurance are met, this helps the banking staff to integrate these services.

Due to computerization, the members are provided with the repayment card which clearly states the amount to be paid by the members and the amount paid by them. Moreover with the help of the printed card, the illiterate members are able to see visibly the amount deposited by them and the interest paid for their amount.

The computer feeding requires only one-time registration and the details of various reports such as those based on age, occupation, loan, number of times loan availed, area/locality, area organizer, group leader, member, groups can be taken at the click of a button.

**Table 4.8**

*Efficiency of Banking Activity after Computerization*

| *Banking Activity* | *After Computerization* |
|---|---|
| Loan product – to make the loan product reach customer it needs to be updated in all the branches effectively. | It can be updated within 24 hours. |
| Loan application processing – to verify the clients' past history and their credits. | Earlier it took weeks to decide but now just in a few minutes one can apply different types of filters (savings, past repayment history, occupation, etc.) and get the list of borrowers. |

*Cont'd...*

*Cont'd...*

| | |
|---|---|
| Monitoring the group of default members | It was very difficult for few staff but now the report can be generated and the work has been made easy for the field staff. |
| Tracking of group loans, individual loans | It was difficult for the banking staff to track the loans. Now it is easy and they can concentrate more on the field. |
| Sanction list – future loan disbursement | It was very difficult to get the list of waiting borrowers. Now within seconds the list can be generated and can forecast the loan requirements. |
| Loan repayment schedule for clients | It was a labourious task for the banking staff to calculate the repayment schedule. But now in a single click it is possible to get the repayment schedule. |

Clearly, computerization has increased the efficiency of the banking operation as Table 4.8 indicates. The reports can be generated more frequently and in a more timely way. The ICT can thus add value by increasing staff productivity, reducing transaction cost and removing physical asset barriers to growth.

Some of the branches that have been computerized are inter-linked through VPN connection. Therefore, the data processing work of the branches is done once in a month in the headquarters in Chennai. As the clients are spread across villages, it is extremely important for the organization to accurately track activity at the micro level. The headquarter staff monitors the activity and clarifies the problem immediately. This improves field-level operational efficiency, helps the institution to provide better service to the clients, reduce redundant work, improves staff productivity, lowers costs, improves loan recovery rate, improves data accuracy by reducing human errors and provides higher level of data security and integrity. The WWF (I) trains only the co-operative staff involved in banking operations in computer skills and not all of its members who number around a million.

The website of WWF (I) has helped them to gain visibility and is evident through the e-mail that it receives from the people both from within and from outside the country regarding the activities/programmes that it imparts to interns and other NGOs interested in setting up a similar outfit in their respective region/state/country. The internet has helped it to network with other NGOs even from countries such as Afghanistan. The organization uses the internet frequently while writing reports and research papers. Moreover, it helps to know what is happening in the area of micro-finance and other activities by browsing the net to update and access current information. It has also helped it to get news of policies and programmes, consult with various ministries websites, etc.

E-mail facilitates the organization in a simple way of communication between people. E-mail has facilitated it to communicate with the donors/researchers to stay in touch professionally and get information and ideas from people; it also saves time and money in communication. It also facilitates them to send their newsletter 'Groots' to a wider audience (volunteers, donors, board members, etc.) with information on programme updates. The WWF (I) maintains e-mail communication with the donors, individuals, higher officials, researchers, academicians, insurance officials and with many who are interested to know about their programmes/activities. Most of the communications between the headquarters and the branches are through phone. Only when records are needed an e-mail is sent. The organization does not maintain e-mail communication with its million members. Most of the members do not have e-mail facility as they are poor, semi-literate and do not have any computer knowledge.

The organization encourages the use of mobile phone as it enables it to get work done faster, but the members are not provided with mobile phones by the organization. Daily collection details are informed by the staff from the field to the head office through mobile phone. The SMS communications between these people is non-existent. Mobile phone communications between the organization members has improved efficiency and effectiveness of the organizational programmes. When borrower meeting is held on a particular date at the office, the information is passed on to the members on their mobile phones that they have to be at the office at the particular time. When a visitor visits WWF (I), area meetings are arranged. Some visitors request for market visits too. As these programmes have to be often arranged within a short span of time, the organizers and area leaders are informed through their mobiles to arrange for the programme. When the staff visits the field to enquire and get other details of the members, they inform them that they are on their way and would reach their place within the time. When a member is not able to pay their monthly instalment they call up and inform the staff that they would pay within such and such days and also inform the reason for the delay. Sometimes members' problems are conveyed to the head office through mobile phones. When a member is out of station and would take time to return, the member informs the banking personnel regarding their outstation trip. The members call up at the office to enquire about their loan dates and also to know about the status of their loan. When a member changes their residence and fails to inform the office, the mobile phone number comes in handy to the bank and they can communicate with them regarding the present address.

Clearly, the adoption of ICT has improved the efficiency of the organization in its microcredit service delivery. While it cannot be categorically stated that ICT alone enabled the organization to reach microcredit to larger numbers, it has certainly made it possible to deliver the services efficiently and expand the range of banking services as more and more women get progressively drawn into the fold of the organization. Many hold sceptical views about the "scaling up" of microcredit as a strategy to combat global poverty under the neoliberal agenda. Organizations like WWF (I) that belong to the NGO sector can not alter neoliberalism even if they may well be a part of the global civil society voicing its concerns. They can at best make a pragmatic judgement of being prepared to handle the emerging challenges. The organization has moved in the direction of this preparedness by enlarging its corpus of loanable funds through drawing credit from big multinational lenders like Citigroup and Rabo Bank. The ICT adoption is also a part of this preparedness to face newly emerging challenges.

**Conclusions**

It is evident that factors that determine the adoption of ICT at the level of the organization are different from those at the level of individuals. But when the two are combined it has a significant potential for empowerment. The analysis clearly suggests that differentiating the ICTs yield insights into the needs of poor women better than an aggregated notion of ICT. Being poor, illiterate informal sector workers, they have no requirements of computer skill or computer use, although they understand that such skills open up pathways of economic mobility which they are eager for their children to access. The mobile phone though serves useful purposes in promoting women's micro-businesses through access to market information and reduces transaction costs and supports what Heeks et al. (2004) had suggested that the use of ICT in "extensive" applications is likely to increase productivity and profitability even when it does not change the labour process. Further, it improves communication in family and social life, and thus the analysis supports the observation of Aminuzzaman et al. (2003) that mobile phones create ripple-effects in the society, increase network density and promote trust and social capital. Most importantly as Alampy (2005) argued, mobile phones increase the "capabilities" and "functioning" of poor informal sector women. The analysis shows how these women are handling multiple roles, how it has fostered their entitlements through business promotion and increased incomes, and has enabled them to access more freedom and choice in different aspects of their lives thus contributing to increased empowerment. The women are able to adjust the cost of mobile phone usage according to their affordability. Clearly in terms of policy, there is a need to move towards a universal coverage of mobile phone, perhaps through free distribution of the equipment for those below the poverty line and provide free help-line services for accessing various services.

# 5

# Culture and Sustainability

## Women and Climate Change

Issues of sustainable development have assumed increased importance as a consequence of the debates on global warming. Sustainability requires that the resource base upon which production and consumption activities are based, is not jeopardized for future rounds of production and consumption on account of unsustainable present levels of production and consumption. Thus, sustainability implies a concern for the future in which present-day greed needs to be curtailed to ensure intergenerational equity and justice over an infinite time horizon. Indigenous cultures everywhere have long practised sustainable modes of living which with modern industrialization and capitalist globalization are being threatened. Here, we examine the role of women in sustainable practices shaped by cultures and how their roles are being envisioned in climate change solutions.

### Global Warming and the Solutions

Climate change poses the most significant challenge to all humanity in the coming century. Scientists have told us that climate change is caused by global warming caused by high levels of greenhouse gases (GHGs) (carbon dioxide, methane, etc.) in the earth's atmosphere caused mainly by inefficient energy utilization on account of the fast-growing industrialization. While the developed countries with advanced industrial base have caused this problem being the early industrializers, fast growing economies such as China, India and the other BRIC nations have increasing levels of emissions in the last decade with their rising economic growth rates. Under the aegis of the United Nations countries evolved the Kyoto Protocol and its future is currently under discussion. Based on economists' reasons, among which there are different views, the UN adopted the principle of pricing carbon and setting mandatory reduction targets for the developed countries. This means that emitters would have to pay a price for carbon emissions above a certain limit, and those emitting less than their quotas could sell their permits to others. A carbon market has thus evolved globally with various financial instruments and their derivative products that are traded on carbon exchanges set up much like the stock markets. The USA withdrew from the UN Kyoto Protocol and developed its own voluntary GHG market. Now negotiations are underway globally about the future of the Kyoto deal and attempts are made to evolve national strategies for cap and trade that would bring both China and India to voluntarily reduce their emission levels. Apart from a price of carbon and the trading of emission rights, economists have long advocated a tax on the polluter, what economists call the "pigouvian tax" which given the global nature of the problem was found infeasible to adopt at a global level (Kalpagam, 2009).

The UN strategy is two-pronged, one of both carbon mitigation and adaptation to climate change. Under the mitigation strategy, the overall aim is to reduce the dependence on fossil fuels for energy and move to renewable energy sources or other forms of clean energy sources. This calls for wide ranging industrial innovation and adoption, almost like a third industrial revolution – from the steam engine to computer chips to clean energy. The other strategy is the adaptation to climate change whereby funds have been earmarked to help economies and communities to adapt to climate change as it recognizes that climate change effects are already being experienced and are likely to do so in the future as mitigation is both likely to be slow and not to the expected scale at least in the short and medium term. Some of the climate change effects currently underway are droughts and floods caused by untimely or insufficient rainfall, desertification, soil salination, unseasonal high and low temperatures causing changes in crop cycles and effects on vegetation growth, ocean acidity causing depletion of marine resources, localized acid rains, rising ocean levels causing erosion of coastlines and so on. Adaptation strategies acknowledge that poorer communities in the developing world are most affected by these climate change effects that increase their vulnerability and push them further into poverty with consequent effects on livelihood, income, nutrition, health and so on, and therefore these communities need to be assisted to cope with such climate change effects through better agronomic practices, protection of habitats and livelihoods, and ensuring food security. It is also acknowledged that poor women are most likely to bear the brunt of these climate effects. Adaptation to climate change also requires scientific research inside the laboratories and on the field to develop and test new varieties of seeds that could withstand higher temperatures and the changed conditions of water availability. Adaptation strategies alone without the mitigation strategies will quite obviously not solve the problem, nor one without adaptation strategies likely to alleviate the sufferings of the poorer communities subjected to climate effects. Nor is it certain that desired results would be obtained even if mitigation and adaptation were followed successfully for lacking complete and predictable knowledge on this issue, we are dealing in the realm of uncertainty.

The foregoing discussion sets clear the current global discourse on climate change solutions. For anthropologists it is important to discern the perspective embedded in this solution. Increased industrialization both intensive and extensive has been taking place globally as a consequence of global capitalism. Modern industrialization has been equated to development as many theories on economic development suggest that with development the share of the primary sector in Gross National Product would reduce and the share of the secondary (industrial) and tertiary (service) sector would rise. The desire for modernity is the desire for industrialism as a way of life, a life in the city with the possibility of consumption and use of a wide range of mass-produced factory goods and not an agrarian one of countryside or village lifestyle. More and more people are migrating to the cities from the countryside in search for jobs and "better" lifestyle leading to sprawling slums and shanty towns that one writer has even called as "The Planet of Slums". The climate change solutions discussed above do not question modern industrialization or global capitalism and the associated ways of life as norm and desire that have spread globally. Although the discourse does refer to pre-industrial levels of GHG concentration in the earth's atmosphere as being far lower than the current levels on account of the last 150–180 years of industrialization in the present developed countries, it does not lay the blame on industrialism as a way of life, rather it is the inefficient use of energy through the use of fossil fuel. It is thus believed that introducing cleaner technologies could reverse the situation even as the human insatiety for goods makes possible the discovery, production and consumption of newer and newer goods and services. While the adoption of cleaner technologies at least recognizes the importance of changing how the world produces goods, there are even some scientists who have launched on visionary experiments like the intentional interventions in climate change through putting up panels in orbit much like the satellites to deflect sun's rays or increasing iron content in the oceans and so on, without any attempt to change either the production processes or human behaviour. The quest for cleaner technologies is predicted to lead to the next industrial revolution as scientists and corporations are now developing new technologies in far-sighted ways. Clean and cleaner technologies are not a one-shot invention but will more likely be a spiral series of inducting better technologies over time. This is expected to extend the limits of planet Earth's sustainability for the industrial way of life.

### Industrialism, Sustainability and Women

The concept of "sustainability" inherent in this approach is sustainability for industrialism, production for profit or capitalism, and a consumption-oriented lifestyle. It is also envisaged that attainment of this sustainability is a dynamic long-term process. Economists now are talking of "green growth rates" – growth rates that would factor in the sustainability through green technologies where earlier they had been only referring to growth rates. All over in the West, there is much hype about promoting "green lifestyles". There are advertisements posted on buses in the New York city to give up eating meat as meat production contributes to global warming. The New York subway system has hoardings on subway cars claiming that its operations are clean and abide by green norms. Banks, companies and universities are all now voluntarily going green which means they calculate their carbon emissions and buy offset carbon credits either from the domestic carbon market or through international projects. The USA has signed agreements with Brazil and India for purchase and sale of carbon credits from sustainable rural development projects. This is outside of the UN system of CDM (Clean Development Mechanism) that allows countries with mandatory compliance under the Kyoto Protocol to buy carbon credits from projects from developing countries which are largely industrial process innovations for carbon mitigation.

Carbon sequestration through afforestation projects also qualifies for carbon credits in the voluntary market segment and many prospective credit buyers are encouraging afforestation programme through tree planting in the developing countries. Many NGOs in India have also taken up tree plantation programmes to earn carbon credit and rural women are engaged in these activities. Barclays, the British bank even decided to offset its emissions through distribution of better cooking stoves in some rural African households which would surely benefit women there. As emissions are not territorially bounded, carbon credits can be sought from areas away from the site where emissions take place. The World Bank and many other banks too have set up many carbon funds and are actively buying carbon credits from projects in the developing countries for reselling it to countries and corporations facing mandatory emissions reduction targets in the developed world. There is scope for speculative gains and money to be made. Not long before the recent meltdown and downturn of the US economy, many Wall Street financial firms had pledged huge amounts of money for climate change initiatives as it was seen to be profitable. The founder-economist of the Chicago Climate Exchange has even remarked that the market for environmental products will sooner or later be larger than the total food market in the USA. It is expected to attract huge amounts of hedge funds and high net worth investors.

From the foregoing outline of the climate change solution where do we envisage the role of women? Women in the developed countries are urged to adopt "green lifestyles" as consumers by choice. Like the fad for organic produce or power yoga a few years ago, this extends to cutting down on meat consumption, recycling products, opt for cars that conform to the latest environmental standards even if they cost a bit more, enquire into carbon footprint in investment decisions as mutual funds, pay for carbon offset for air travel, paying up a few additional taxes wherever those are imposed for environmental pollution, sign a few petitions of Green Peace and other environmental groups for say Dolphin or Shark protection, don a few T-shirts saying they are climate activists and lobby to get the governments to tackle global warming seriously at best. Such appeals for "green lifestyle" do not entail any ethical or political responsibility for a radical or even a moderate change in their existing lifestyle of industrialism. It does not for instance restrict the number of cars a family could own, the mileage covered weekly, pooled and public transportation options, unnecessary high-tech innovations, do away with the no-repair-throw-away culture for goods and gadgets, processed and canned foods, multiple sets of clothing and footwear to keep up with fashions than what is required and so on. Non-political economists would call this the "want-based economy" wherein production and reproduction in the economy are geared towards an ever-increasing set of wants, while the political economists term it simply as capitalism. A "need-based economy" is one where the production and reproduction of the economy are geared towards needs. Such economies are called pejoratively as "subsistence", "backward" or "underdeveloped" economies. Without a shift from "want-based" economy to a "need-based" economy (which seems unlikely on a large scale and most would consider such a move as regression anyway) the green lifestyle movement in the West seeks to protect industrialism as a way of life and seeks sustainability within that mode. This is a delusional solution for it does not acknowledge that the industrial form of life has already seriously eroded sustainable lifestyles in the subsistence economies of the world. Women in the developed countries on the fad of adopting "green lifestyles" do not realize either, the connections and causation between their industrial mode of life, and the erosion of sustainable lifestyles elsewhere. Nor do they understand the commonalities between them and women from the third world subsistence economies in terms of the commonality of the mode of oppression that has rendered capitalist power as also a patriarchal power.

There are many women from the developing countries as immigrants in the developed countries and even such women whom one would expect to understand the global connections between Western lifestyles and subsistence economies elsewhere fail to grasp the connection. Even the developing countries' arguments such as the Indian government's position against it being covered under mandatory emissions reduction targets is based on the logic that not only is India's per capita emissions low but that it would affect the country's growth and development adversely, meaning thereby its industrial development and its transition to the industrial mode of life. The Indian nation itself is now viewed by many as composed of two segments – India and Bharat. While India is governed by the logic and values of global capitalization, Bharat represents village India with its logics and values of subsistence peasant orientation. The social, economic and cultural distance in the India-Bharat divide has increased in the era of globalization and the erosion of sustainable agrarian livelihoods is most evident in recent years in the rise of farmers' suicides in the country on account of commercial farming, market fluctuation and indebtedness. More and more farmers in the country are complaining that farming has become an unviable economic activity and a leading agricultural scientist has even said recently that in the future we would have to depend more on industrial processed ready-to-eat food, some of it imported perhaps, than depend on the crop output. No doubt, women and men by participating though not necessarily by choice in this industrial mode of life bear responsibility for global warming and climate change.

**Modernity and Domination Over Nature**

Many feminist scholars have emphasized that the industrial mode of life has been made possible by man's domination over nature (Merchant, 1980; Mies, 1986; Shiva, 1989). It was philosopher Francis Bacon who had noted that the role of modern science was to intervene in nature and make nature reveal "her" secrets. It was such an interventionist approach to nature that has contributed to the rapid development of science and technology, and global warming as its unanticipated consequence today. Metaphorically, we could say that "mother nature" is now resisting her rape and plunder by expressing her anger through global warming. Such metaphorical language would appeal to people with pre-modern attitudes who have often attributed natural calamities to god's fury. Merchant (1980) and others have noted that the modern conception of nature is mechanistic and that conception has made possible that nature can be intervened and manipulated upon in calculated and predictable ways which is different from the pre-modern conception of nature that was organic and treated it as a living being. In the organic conception, the man-nature interaction is not one of domination but of complimentarity that beckons mankind to acknowledge that the cosmos is a living spirit and that all animate and inanimate entities in the cosmos are connected and imbued with the spirit of the cosmos. This no doubt is a simplification of a more complex history of Western thought on nature. Up until the 16th century, pre-modern Europe did not approve of deep mining but with the beginning of the modern era and with the development of capitalist industrialization things changed.

Smith and Harvey, in their work on uneven development argue that uneven development "is the concrete process and pattern of the production of nature under capitalism" (1984/2008: 8). They observe that capital transforms the shape of the entire world in its constant drive to accumulate larger and larger quantities of social wealth under its control. "No God-given stone is left unturned, no original relation with nature unaltered, no living thing unaffected. To this extent the problems of nature, of space, and of uneven development are tied together by capital itself" (ibid.: 7–8). Smith and Harvey further note, "Yet, despite the centrality of this experience, at the level of individual daily life as well as that of society as a whole, our current conception of nature is not simple, nor is it at all a mere conceptual reflection of this relatively recent social experience of nature … the social concept of nature has accumulated innumerable layers of meaning in the course of history … Industrial capitalism has cut into the accumulated meanings of nature so that they can be shaped and fashioned into concepts of nature appropriate for the present era. Old concepts of nature are less vanquished than co-opted to the present purpose" (ibid.: 11).

Smith and Harvey are referring here to the Western conception of nature. The modern conception of nature that is attributed to Bacon has also many meanings to it in the Kantian scheme. For Kant, nature is external, which is the Bacon sense of it being amenable to intervention and manipulation. It is also universal. Another meaning is that it is internal, something intrinsic to humans as essence that determines behaviour. It is in this sense of it being intrinsic as human nature that woman are seen to be closer to nature. Bloch and Bloch (1980) indicate the multiple meanings of nature in the 18th century Europe. "In the first, the state of nature refers to a chronologically pre-social state. In the second, nature means the internal processes of the human, especially instincts and emotions but also reproductive processes. Thirdly 'nature' is taken to mean the universal order which implies the harmonious coexistence of human nature and the external world of plants, animals and the countryside. Fourthly, nature is used to qualify the way of life of primitive peoples whether real, imaginary or a mixture of the two" (ibid.: 27).

Merchant (1980), following the ideas of the Frankfurt school social theorists Horkheimer and Adorno, argues that man's domination of nature paralleled domination in social relations and both nature and women were subjected to domination and violence simultaneously. Mies (1986) also corroborates that the domination of nature and women went along simultaneously and that capitalist power is both class power and patriarchal power. In both the mechanistic and organic conception of nature, nature is often referred in feminine terms such as "mother nature". The mechanistic world view is that just as the wildness of nature needs to be tamed, women must also be tamed and subjugated. Ortner (1972) in her article "Is female to male as nature is to culture?" highlighted that nature and culture are set up as a hierarchy with culture above nature and similarly male above female. She further observed that women were universally subordinated to men which she noted was on account of reproductive functions which were seen closer to nature, although she also concluded that both "nature" and "culture" were themselves cultural constructions. MacCormack (1980) challenged Ortner's ethnocentric view to argue that in some cultures men are equated with wildness and that there are cultures where women do not think they are subordinate to men although they may acknowledge the sexual division of labour, nor is nature considered inferior to culture.

I have given a brief gist of these anthropological debates because they are indeed relevant to what is at stake here. First is to acknowledge the domination of both nature and women under capitalist industrialization. Second, with the spread of the capitalist industrialized mode, the domination of nature and women now appear to be universal, although much like uneven development, there may be variations in the degree of domination and subordination. Both Western and non-Western cultures had prior to this mode a different kind of man-nature interaction. In the non-Western world, the two modes of man-nature interaction still persist although the predatory tendencies of the capitalist mode of man-nature interaction is progressively destabilizing and rendering the older modes vulnerable and putting in place unsustainable practices.

### Nature in Hindu Thought and Practices

Let me recapitulate here the conceptions of nature that can be gleaned from the Hindu religious beliefs and practices because these have shaped cultural practices in India for long. The Hindu gods and goddesses are those of nature. All the elements of the cosmos – sun, fire, earth, water, food are personified as divine beings and worshipped. While Hindu practices do undergo changes over time, the basic tenets of religious beliefs and the Hindu pantheon remain unchanged. If nature is personified as divinity and the Hindu culture and way of life have evolved on these beliefs, then nature is not clearly perceived as inferior to culture as the modern Western conception. Vegetarianism of certain upper caste Brahmins and of Jains is based on the sanctity of non-human living beings whose life cannot be taken away. Associated is the worship of cows. Hindu mythological stories are replete with many animals sharing space with humans and Gods, and some like the monkey-God (Hanuman) and the elephant-God (Ganesha) are pre-eminent deities in the pantheon. The Hindu liturgical practices such as the various Homas mention so many plants, herbs and flowers found in nature. Associated with the Vedic religion are the Vedic sciences like Ayurveda, an advanced medical system that uses natural products such as plants and herbs and some metals in healing and curing. Once again, it is a culture that has evolved not by dominating nature but through knowledge of nature gained through non-instrumental, non-dominating or non-extractive ways. Even the Hindu way of disposing the dead human by cremation indicates that the mortal body inhabits the earth only temporarily and the ash remains are thrown in large water bodies such as rivers and oceans to merge and mingle with nature.

Many seers and sages of Hindu philosophy have tried to expound the relationship of the human self to the cosmic spirit. Even the planets are worshipped to indicate this cosmic unity and harmony. Hindu kings ruling by divine right always blamed themselves and their kingdom for *adharma* (wrong conduct) for nature's fury and visitation of droughts and floods and sought both to appease the gods and to promote *dharma* (right conduct)in their kingdom. So it was both individual and collective behaviour modification rather than controlling nature. Hindu astrology may not meet the norms of modern science but it bases its predictions on the influence of planetary positions and constellation clearly signifying that such influence of nature on humans cannot be tamed by modern science, calculating logic and human intervention. It is immaterial whether Ptolomey or Copernicus was correct to the Hindu astronomers who since time immemorial evolved accurate calendrical systems, planetary constellations and eclipses. It is because of such time-tested knowledge that modern science of the more recent historical period could not fully supplant the pre-modern under-standings of nature in India. Correspondingly, the conception of femaleness is not one of inferiority to males as the way Ortner assumes it to be universal, rather the feminine (*Prakriti)* and masculine (*Purush*) are complementary, and like the Chinese philosophy of *Ying* and *Yang*, femaleness and maleness mark not only sexual difference in humans and animals but is the fundamental organizing principle of complementarity of both nature and cosmos as well. Historians of science have long been puzzled over the question as to why despite an advanced state of knowledge in many sciences like medicine, metallurgy and astronomy, the ancient civilizations of China and India were not able to develop modern science and technology like the Western civilization. This may have been inherently due to their conception of nature and of the complementarity principle of *Ying* and *Yang* or *Prakriti* and *Purush* in nature that did not allow for the emergence of a conception of nature that could be dominated and manipulated.

With this conception of nature, the feminine principle was viewed as complementary and hence women were not viewed as inferior to men on account of their reproductive function the way Ortner assumes it to be universal. The reproductive process was perceived in terms of fecundity of both mother and mother earth, such fecundity leading to prosperity. The biological symbolism of seed and earth in the folk cultures of India is an instance of the fecundity of both earth and women. The Hindu trinity of Gods – Brahma (the creator), Visnu (the protector) and Siva (the destroyer) – symbolizes creation, destruction and reproduction as an ongoing and eternal principle of life, which gave rise to the phallic symbol of Siva (the Sivalinga). In social practice, the worship of the principle of fecundity no doubt led to notions of auspiciousness and inauspiciousness that bore on the status of women in the society such that marriage and childbearing were associated with auspiciousness, and singleness and barrenness stigmatized as inauspiciousness in the Hindu culture. Modern Indian women are still struggling today to overcome these notions and stigmatizations.

Sociologists of religion have identified a divide in the Hindu religious practices, what they refer as the "great tradition" which refers to sanskritized forms of Hindu religion and the popular religious traditions informed by folk culture in what is described as the "little tradition", with the latter constantly borrowing from the former, but never fully engulfed by it. The conception of nature and the unity of the feminine and masculine principle analysed above no doubt pertain to the "great tradition" of Hinduism. The folk religion of the little tradition is closer to nature in a less abstract sense than the sanskritized Hinduism. In the little traditions trees, animals, snakes are worshipped. There are folk deities (*devatas*) that guard natural resources such as forests, lakes and rivers. Every traditional occupation such as carpentry, pottery, agriculture has its specific gods to whom they offer worship for their livelihood sustenance. The folk gods and goddesses are personified as easily susceptible to anger and who punish wrong doers immediately. Wrong doings are generally acts and behaviour that fall outside of the community and village norms which could be felling trees from sacred groves and so on. Folk gods and goddesses have the power to invoke the fury of nature in circumstances that displease them and can bring in bountiful harvest and prosperity or drought, disease and misery. Folk religion therefore becomes a kind of social discipline to reinforce community norms of nature, culture and gender.

Although the principle of fecundity is not sacralized as in sanskritic Hinduism, Mother Goddess, sometimes personified as earth, is considered the primeval energy, the source of all Shakti (power/energy) and the mother of the trinity of Brahma, Visnu and Siva. This primeval energy that is the source of all life is female energy. The worship of mother goddess in the folk traditions is still very popular among peasants, artisans, fisher folk and other poor and marginalized communities. The conception of nature in the folk tradition is not one of the unity of all living beings with nature and cosmos as in Vedantic thought but a conception of nature as the source of all sustenance.

## Sustainable Practices in Pre-colonial Times

Given these conceptions of nature in the great and little traditions of Hinduism, let me briefly examine some of the sustainable practices of man-nature interaction that were followed in the pre-colonial past of India before private property in land was established and before modern industrialization began. There was communal ownership of agricultural land. Farm plots were rotated among the farmers so that all of them got their turns to cultivate the best lands located at the head of the water source. By this, tendencies for inequality and accumulation were minimized. In most other parts of un-irrigated lands, field rotation was practised so that land was not used intensively so as to exhaust its fertility. Certain lands in the village were set aside for the poorer groups for their sustenance through grazing of animals, collection of trees products and fodder, etc. Methods of making organic manure were developed to fertilize the land. Multiple cropping and crop rotation were practised as well. Seed selection was based on identifying the appropriate seed strains for particular soil types that maintained high nutrition levels and that could withstand weather changes. Community granary was set up in villages to ensure food security. *Women played important and significant roles in all these sustainable practices of agriculture.* Although largely oriented as a need-based economy, agriculture did produce surplus to support the rulers as well as the non-agricultural classes and the growing urban settlements. Farm women supplemented nutrition from cereals with a collection of a wide variety of plant products of which they had good local knowledge. Such knowledge exists among poor tribal women even to this day (Sen, 2008). Tribal communities and forest dwellers used forests and forest resources for livelihood and sustenance without disturbing the eco-diversity. Sections of forest areas were marked off as "sacred groves" where no felling was allowed to retain the bio-diversity. As modern industrialization had not developed, the wood from trees was used for construction and making of implements, and not for the paper industry. Communities practised sustainable forest practices while retaining their rights of livelihood, habitat and usufruct in forest that they had held for a long time. In the case of water resources too, it was largely the use of surface waters from flowing rivers, lakes, ponds and tanks. Small earthen dams were constructed for water storage for small irrigation works. Fishing being small scale then, the communities fishing in water bodies and along the coast practised sustainable fishing practices.

Almost all rivers in India have some sacred significance to them, the most sacred being the Ganga, which is mentioned in Vedic and many texts of Hindu religion. One of the Vedic origin myths that has made these rivers sacred relate to the churning of oceans and how the nectar collected from the churning process was brought in an urn, and how in an ensuing fight between the gods and the "asuras" (demons), the nectar spilled at four places in India from where the rivers flow through and the Vedic civilization began. It is indeed remarkable that this origin myth of the churning of oceans bears a striking resemblance to what scientists are now telling of carbon "burb" from the oceans at the end of last ice age that started the global warming and that during the ice ages huge amounts of carbon dioxide got stored in the deep oceans.

As there was no industrialization except some metallurgical work in artisanal workshops, all commodities in use were generally madc of natural products that were "biodegradable" and so waste accumulation and disposal was not a problem then. There were always marked social differences and inequality in the society and so luxury consumption did exist in the form of fine jewellery, silken textiles and carpets although the bulk of the economy was oriented towards the production of needs. Luxury production was also only artisanal production by skilled craftsmen and so did not lead to the exploitation of nature and there was considerable long distance trade for luxuries, bullion and other goods.

## Colonial Disruption of Sustainable Practices

All this was to change under colonialism, and capitalist industrialization brought in its trail. First, private property in land was established and land revenues were increased. This led to an intensification of cultivation by tenant farmers. Private property also clearly established classes of people who had no usufruct land rights as well and farm women overwhelmingly were deprived of land rights. The process of privatization set in motion the appropriation of common property that provided sustenance to the poorer classes by the landed elites. The periodic cycles of drought and famine caused migratory movements of poor peasants both within and outside the country. Thus, many peasants lost their traditional ties to their land. The growth of plantation crops such as indigo, tea and coffee for export markets and of commercial crops such as cotton brought far-reaching changes in the peasant agriculture. The export of raw cotton and the import of manufactured textiles from the mills of Manchester ruined the Indian countryside by throwing out millions of home-based female spinners in what has come to be known as the "de-industrialization" process. Alienation of land from tribal groups by the colonial state for the setting up of plantation estates disrupted the local sustainable economies of many tribal groups in the hill areas who were forced to join the ranks of the peasantry as landless agricultural workers. The colonial state made very little investment in irrigation till the last quarter of the 19th century and traditional systems of irrigation fell into disrepair on account of the disruption of agrarian economies and the lack of maintenance as private property in land and the *zamindari* (landlord) system, and commercial agriculture dismantled community-level organizations that were previously voluntary and cooperative. These undermined sustainable agriculture. As elsewhere in the colonies, commercial agriculture progressively marginalized women's independent roles in agriculture and they became involved in subsistence activities that made them both invisible and categorized as "dependent women". Women left behind in villages on account of male migration found it difficult to carry on sustainable livelihoods in the villages and migrated to urban areas to work in factories as "coolies".

The colonial disruption of forest communities and their sustainable livelihoods and practices is by now well known. Forest dwellers were progressively denied the use of their forests through the take-over of the forests by the colonial administration. In their attempt to introduce practices of scientific forestry, they made forestry into a masculinist project and marginalized women forest dwellers of their traditional roles and rights in forest life. Forest dwellers were shifted out to the peripheral areas of the forest and they lost their autonomy and independence as they now had to work for state agents as collectors of forest produce. Many trees and forests were cut to meet the growing demands of railways, paper industry and construction as urbanization and industrialization took off, a phenomenon that has become more intense in the post-colonial period.

**Unsustainable Development Trajectory After Independence**

All these changes did not take place without fierce resistance from the peasants and tribals. But in the end, the changes ushered in by capitalist industrialization and commercialization altered the sustainable lifestyles and practices of the masses. The choice of hand-spun Khadi as the garment to be worn by the nationalists in the Indian National Congress and the spinning of Charkha adopted by Gandhi and the Gandhians were the symbolic statements of the destruction wrought upon the country by colonial and capitalist industrialization. With the maturing of the nationalist movement and at the time of independence, there was a debate as to the kind of development path the country should adopt. Mahatma Gandhi was not in favour of modern industrialization and preferred the idea of sustainable village republics based on rural industrialization and decentralized forms of governance. But by then, the world had begun to equate modern development with modernization of economies and modern industrialization. Leaders such as Nehru and Ambedkar clearly favoured a decisive shift to modernization as the development path to be adopted.

Thus, with the launch of planned development, the country focussed on large scale industrialization like putting up steel plants in the public sector, and the building of large scale multipurpose dams and irrigation projects, with Gandhian approaches and concerns being considered only in a tokenistic way. It is not altogether clear whether demographic considerations decided the choice of the development path, but it was a significant factor in the agricultural modernization in the 1960s. The need to feed the growing population under conditions of uncertain agricultural output on account of wars and drought years hastened the introduction of the green revolution, i.e., the use of HYV seeds, fertilizer and irrigation combination to achieve higher levels of agricultural output. These developments paved the way for an unsustainable development trajectory that was probably unanticipated.

The increased application of chemical fertilizers affected the soil quality and the use of water for intensive cultivation through tube-well irrigation has led to a severe depletion of ground water in many parts of rural India. As the village commons have been appropriated by the dominant groups in the villages, the poorer classes have lesser access to common lands for grazing and collection of fuel, fodder, etc. This combined with demographic pressure has led to overuse of whatever land is available to them causing further land degradation. Deforestation has been rapid and green cover has reduced considerably on account of indiscriminate felling by forest contractors and others. Yet, forest dwellers have been increasingly denied their rights of livelihood through forest-based resources and have been progressively pushed out. Social forestry schemes to improve access of the poor to forest resources paid no heed to eco-diversity and encouraged only the cultivation of Eucalyptus trees that pushed ground water levels down even further.

Water scarcity in urban and rural areas is becoming worse as demand outstrips supply on account of inadequate rainfall, poor rain harvesting, water run offs, etc. In urban areas, air and ground water pollution on account of rapid urbanization, industrialization without adequate environmental protection safeguards, and poor quality fuels for urban transportation have caused much environmental damage. All these have undermined sustainable development in a big way. These have impacted on women's lives and livelihoods. Non-availability of water, fuel and fodder in proximate distance has forced rural women to traverse long distances everyday to collect these thus increasing their workload and the amount of time spent on these activities. Water scarcity in urban areas has made the lives of women in slums and low-income neighbourhoods even more onerous, even as young girls in families now shoulder more housework such as water collection. The health effects of environmental degradation and pollution are only now beginning to be cognized. As more and more industrial goods are being consumed, waste disposal has become a problem posing health hazards. Apart from toxic waste exported to India by some developed countries, there are now huge amounts of e-waste to be dealt with, as well as the problem of non-degradable plastic and industrial waste. Aquatic life has been affected by the disposal of industrial chemical effluents in water bodies on account of improper regulatory standards. If cobalt sticks causing radiation can be mindlessly disposed in the scrap market in the nation's capital causing grave health problems to those exposed, the situation of environmental standards being flouted is indeed very serious.

**Globalization and the Intensification of Unsustainable Practices**

All these problems have been aggravated and intensified in the post-liberalization period (after 1991), the period being widely perceived as one of fast globalization. Agricultural land is now being taken over for mega-industrial projects by multinational companies such as building factories, airports and Special Economic Zones (SEZs). All of these activities leave big carbon footprints. Tribals and peasants are increasingly resisting these land acquisition moves, often made through the misuse of law by the governments, as the law permits such acquisition for "public purposes". The displaced tribals are given a pittance as compensation and relocation of those displaced is tardy. Even if both compensation and relocation were satisfactory, people's ties to land are stronger and emotional, especially if they have been there for a long time. Even tribals who were displaced in the 1950s and 1960s to set up public sector projects have not been rehabilitated till now. In the era of neoliberal globalization, promoting the interest of capital has now become "public purpose", while dislocation of tribal people, rendering them vulnerable and making their livelihoods and lifestyles unsustainable is of no consequence. The tribals in central India are now waging a war against the Indian state through a violent Maoist movement to resist the mining of minerals by multinational companies and the cutting down of forests to put up industries in the region that renders their livelihoods and lifestyles unsustainable. Illegal mining has become rampant everywhere on account of its profitability. There is also mindless export of resources. It is alleged that on gathering information about soil nature from satellite imagery, the Chinese ordered for bricks made of that soil from a region in Karnataka in south India for construction during the Beijing Olympics. Eager to cash in on the opportunity, the brick manufacturers even dug up vast areas of fertile agricultural land. Natural resources have now come to the forefront as a contested terrain at local, regional and international levels. While nationalism and territoriality propels China and Japan to conserve and stockpile rare earth minerals, China seeks to exploit Africa's mineral wealth. As global warming is not territorially bounded, predatory strategies of using non-renewable natural resources affects globally even as it appears to give national gains.

With the rapid spread of urbanization, more and more agricultural lands are acquired for urban residential, factory and office construction. Thus, cultivable land is progressively being diminished which leaves no other option but intensification of cultivation through modern scientific methods of HYV seeds, chemical fertilizer and increased use of water. There is no long-term foresight on the extent of cultivable land required for sustainable agriculture to feed the growing millions. Urban constructions do not abide by any green norms and are huge guzzlers of electricity.

Globalization has increased economic opportunities for a growing middle class whose aspirations and desire for commodities and consumption emulate Western lifestyles. More and more car manufacturers are putting increased number of cars on the roads, which have been characterized by some as a "green nightmare". Flyovers and parking lots are constructed everywhere to ease traffic congestion; all of these are carbon-intensive activities. Small scale retailing and petty shops are being replaced by huge multi-storeyed shopping malls which are to increase rapidly in the next few years as about 800 small towns are slated to have shopping malls. All these activities of want-based consumption increases carbon emissions, even as groundwater levels everywhere are depleting rapidly owing to high unsustainable consumption levels and is everywhere getting increasingly polluted. Some television news channels provide details of air and water pollution everyday much like the weather details, a feature that was non-existent a few years ago. It gives the misleading impression that the environment is constantly monitored by the authorities and that something is being done about it when in fact the root cause of such problems is not addressed at all.

The problem and the solution proposed for climate change is now placed in a broader framework of sustainability. Trying to find sustainable solutions keeping intact the industrial mode of lifestyle is a problem as such a mode of life is constantly undermining sustainable livelihoods and lifestyles in those areas where the non-industrial mode of life still struggles to exist supporting large masses of poor and labouring populations, and for whom the industrial mode of life only signifies displacement, casual work at low wages and indecent life in urban slums. The climate change solution through the carbon market now appears clearly to be limited. For one, it seeks to preserve the industrial mode of life and even the adoption of cleaner technologies which is a long-run dynamic solution will constantly propel lifestyles everywhere into the industrial mode. The mechanism of carbon offsetting does not factor this and merely takes into account the emissions of one industry or factory and not the spiralling effect of emulation with a time lag elsewhere. It is also not a dynamically feasible solution to have both mining and land acquisition by multinational companies and significant afforestation programmes for carbon sequestration. The issues of sustainability have to be viewed as a whole in both mitigation and adaptation to climate change. The adaptation solution has to take into consideration the on-going process of rendering life-worlds unsustainable as the process by which capitalist industrial mode spreads globally.

In envisioning solutions to climate change, it is necessary to abide by certain principles to guide practices. Nations and the global community of capitalist corporations included have to evolve a consensus on natural resource use in ways that address issues of intergenerational justice. Can we allow the present industrial mode to exhaust the earth's supply of non-renewable resources in the next few generations or is a longer term perspective required that would curtail the greedy use of it (Shiva, 2006; 2009). It is utopian to think that the industrial mode life can be reversed, but restricting the exploitation of natural resources would certainly slow down this hurtling pace of the industrial mode. If consensus has eluded for the Kyoto protocol for capping emissions or for nuclear non-proliferation, it will be much more difficult to get a consensus on resource use that undermines the interests of capital.

## Women, Climate Change and Sustainability

As Dankelman (2010) observes, climate change affects all but the extent and the manner in which it affects vary as such effects tend to accentuate inequalities and vulnerabilities. Poor women in the developing countries in India are affected much more than others as their pre-existing vulnerabilities are exacerbated as a consequence of climate effects such as extreme variations in temperature, desertification, floods and rising ocean levels to name a few. On account of inadequate food security provided by the state, poor rural women in India bear the responsibility of ensuring food for the family in times of crisis through collection of whatever edible products such as leaves, fruits and small catch are available in their local neighbourhoods. Climate effects of extreme temperature variations will affect crop cycles and crop production. and accentuate the scarcity of food availability in poorer households thus increasing women's burden. New agronomic practices that may be required to cope with climate effects such as new varieties of seeds developed in laboratories may further marginalize women's traditional agronomic knowledge and practices. Desertification and increased scarcities of fuel, fodder and water on account of climate effects means increased burden on women who are engaged in collecting these. Already, women in many rural areas and urban slums spend considerable number of hours in water collection for household needs. Disasters such as floods that would likely be caused by increasing sea levels are also likely to affect poorer households in low-lying regions and many disaster studies have indicated that women everywhere bear a greater burden on account of these. Clearly, the capacity building of women to cope with ecological insecurities is needed by evolving a comprehensive and holistic programme of ecological security (Larson, 2002). But efforts towards that first require a mapping of women's vulnerabilities on account of ecological changes and insecurities for each local community in the domains of livelihood, food security, health and resource-base sustainability. Gender equity and gender justice have to be cognized in all climate change solutions (Terry, 2009).

6

# Evolving Multiple Securities and Securing Gender Needs*

Formal/informal sector debates in development in the 70s and 80s of the last century were a part of the ongoing discourse on the dualistic nature of the development process that was under way. As such, the debate in the 80s sought to understand the nature of the linkages between these two dichotomous worlds of widely differing wages, working conditions, opportunities, growth, etc. It was hoped that even if these two worlds – the formal/informal, the organized/unorganized, the traditional/modern – could not be completely overcome under conditions of third world modernization and capitalist development, our progressive visions did not allow us to tolerate the vastly different working conditions and the quality of life. The state-sponsored capitalist industrialization process and the developmental roles of the state enabled us to envisage the plausibility that more efficient regulatory measures could progressively bring sections of the informal sector under the benign governance of the state. Legal and statutory provisions that existed could be made applicable to more and more workers through trade union initiatives and struggles, and the vast field of the informal sector was left to the imaginative initiatives of trade union-like organizations. Even then it needed little intellectual effort to comprehend the fact that there were two circuits of production-exchange-accumulation in the economy. One, the capitalist circuit in which capital accumulation and growth or extended reproduction was possible and the other, the circuit of subsistence in which commodity production was of the simple reproduction scheme that

* An earlier version of this chapter was published in Kalpagam, U. (1999) 'Globalization, Informal Sector and Gender Needs', *Man & Development*, March, Vol. 21, No. 1, pp. 1–12.

nevertheless permitted the survival, and biological and social reproduction of the vast majority dependent on that sector. But no capital accumulation took place in the circuit of subsistence to enable it to break out of the subsistence circuit, nor did the expansion of the capitalist circuit progressively absorb this circuit (Kalpagam, 1994).

With globalization, the circuits of accumulation and subsistence are no longer seen as separate and connected circuits, as analysts did so earlier, but are clearly a single complex with simultaneous processes of both strengthening and weakening the nodes of accumulation and subsistence. This is evident in the whole array of empirical cases that were highlighted in the earlier chapters. Vulnerabilities and insecurities of the workers are likely to be generated dynamically as processes of strengthening and weakening go on. It is therefore necessary to understand how vulnerabilities are constantly engendered and evolve ways that enable workers to stave off insecurities and overcome vulnerabilities.

**Formal and Informal Distinctions Become Fuzzier**

The fundamental principle of globalization and liberalization is to ensure competitiveness in the world economy. This is sought by ensuring the prevalence of market prices in national economies that are in tandem with the world market prices, and of external trade acting as the engine of growth. Developing countries that had earlier embarked on import-substitution industrialization strategies now have to move to export competitiveness as well as make the economies attractive for flows of foreign investment. Stabilization and structural adjustment policies sought to deregulate the economy and privatize the public sector.

If in the pre-liberalization pro-statist regime of development, it was possible to divide the economy into two sectors – formal/informal, the post-liberalization pro-market situation calls for a four-fold classification. For simplicity we say Fd (Formal domestic), Ff (Formal foreign), Id (Informal domestic) and If (Informal foreign). The foreign sub-sectors may be construed as sectors of the economy, which have greater non-domestic links than the domestic sub-sectors. These links may be in the nature of export markets, inflows of capital, technology, management, etc. The dynamics of production-exchange-accumulation in these four circuits are now more complex than in the earlier two circuits. The nature of the dynamics depends crucially on the nature of linkages between the four and with external economies as well.

Literature on informal sector in the country has so far suggested the coexistence of a dependent and an autonomous informal sector. The dependent sector is linked to the formal sector by a variety of linkages, subcontracting linkages being a pervasive feature. In fact, subcontracting is an important feature of the era of "flexible capitalism", with offshore production and on-shore assembly that is so common in the developed market economies. There is, therefore, no reason to believe that sector Ff would not also revive and reconstitute subcontracting relationships both of the old and other newer forms with firms in the If sector, such relationship would be varying according to the industry requirements. There is, as well, a need even to modify our conception of the Formal sector, as one that provides greater security and stability under the changed context of flexible capitalism. Flexibility, mobility and the efficient management of cyclical fluctuations of the market are basic to the success of flexible capitalism. Structural rigidities in labour-surplus developing economies signify the possibility of only a grossly altered form of flexible capitalism to prevail. Interdependence in the world economy may translate events that are cyclical in the originating end into structural effects at the impact end. Developing economies with structural rigidities face the challenge of ensuring, for instance, a temporary fall in demand in the export market is not translated into a permanent loss of market say to other competitors, when the market revives. If hitherto we characterized the Indian economy as a multi-structural one, with a variety of forms of production distinguished in terms of the nature of technology and labour relations, it will now be necessary to note that some segments of these will be governed by norms of flexibility, not only in respect of labour-use but a wide range of other strategies as well (Kalpagam, 1994).

The former understanding of formal/informal sector needs to be augmented. In some segments of the formal sector, the distinction between formal and informal will become fuzzier as flexible labour contracts become more pervasive. Unless regulatory mechanisms are set in place that acknowledge this feature of flexibility, this segment may suffer the same neglect as labour under non-registered enterprises. Firm-level regulatory mechanisms that have so far been in place for the formal sector, such as compliance with labour laws and surveillance by Factory Inspectorate (not to mention all the lacunae in implementation) are both outdated and/or inadequate and need to be augmented by other mechanisms. The norms and ethos of flexibility will in course of time govern private sector firms in the formal sector that offered relatively greater security of employment. While developed market economies practice hiring and firing – corporate downsizing and all that – they have also in place fairly efficient systems of unemployment compensation and monitoring. Systemic biases in employment, with respect to factors such as caste, gender, education and skill will be further strengthened under a non-regulated system of hiring and firing by the private sector.

For the vast segment of the informal sector that is relatively autonomous of the formal sector and providing subsistence employment for millions, the prospect of seven per cent or nine per cent growth rate of the economy means that there will be greater opportunities to multiply subsistence employment with increasing population. The symbiotic relationship between subsistence sector and the rest of the economy is all too apparent although research has not clearly established the co-integration of informal sector with macro-policy variables, unlike the formal sector. There has been some thinking in recent times on the nature of savings, investment and capital formation in the informal sector. The contribution of the informal sector to the total net value added by industry has been estimated in 1992–1993 to be around 63.5 per cent (Kantor, 1997). Much of the investment in the informal sector is only inadequately estimated in national accounts statistics, is in the nature of working capital rather than fixed capital, financed by household sector savings and estimated as a residual category.

Such prospects for the economy and for the informal sector under conditions of liberalization and globalization means that for the bulk of the women workers, subsistence employments that they have been engaged in so far will prevail and empirical evidence now points to an increase, and employment in modern manufacturing, such as export-oriented factory production in garment, electronics, food processing that they have been engaged in will continue under a more stringent ethos of flexibility. Research has established that women serve the role of a reserve army of labour, being absorbed and dispensed to suit the requirements of capital (Kalpagam, 1994). Under flexible capitalism, capital acquires a greater justificatory rationale for continuing to treat female labour as dispensable. But under what increased costs to women workers will the efficiencies and benefits of globalization and flexible capitalism be secured needs to be taken cognizance of.

Using macro level data, studies have shown an increase in the casualization of work force, declining organized sector employment, declining levels of poverty, feminization of poverty and greater regional disparities. There is increased casualization for both male and female workers in both urban and rural areas (Dev, 2000a; Chadha and Sahoo, 2002; Bhalla and Hazell, 2003). The availability of large numbers of workers, who are unable to find regular, permanent employment has fuelled the increasing use of contract/casual labour in industrial activity. As a part of liberalization and privatization policy, the government has attempted to curtail the rights of formal sector workers (Bremen, 2004). On the part of multilateral institutions, which have led the globalization agenda, the recognition that reforms have a dislocating impact upon labour has been quickly channelled into a larger discourse over "structural adjustment with human face" and more specifically into policy discussions on social security (Roy Chowdhury, 2004).

**Evolving Multiple Securities**

Analysis of industries and occupations under liberalization has highlighted the extreme fragility of livelihoods in many instances. It is of foremost importance to identify and evolve livelihood security mechanisms across a range of occupations to ensure that masses of workers can earn "decent" livelihoods in their preferred occupations. Traditional workers in many occupations face the greatest threat of survival and new jobs that come up often do not absorb the displaced workers. Tribals and marginalized communities are losing their traditional usufruct rights to forests and pastures, their lands being taken up by MNCs and big capital, mining industry and so on that they more often suffer the consequences of displacement with their lands being forcibly acquired.

Livelihood insecurities have affected women as well. With the shift from subsistence farming to commercial and cash cropping, women have lost both work, access to land for cultivation and control over their earnings. With greater appropriation of village commons and forest tracts, women have lost the work opportunities and income supplement through collections of fuel, fodder, minor forest produce, etc. As traditional industries like handloom face competition under conditions of globalization, women engaged in these industries as waged or family workers lose their livelihood.

It is generally assumed that women migrate on account of marriage, but they also do for employment and livelihood. Marriage-related migration of women is undoubtedly significant as almost every daughter of a village is married out of the village as dictated by the social conventions of marriage. But women also migrate for employment and this includes both young and older women, skilled and unskilled, educated and uneducated. The contribution of migrant women varies by economic class ranging from subsistence support to family to upward social mobility. Young high-school educated women migrate from villages and small towns to EPZs to work in export-oriented industries and stay in the numerous hostels that are coming up in many towns. In recent years, women have also been migrating to overseas countries for employment. The different categories of migrants face different insecurities and vulnerabilities. While a policy to provide *migrant security* may not cover all aspects, it is necessary to evolve mechanisms to provide security of employment free from harassment and exploitation, basic amenities, healthcare for migrants and their families, education for migrants' children, old age pension, etc. It is also necessary to extend the reach of microcredit to them wherever possible as microfinance institutions are more likely to view them as high-risk clients who cannot be traced to recover the loan amount.

The importance of *employment security* can never be overstated and it has been lately recognized by the legislative enactment of the Rural Employment Guarantee Act (NREGA). In Chapter 2, we highlighted the intermittent nature of employment in rural areas and the significant underemployment that exists as persons do not obtain adequate days of employment during the week as indicated by the current daily status and current weekly status employment and unemployment data from the NSS data. The employment security provided by NREGA ensures 100 days of employment per annum for one member of the rural household and the administrative modalities are innovatively designed so as to avoid leakages and corruption like social audit. Surprisingly, NREGA wages are delinked from the legally notified minimum wages and NREGA workers in many states are not being given the legally stipulated minimum wages. Economist Jean Dreze, the architect of NREGA programme has noted that it is unfortunate that NREGA was being misused to undermine the provisions of the Minimum Wages Act, while he thinks it ought to be a fantastic opportunity to reactivate the minimum wages (*The Hindu*, 7 November, 2010). NREGA is a logical culmination of a much older and tardily implemented programme in some states called the Food for Work Programme and Employment Guarantee Scheme. There is now mixed evidence of how NREGA is being implemented. While in some regions wage rates in NREGA are higher than the prevailing market wages, in some other regions the workers were paid ₹ 1 per day of work, or far less than the stipulated wage. Yet, the stipulation that only one member of a household can avail employment under NREGA is most likely to keep many women who need the jobs out of it. The NREGA emanates from the perspective of rights-based development and acknowledges the right to work. While it is an important move in actualizing the right to work, there is a need to acknowledge other dimensions of the right to work.

The right to work should imply "decent work" and not any work, and decent work is one that is hazard free, provides good working conditions meeting all the stipulations of factory laws and a wage rate that allows a decent living standard. In this sense, there is still a long way to go in making right to work a reality in the Indian context. There are indeed specific issues relating to women's right to work. In a patriarchal society as India, women's work is perceived as supplementary work in most regions and men are viewed as the bread winners of families. This perception of women's work has not only kept female wages always lower than male wages but has also led to the practice of withdrawal of women from labour force on status considerations as household income goes up in those sections of the population where women do not acquire high education standards. We had earlier noted in Chapter 2 that many women engaged in domestic duties have indeed expressed their willingness to work at home if work is provided to them. Much more innovative thinking is necessary to conceive the right to work for women.

Along with livelihood and employment security, it is necessary to ensure that the poor and marginal informal sector workers are provided with *food and nutritional security* as well. Food security issues in the country have so far been discussed regarding the nature of the public distribution system (PDS) that provides subsidized cereals such as wheat and rice, kerosene and sugar to households below the poverty line. While some recommend universal coverage and want to do away with the BPL and non-BPL distinction as such distinction only encouraged corruption and siphoning of benefits by those ineligible groups, yet others argue against universal coverage. To a recent suggestion that cereals be distributed free to the poorer classes as food stockpiles rot in the godowns, the government has rejected the suggestion as it would act as a disincentive to farmers who would reduce cultivation. But there is increasing evidence that globalization and liberalization have increased disparities between the rich and poor affecting the latter nutritionally and unless long-term effective measures are put in place the situation will only deteriorate. The PDS system has focussed only on cereals distribution and not pulses and cooking oil. Some states have recognized this lacuna and are assisting in those as well and also providing other required condiments at subsidized rates. This needs to be expanded at the national level to ensure balanced and nutritive food. With food prices soaring and especially of pulses, the diet of the poor has much lower protein content. Micro-nutrients are another area of deficiency for the poor. Nutritional security is sought to be provided for children, pregnant and lactating mothers through the Mid-Day Meal Scheme that has been made mandatory by the Supreme Court. It has been established that wherever the Mid-Day Meal Scheme is running efficiently, school enrollment and attendance have improved. It is necessary to have a more broad-based meal scheme in every village. The reduction of food subsidies has put pressure on the food security of poorer households and women are typically losers because of culturally determined intra-household food distribution patterns that are disadvantageous for them. Women are expected to eat last after feeding men and children, and there is usually only insufficient amount left for them.

Deshmukh (2008) has argued that it is difficult to take right to food inside the family where gender discrimination takes place. For changing such cultural norms, there has to be a significant and convincing change elsewhere that makes it possible to change norms. In the case of food security, it is necessary to explore how best the Panchayati Raj system could be used for an efficient and accessible public distribution system that could provide nutritional security to the vulnerable groups. Civil society organizations, panchayats and governments should try and evolve a blue-print for free Meal Scheme Centres to be set up in each and every village. Such a scheme should seek to provide two hot nutritious meals to every person in a village every day if they so desire. The cultural resources for starting such an activity is very much there in terms of religious philanthropy that needs to be mobilized and channelized at a scale that could make such an activity possible. Churches all round the world run soup kitchens for the destitute and homeless, Hindu temples have since a long time free-feeding of the devotees and the poor, the Sikhs have their *langar* in the Gurudwaras and so too the Muslims. Through a system of grants to each village panchayat from the state government and a matching grant from religious organizations such as temples, ashrams, churches and so on decreed by a law to that effect, it is possible to operationalize the scheme through village panchayats using local labour under the NREGA and so on. When poor and needy women can access their nutritious meals under such a scheme, gender discrimination within the family too will diminish, as public acknowledgement of their needs and entitlements will diminish their non-recognition in the private sphere of the household on account of scarcity.

*Housing security* has not received its due share of importance in public policies. Lack of adequate and proper housing affects migrant populations who suffer the most, and also all poor people in rural and urban areas. Policy support through financial assistance for housing for the poor is far too inadequate. Even some progressive state governments that took laudable initiatives for slum improvement in the 1970s and 1980s seem now to have lost the momentum and initiative even as they are grappling with the issues of relocation and rehabilitation of families displaced on account of development projects and for other reasons. It is because of lack of proper housing that many die during recurrent storms and rains when trees fall and buildings collapse. Housing security also complements facilities for clean drinking water, water availability within accessible distance and sanitation facilities. Women suffer on account of lack of these amenities much more as the responsibility of household chores are generally borne by them.

The decline in the resources and efforts expended upon the education, training and skill development of women and girls, which are crucial if women are to arrive at some degree of equality of social and economic opportunity, are another consequence of liberalization and economic reforms. Adult education programmes that earlier were targeted at illiterates, especially women, are now not popular with government agencies as greater importance is given to enhancing income-earning capacities of illiterate women through microcredit programmes. While the state has enacted the Right to Education and is making efforts to make primary and secondary education compulsory, it is necessary to fit in the Right to Education and Right to Work in a complementary manner such that at all levels and types of education, jobs are available and the right to work is also actualized in terms of appropriate employment. This would require better foresight and planning for vocational education and skill training. If illiterate and semi-literate women are to be able to move out of low-paying informal sector work, such complementarity at the level of policy design would be required.

*Health Security* must also be ensured through universal healthcare access. Although public health in India seeks to do so, its coverage and efficiency leaves much to be desired. Also, there are urban and rural differences as well as regional differences in public healthcare facilities. The health indicators of poor women in rural and urban areas are quite appalling in terms of mortality, morbidity and nutritional deficiencies, and it is also evident that the linkages between women's work and health are quite unfavourable to women.

A broad-based Social Security Programme covering, health, education, skill acquisition, widowhood and old age should be comprehensively addressed. The Second National Commission on Labour (2002) had a mandate to suggest umbrella legislation for ensuring a minimum level of protection to the workers in the unorganized sector. It is necessary to consider a holistic security system. The report of the National Commission for Enterprises in the Unorganized Sector (NCEUS, 2008) suggests a more inclusive group of unorganized/informal sector workers which apart from the usual regular and casual wage workers, and the self-employed in the unorganized sector and home-based workers would also include the unprotected wage workers in the organized sector which in the era of liberalization is a growing segment in the organized sector. The NCEUS has taken the position that the conditions of work including a minimum of social security should be in the nature of entitlement backed by national legislation as well as a public programme for promoting livelihoods backed by a dedicated National Fund. It has advocated the introduction of a National Minimum Wage related to the requirements of subsistence and minimal health, education and housing requirement, and advocated parity of wages between men and women, and between time-rated and piece-rated wages. Based on the suggestions of all earlier committees, the NCUES proposed a National Social Security Scheme in 2006 that covered life, health and disability benefits and old age pension for poor workers.

The approaches and schemes to actualize all the different security measures should have a built-in flexibility and be innovative about ways that can involve the civil society organizations along with the state institutions. As these security measures are constitutive of a new bundle of economic rights deemed necessary under neoliberal conditions of market-led development, it is necessary to involve a wide array of agents other than state institutions, which will go a long way in deepening democracy in the country. Working women have to be included in this process as decision-makers, beneficiaries and agents in the democratizing project.

All the different securities listed above will be effective only if simultaneously steps are taken to reverse the increasing informalization of work and to increase secure jobs for all. It is necessary to ratify and implement, as a minimum measure, all core ILO conventions and conventions which protect the rights of women workers, particularly conventions regarding maternity rights and home-based workers, and extend these rights to all other marginalized categories of workers. As well, recognition, support and protection of all organizations of workers, including organizations of informal sector workers, women's trade unions, community organizations and migrant workers' organizations is necessary. Setting up social safety nets for workers that would include a living wage, benefits for the unemployed, reproductive health, childcare, education and housing for women workers ought to be a priority issue. It is necessary to enact and implement equal opportunity laws that would ensure that there would be no discrimination based on gender, age, disability, ethnicity, religion, nationality status or sexual orientation. These policies should be promoted at an international level and it is necessary to reverse all the current policies that undermine them.

## Women as a Separate Category

Many still question as to why women should be treated separately and why an analysis that holds for men in the society should not be considered adequate to explain women's situations as well. Although a little awkward to make a case at this stage for treating women as a separate analytical category when "Women's Studies" has now established itself world-wide in the curriculum, the attempt here is to elucidate the multiple roles that women unlike men perform, which need to be brought into every analytical framework that seeks to explain labour-market behaviour and outcomes of women.

In all the societies, women perform reproductive functions, although the nature and extent of reproductive tasks (primarily child-bearing, child rearing and nurturance tasks) do vary across societies and classes of women. A whole or part of the reproductive tasks is not performed by men in any society. Women's reproductive tasks are crucial for the maintenance of social reproduction, since social reproduction requires biological reproduction as well. With the advent of capitalist industrialization, statistics on the labour-force began to be collected throughout the world. But in over 150 years of censuses, statistics on time spent by women in reproductive tasks have not been considered necessary either for policy purposes or even as a matter of social knowledge. This in part has arisen because reproductive tasks are seen to be private tasks performed in the private realm having no bearing on labour markets and public policy. In fact, even the few modifications made, upon insistence by feminist scholars and activists, in the Indian NSS data on time spent by women in fuel and water collection, etc., came through the logic of capturing all non-marketed production in agrarian economies such as India, rather than through the logic of reckoning reproductive tasks. There exists, therefore a clear case for giving importance to reproductive work in systems of national statistics.

Moreover, in all the societies, women combine these reproductive roles along with other roles, the extent and nature varying as well across societies. These roles are productive roles that are too well known to be elaborated, as well as the roles of home-managers and community organizers. Although the "Home Economics" of Gary Becker gave importance to household production, the tasks of household management, which is much more than household production has not been adequately acknowledged. Moreover, households do not exist in isolation. In most regions, inter-household social relations either organized around community or otherwise are maintained largely by the women of the household. Captured under the telling phrase "family status-production" by Papanek (1979), this too is an important aspect of social production for the social and cultural life of the community. This activity often gets categorized as the leisure activity of women. A study comparing rural women's activity patterns in four states (Gujarat, Meghalaya, Mizoram and Kerala) reported that nearly 22% of women's time in a day was spent in household activities, either indoor or outdoor, and leisure accounted for 9–10% during which time anyway women are engaged in community activities. These two together accounted for a significant 30% of time, only slightly lower than the time spent in fieldwork (Sriram and Ganapathy, 1997).

While it is generally accepted that these multiple roles impinge on women's labour-market participation, these have not been adequately brought into an analytical framework that would be useful for analysis. Moreover, these roles do affect and are in turn affected by social norms. Social norms embedded in institutions and practices translate cultural beliefs and expectations into modes of acceptable behaviour. Thus, rational behaviour and rational action in social settings are in fact authorized by and through cultural discourses. Not infrequently, these social norms themselves are bearers of gender and thus become gendered. For instance, the social norm relating to female responsibility for child-care constrains to some extent women's participation in the labour force, which in turn relegates them to a secondary status when it comes to wages and other benefits. Norm violations, especially of the gendered social norms, seen often as transgressions or deviance, evoke many disciplinary measures, of which violence forms an essential part. Women's participation in market and non-market activities is thus conditioned by the multiplicity of roles they perform and by the gendered social norms.

Not only are the multiple roles of women governed by gendered social norms, but these also serve to allocate power, prestige and status. Intra-household allocation of resources and the decision-making power over resources, income and consumption guided by these social norms render women as subordinate agents in patriarchal households. This is true of women's roles in other institutions as well, whether market or community. Patriarchy thus permeates all layers of the society, though in a society structured along caste and class lines, it would be more appropriate to use the notion of "multiple patriarchies".

While it is being increasingly acknowledged that labour-market analysis is best done in an institutional framework, the evolution of norms in institutions which is so crucial for institutional analysis is yet to be recognized. Such analysis would also need to account for the presence of gendered social norms and their impact on behaviour and outcomes. The thrust of the argument so far has been to reinstate "women" as an analytical category and to move to an incorporation of "gender" into economic and social analysis containing within it the many asymmetries of social relations (Kabeer, 1994).

**Liberalization, Economic Reforms and Women**

The economic philosophy of liberalization is that the market is the most efficient allocator of resources, and therefore it is necessary to allow the market forces to operate in an unhindered manner. State interventions in the allocative mechanisms have, it is argued, generated market "distortions" in resource prices. The costs of capital, foreign exchange and labour in pro-statist regimes of development did not reflect their true market prices. Currencies were over-valued, interest rates were kept artificially low to benefit the local capital and organized labour unions created themselves as "labour aristocracy". "Getting prices right" is seen as the panacea for all evils. Liberalization policies hinge crucially on the following three features: fiscal deficit reduction, increase in export growth and divestment of the public sector through privatization.

Fiscal deficit is sought to be reduced by demand restraint in the economy. More recently with a targeted nine per cent growth, it has been realized that demand restraint is not a prudent policy, and incomes policy in the modern sectors has been designed to spur demand and growth. Reduction of subsidies, especially for the agricultural sector, and cut backs in social expenditure affect the poor and vulnerable. Women in particular bear the brunt of reductions of expenditure on food subsidies and health. As trade is seen as the engine of growth, liberalization and economic reforms emphasize increase in export growth. In an increasingly interdependent world, there may be some truth to the logic of trade-led growth, but in the context of unequal power in the world economy, trade-dependent growth is likely to subject the economy to greater fluctuations. Global integration through trade implies greater integration of financial markets as well. Fluctuations in the production and trade sector is magnified in the financial sector causing greater instability, without forgetting the fact that financial instability as reflected in stock market behaviour can be quite independent of the trends in the real (production) sector.

Divestment of the public sector through sale and privatization follows logically from the idea that the market is the most efficient allocator of resources. What does seem surprising is that the logic of the public sector so well argued in economic theory till recently has been cast aside into the dustbin, replacing it with pious assertions of the efficiency of the market. The argument of "market failures" is now replaced with "state failures", and "rent-seeking" is made a greater vice than "profit-seeking". In all this, an impression is created that the state is redundant to the functioning of markets. A discourse that renders state and nation as anachronisms is an attempt at persuasion on the need to throw open the vast domestic market to global capital.

The emphasis on non-traditional agro-exports, textiles, apparel and electronics, in the new export strategy means greater opportunities for women's employment, although innumerable studies on these industries as discussed in Chapter 3 have shown that there is a great deal to be desired in terms of the nature of work and working conditions. Women's employment in the formal sector is quite insignificant. A reduction in public sector employment means less of formal sector employment for women. With the private sector adopting the norm of flexibility, formal sector women in the private sector are seen by management as the least flexible workers, and hence less desirable, while informal sector workers who are perceived as the most flexible are also the most desired (Gothoskar, 1997). The prospects of formal sector employment for women in the context of a diminishing role of the public sector and flexibility criterion are not very bright.

While arguing for social protection for informal workers, Unni and Rani (2001) observed that the growth of the informal sector in the emerging labour market is inevitable. The process of globalization, export-oriented industrialization and relocation of industries from developed to developing countries also leads to the increase of employment in the informal sector. Women's employment in the informal sector is also likely to rise due to various reasons. With the adoption of liberalization policies, women tend to be concentrated in certain sectors of the industry and certain status categories, which are generally concentrated in the low skilled, repetitive kind of jobs, thus the gender dimension of work leads to specific insecurities faced by women. A woman's double role in both the productive and reproductive spheres also leads to special social security needs (Unni and Rani, 2001).

Thus far, the basic features of economic reform process and some of its effects have been highlighted. There are, however, many assumptions of the liberalization approach that need to be questioned. The assumption that markets provide "proper costing" of resources under all circumstances is questionable. There are in fact factors intrinsic to the market, which limit its ability to provide "complete and proper costing". The well-known situation is the incompleteness of contracts through uncertainties and information asymmetries. Social customs and norms also play an important role in efficient resource allocation; in fact, as has been argued before, social norms are embedded in institutions. For instance, cultural practices that foster trust and cooperation among members of a social group reduce transaction costs and internalize externalities (Elson, 1994).

The idea of trade being an engine of growth has been caught in the debates on proving and disproving the neoclassical assumptions of automatic adjustment to full employment (Patnaik, 1997). Stylized thinking is often unhelpful in analysing the ground realities. Liberalization and economic reforms are based on the unrealistic assumption that resource transfers can be smoothly and costlessly effected from the non-tradable sector to the tradable sector. This neo-classical assumption of factor mobility flies in the face of reality. Take a factor such as labour. It is quite unrealistic to assume that a male construction worker can be made to work in an export garment factory. First, the construction worker needs to be trained to become a tailor, and the success of the training depends on motivation, ability, age, etc. Moreover, imparting skills entails a cost. Even if we grant that structural adjustment of the economy is made aware of skill and training components, there is an inherent male bias concerning the gender division of labour that is unstated. After all, it is well established that what is "men's work" and "women's work" is socially constituted.

Such assumptions about the malleability and flexibility of labour are particularly detrimental to women's work. Unpaid domestic work necessary for producing and maintaining human resources is not reckoned at all in macro-economic thinking. Structural adjustment policies are premised on the assumption that women have an unlimited capacity for domestic work. All reductions in social expenditures imply substitution of domestic labour. For instance, reduction in healthcare services means the sick are taken care of for a longer time at home. Further, the greater the reduction in incomes and more the inflation, the lesser would be the dependence on readily available processed or cooked foods. This implies that store-bought food is replaced perhaps by some kind of food cooked at home, thus increasing women's domestic labour. Given the deplorable situation of poor women's access to basic services in rural and urban areas as regards fuel and water availability and sanitation, women's and girls' domestic burden are already very high and increasing.

The assumption that women can be pulled out into the labour force and pushed back into the household at the whims of the market is the outcome of male bias and capitalist bias working in conjunction. For the already overburdened poor informal sector workers, increases in domestic burden are at the cost of their already poor health. There is overwhelming evidence that women and children's health are suffering in the post-reform period, despite all the talk of "health for all", and attention to the girl child. The most outrageous expose has been the sale of kidneys by slum women (and also men) in Chennai, Bangalore and elsewhere, for nearly ₹ 30,000 as a consequence of poverty and indebtedness (*Frontline*, 1997).

The "gender distortions" of structural adjustment policies are not limited to a lack of understanding of gender division of labour and women's unpaid domestic labour, but more importantly about the household itself. The household, while recognized as a basic unit of analysis, is viewed as one with unitary interests exhibiting homogeneity of behavioural responses among its members. Thus, the internal functioning of the household required no further analysis. There is now convincing and abundant evidence that the household is a site of conflict as well as cooperation; of inequality as well as mutuality, and these are structured along gender lines (Dwyer and Bruce, 1988; Sen, 1990).

It is no wonder that given these assumptions, the effects of structural adjustment policies on women have been uniformly negative according to a wide range of country experiences (Sparr, 1994). More women become unemployed, their working conditions deteriorate, male-female wage differentials widen, women become poorer, their unpaid work increases, their education and that of girls' suffer, their health deteriorates, they suffer greater domestic violence and stress, women-headed households increase and food security gets undermined. Overall, the implication of the structural adjustment programmes have been typically negative in terms of reduced real incomes and standard of living for most women, along with a greater burden of unpaid work. In fact, one very common gender specific result of such policies is the increase in the unpaid labour of women. The reduction of government subsidies to energy sources and to basic amenities such as sanitation, water supply, public health and education services has not only reduced wage earners' household incomes, but has put a special burden on women who generally bear the responsibility for providing these to the family.

Recognizing these negative effects, the Commonwealth Secretariat in its report noted that greater support needs to be given to women in all their multiple roles. It also recommended full integration of women into the decision-making process and suggested the need to create a supportive international environment. Action was suggested on the following fronts: Employment, credit, foreign exchange, infrastructure, marketing, training, extension and technical services, technology, land, environment, legal issues, access to basic goods and services, education and health among others. While this shopping list is certainly better than none, and some consider it far more gender sensitive than the UNICEF's *Adjustment with a Human Face*, it still falls short of a full and complete feminist critique of structural adjustment policies. In fact, even the World Bank noted in its report *Women in Development* (1987) that the policies' effects on women should be mitigated and that measures on the following four fronts were necessary: (i) legal and regulatory measures to ensure equal opportunities to men and women, (ii) investment on their health, education and nutrition, (iii) improving their access to credit and assets, and (iv) targeted public interventions for promoting women's skills, employment and work. In the last two decades, feminist scholars working in the World Bank are increasingly sensitive to carry into the Bank-Fund approach some of the concepts and ideas generated by the progressive women's movement and to consider the inclusion of NGOs in their dialogue.

A feminist understanding and activism should attempt at the restructuring of market relations, restructuring of political and bureaucratic relations, and restructuring of relationships within households and communities so as to reduce the inequalities of power. However, the useful insights that feminist pragmatism has yielded so far, and they are very significant in our trajectory of ideas is the notion of "gender needs" and the much debate-inspiring concept of "empowerment" (Antrobus, 1989).

### Securing Gender Needs

Gender needs, it was noted by Molyneux, can be classified into practical gender needs and strategic gender needs (Molyneux, 1986). Practical gender needs refer to those needs of women that would enable them to perform their varied roles – production roles, reproduction roles, home managers and community organizers. Fulfilling these gender needs would not challenge the status-quo in the society. Strategic gender needs are those needs of women which would challenge their subordinate position and seek to ensure greater equality. The clear specification of these two sets of needs has served an amazing role in studies on women and development, in gender planning exercises, and helped to bring to focus and debate the idea of "gender empowerment" (Moser, 1989; 1993). The experience of women's NGOs has been that by taking up issues of practical gender needs they could also sensitize women about their subordinate position. There is also a contrary opinion that by concentrating too much on practical gender needs, the women's NGO movement has exhausted itself of all energy to take up strategic gender interests.

A book on women's economic empowerment covering organizations like SEWA in Gujarat, construction workers union in Chennai, and Cooperative Development Foundation in Andhra Pradesh and others indicates the range of strategies adopted by women's NGOs in working with the informal sector workers (Carr et al., 1997). There are many more written and unwritten stories of various kinds of NGO strategies. The report "Shramshakti", brought out by the National Commission on Self-Employed Women and Women Workers in the Informal Sector (1987) identified the range of problems and a set of sector-specific strategies for informal sector workers, all of which still continue to be valid, and has also been validated by the recent report of NCEUS (2008). Recently, some scholars have expressed the view that a move from sectoral approach to "livelihood strategies" is likely to fully account for women's multiple occupations and multiple roles, and also take into account the shifting goals of "survival, stability and growth in response to external conditions and internal constraints" (Rao, 1996). No doubt, strategies of economic and social empowerment did attempt, in howsoever limited, successful or unsuccessful ways to restructure market relations, political and bureaucratic relations and household relations in women's favour. However, these attempts at tilting relations favourably towards poor women have not made a significant dent in the overall problem.

One has to agree with the assessment made by a scholar that the search for empowerment makes contradictory demands on grassroots organizations, for they have to confront the forces that disempower them and yet, at the same time remain in the "mainstream" to ensure access to governmental resources (Sharma, 1991–1992). With government resources and role progressively shrinking, there are more actors on the scene to reckon and appease. The challenge is to break out of these contradictory pulls, which can only be done by reimagining empowerment in radically new ways.

Although globalization and markets are going to be with us, they need not have to be what they are. Radical critiques of development have always argued for alternative development paradigms that are eco-friendly, equitable to women, other vulnerable groups, etc., but nothing that could reverse the on-going development process has come into existence. Yet, we know that grassroots organizations have in the

Indian context at least generated a substantial body of "local knowledge" of development, of micro-impacts of macro processes, and have shown both the tenacity and creativity for both local action and global struggles.

It is this creativity of the people that has to be harnessed to evolve a political vision, over the next few decades; this cannot be a quick-fix solution. If "socialism", "planning", the "welfare state" and the "developmental state" that provided hope in the middle of the 20th century have failed to meet our expectations, what we need is an imaginative and creative replacement of those ideas. The challenge ahead is how to restructure our democratic system to truly empower the poor and marginalized, women, Dalits and minorities. It is necessary to set in place the notion of grassroots consensus for development governance by promoting a "rights-based community-oriented democracy" in which consent at the community level will become necessary for allocative and distributive mechanisms to operate. The market will then be transformed into a social institution that all social actors can shape, control and negotiate. There is perhaps some scope in moving the Panchayati Raj system to this conception of a political community.

# 7

# Social Protection for Women in the Informal Sector*

Globalization has added to the woes of the informal sector workers as there are now greater market induced livelihood risks. For instance, as agriculture is increasingly brought under the orbit of global market forces through commercial and contract farming, agro-exports, modern farming using HYV seeds and fertilizer use that are part of the bank-loan packages and futures trading, farmers in some regions who thought commercial cropping would be more profitable landed themselves in debt when price movements turned unfavourable. In the liberalized regime of markets, lending banks pushed ahead with loan repayments and foreclosures that forced farmers in some regions to commit suicide, a phenomenon well articulated in the recent Hindi film Peepli Live. The recent global recession also affected millions of handicraft workers whose export markets have dwindled causing livelihood insecurity; such insecurity was caused on account of liberalized imports of silk yarn and textiles, and toys from China in the last decade. The government was compelled to announce a ban on import of toys from China recently. Natural disasters such as floods, drought, earthquake and tsunami destroy both livelihood and habitat bases of the poor. Other global changes such as climate change are also causing greater livelihood insecurity.

The vast bulk of informal sector workers lack any kind of social security such as health, disability and old age pension, nor are they covered for occupational hazards and accidents, except where in some states, governments have introduced some measures that anyway lack universal coverage. Sakthivel and Joddar (2006) analysed the NSS 55th

* A version of this presented jointly with Sudersena of WWF (I) at the Second Global Labour Forum held in New Delhi in December 2005.

round data for 1999–2000 on coverage of workers under provident fund and observed that irrespective of the income group, the non-farm unorganized sector workers have been left out of social security arrangements. As far as the organized sector was concerned, while 90% of the richest group availed provident fund facility, only 55% of the poorest among non-farm organized segment of the workforce were covered under the provident fund system. Overall, in the non-farm sector, as against a paltry 5% of poorest, 33% of the richest workers avail provident fund facilities.

The period of liberalization has also witnessed the growth of new industries in newly emerging townships. This new industrialization has spawned a new set of employment relations that build in both old and new insecurities for the workers. Vijay (1999) has shown how flexibilization is operationalized in the organized sector through casualization and contractualization of jobs. The extensive employment of contract and casual labour, of mostly migrants including women from rural areas, without any kind of social security compels the workers to source for themselves different modes of collective and individual help in times of need which take different forms "such as solidarity, patronage, coercive protection, transactional support, political support and trust, and is expressed through various institutions", not all of these conferring dignity to the workers (ibid.: 12). He rightly observes, "Dignity is to be viewed as the limit of social security, the presumption being that where the labourer is ensured of his/her social security, he/she aims at dignity" (ibid.: 14). Kabeer (2002) pointed out that households may face a trade-off between their search for security and the value they give to the dignity and self-respect of members.

The plight of women informal sector workers is worse. Arunachalam (2005b) observes that the women workers in the informal sector, both in urban and rural areas, face more or less the same kind of oppressive situation. The series of economic problems that confront women in this sector are abysmal living conditions, exploitative and harsh working conditions, low and discriminatory wages, invisibility and powerlessness, disposition of assetlessness and landlessness, monopoly of moneylenders and middlemen resulting in heavy indebtedness and impoverishment, low skill levels/technology/productive inputs/caste inferiority, male dominance, isolation and physical weakness due to large families. Poor women in rural areas not only lack social security but they are more often responsible for providing security in times of severe crisis such as when shortages of food occur.

Rural women have to come up with strategies for survival and ensure minimum sustenance for themselves, their children and aged ones when male members are forced to seasonally migrate in search of work elsewhere (Agarwal, 1990). Often aged widows in rural areas are compelled to eke out a living when they have no family member to provide for them (Chen, 1998). Poor women, both the young in their reproductive years and the older women suffer from problems of ill-health that affect their work life, and the nature of the work also in turn affects their health. Reproductive health problems are also very rampant in certain regions causing high maternal and infant mortality rates. But women lack health security and with overstretched public health infrastructure and gender discrimination in households, poor women face difficulties of access as well. During times of disaster, aid and relief measures do not reach poor women as they are more often cornered by the powerful.

Recognizing that many of the traditional social security mechanisms have been whittled down with the breakdown of the *jajmani* system in rural India (although other kinds of patron-client relations continue to exist), there has been much discussion since the 1990s on social security measures for the poor, deprived and unorganized sector workers (Dreze and Sen, 1991; Guhan, 1994; Ginneken, 1998; 1999; Thorat, 1999). To cover the various threats, vulnerabilities and risks that women workers in the informal sector face, it is necessary to broaden the scope of social security that is usually a scheme-based policy to cover one or two contingencies. What the poor informal sector workers require is broad-based social protection that could cover all contingencies over their entire lifecycle. For women, such social protection would be a long-term empowerment process for if their numerous contingent problems are covered under such a protection policy, poor women would be strengthened economically, making it possible to enhance their social awareness of gender and other systemic inequities through various means that would make them active participants in a gender inclusive, transformative and participatory development.

Jhabvala (1998) noted the tendency of a shift in the target group for social security from the "worker" to the "poor" or "deprived", and rightly suggests that it needs to be "worker or producer in his/her times of vulnerability, both chronic and contingent". This approach confers dignity and the right to social security acknowledging their contribution to the society as workers at some phase of their life. Unni and Rani

(2003) also observed that many different terms are being used such as "social security", "social insurance", "social assistance", "safety nets", "social funds" and "social protection". As noted by Jhabvala (1998), social security in the context of India and other developing countries must encompass both "'protective' aspects of preventing a decline in living standards; and 'promotive' aspects of enhancing normal living conditions by the requirement of 'income maintenance' and 'income support'". Further, she proposes that the programmes and activities connected with provision of employment, income and assets be termed "economic security" and those connected with other basic needs such as healthcare, child care, maternity care, old age pension, food, etc., be termed "social security". Economic security and social security together is often referred to as "social protection" which is considered a broader notion of social security (Jhabvala and Subrahmanya, 2000; Dev et al., 2002; Unni and Rani, 2003).

Some non-governmental organizations (NGOs) and community-based organizations (CBOs) have tried such a social protection approach towards women informal sector workers that could serve as a model for devising policy approaches. Unni and Rani (2003) noted that it is a challenge to evolve institutional mechanisms for social protection that can create instruments and deliver them to the vast numbers of workers in the informal sector. In what follows, the social protection approach of Working Women's Forum (India) is analysed as a case study. Policy inferences are then drawn from this illustrative case.

Arunachalam (2006) notes that WWF's microfinance is an inclusive process of various activities such as group formation, entrepreneurial assistance through micro-loan, skill/empowerment training, social security/occupational safety and healthcare benefits to the members. Further she notes, micro-insurance programme of WWF (I) is protection of assets and lives of the clients against insurable risks of target population. Micro-insurance is linked up with micro-savings and microcredit thereby facilitating them to allocate their scarce resources to micro investments with high marginal return.

## An Assessment of Working Women's Forum's Initiatives

Working Women's Forum (India) (WWF) is committed to empower poor women workers economically, socially and politically. It has found that the main roadblock faced by the poor women is the lack of access to credit for their livelihoods. On recognizing the wider social, political and economic considerations of poor working women, the broad objectives of WWF (I) are to provide a social platform for women employed in the informal sector by organizing them on trade lines, to bring in a structural change by establishing an innovative organizational structure where poor women can participate at all levels, to make the social movement totally women intensive, to identify and address the critical needs of poor working women like credit, social security, training for leadership, skill, healthcare and child care, to provide opportunities for leadership to poor women to mobilize themselves and others, for joint economic and social action by exerting group pressure to demand their social and political rights. Comprehensive accounts of WWF (I) objectives and activities can be found in Arunachalam and Landwehr (2003), Kalpagam and Rajagopalan (2006), Somasundaram (2006) and Nachiappan et al., (2008).

The WWF (I) has promoted two other institutions to work in unison towards poor women's development and progress. Indian Co-operative Network for Women (ICNW) which is the credit wing that enhances the social and economic independence of poor women by providing them microcredit, thereby encouraging their entrepreneurship. Using credit as an entry point is effective in serving the poorest of the borrowers, while acting as a social catalyst. Women are given better choice of livelihoods. Training in women's empowerment, health and skill is a central part of the loan process. The National Union of Working Women (NUWW) is the trade union wing which facilitates poor women in the social action process – to fight for labour, land, housing, representation in local governance, human rights, issues like domestic violence, female feticide, female infanticides, child prostitution and child labour. It upholds the rights of women through collective action and solidarity.

**Need for Social Security**

Arunachalam (2006) has noted that insurance is a security/protection to poorer households against those risks that they are unable to protect themselves through savings/credit/income/or other mechanism. There is a degree of uncertainty among these various sources particularly in the low-income households on account of vulnerabilities caused by contingencies such as lifecycle events like marriage and death, sickness, accidents, disabilities, loss of property, business losses, etc. Poor households may inevitably choose to spend from their meagre income/profits or manage the risk with a loan and get into continued indebtedness. While for most of the lifecycle events the amounts required may be negligible, there are occasional events such as epidemics, environmental natural disasters that are all considerably more risky than ordinary lifecycle events. Lifecycle events are relatively predictable when compared to disability, illness or losses to property resulting from accidents and other disasters, etc. Correspondingly, the resulting losses or costs for each of these vulnerable events can vary from small to very large, but as risks tend to get more and more uncertain, the losses increase and simple savings/meagre income or loan activities may not be able to manage such losses. Social security and micro-insurance are products of microfinance and therefore the micro-insurance is a viable support system to help the poor to get themselves to stabilize in their life and safeguard their income as a livelihood security.

The WWF (I) understood that social security measures are the "lifelines" of its members through the findings of its periodic needs – assessment surveys. The structure of the organization revolves around providing security – both social and economic to its members. It defines social security as being "Empowered" which includes credit facilities, leadership, health and skill training, retirement benefits, healthcare, disability coverage, child care, unemployment benefits, business loss, maternity benefits, coverage for expenditure like marriage, education, house construction and repairs, loss due to natural calamities, etc. The members are home-based workers for whom there are contractors or sub-contractors; vendors and hawkers both in urban and rural areas; handicraft workers and artisans who work for others on piece-rate wages; and construction workers and wage labourers.

The WWF (I) defines social security not only in economic terms but also in non-economic terms. Access to credit, being part of a group, training provided for health and for women's empowerment, the organizational structure all form part of the wider concept of social protection. The social movement of WWF (I) is by itself a manifestation of social security for its members. Anjugam, a 35–year-old member from Chennai, observes that being a member of WWF (I) or "the sangam" has been a turning-point in her life. After her husband deserted her and her two children, she met with an accident. With the insurance claim she received, she set up a petty shop. She then met an area staff or organizer from WWF (I) who appraised her of the activities of the Forum. Now, Anjugam proudly operates a tailoring school with 15 students. She credits her empowerment to the "sangam". This is an example of the social movement of WWF (I) being transformed into a movement for social security. Yet another example of the vulnerability of women is that of Thangarani who lost her business to the tsunami waves that struck Chennai on December 26, 2004. With the financial assistance she received from WWF (I), Thangarani was able to restart her business. These are just two examples exposing the vulnerability of the poor women members of WWF (I) in the metropolis of Chennai and in the 15 branches in the three southern states. The need for social security is also felt by the beedi-rollers of Vellore who are out of work during the monsoon season, the agarbathi-rollers of Bangalore who are susceptible to asthma and TB, the silk weaver artisans of Kanchipuram who face competition from the "polyester culture", the fisherwomen of Adirampattinam who are at the mercy of nature, and the dairy farmers of Dindigul who often face severe drought.

**Social Security Schemes of WWF (I)**

The WWF (I) has a tie-up with Life Insurance Corporation of India (LIC)[1] and Royal Sundaram Alliance Pvt. Ltd. (RSA)[2] for providing social security coverage for its members. This insurance cover to all the clients is being catered through the Indian Cooperative Network for Women (ICNW). The insurance programmes are for life, accident, disability, and health. The health programme also organizes preventive health check-up camps in all the service areas of WWF/ICNW operations.

The WWF (I) plays an intermediary role in the social security model it offers to its members. It collects premiums on behalf of its members, either voluntarily when the member opts for the LIC scheme or involuntarily as part of the microcredit loan given by ICNW, and deposits the premium with the insurance companies. In cases of claim, the WWF (I) verifies the supporting documents and submits it to the insurance company. The claims are received by it, which are then handed over to the insured or the nominee, after verification. In case of hospitalization, the insured avails healthcare in hospitals or nursing homes fulfilling specified requirements, pays for the healthcare, which is reimbursed by the insurance company to ICNW, which in turn reimburses the insured member.

As on December 2007, over 8,80,868 women benefit through the LIC Programme and nearly 38,487 women benefit through the RSA scheme. Nearly 86.66% of the policy holders belong to LIC Social Security Scheme (LIC-SSS), 9.15% of the policy holders belong to LIC-JBY scheme, 3.46% of the policy holders belong to Royal Sundaram Sakthi

Security Scheme (RSA-SSS) and 0.72% belong to the Royal Sundaram Health Insurance Scheme (RSA-HIS). While the highest number of policy holder belongs to the LIC Social Security Scheme (LIC-SSS), presumably due to its small premium and the involuntary nature of the scheme, the lowest number of policy holders belongs to the health insurance. This low coverage may be due to the fact that health awareness among poor women is given a low priority and/or the awareness of the scheme is poor. Schemes and premiums vary across the different branches of WWF (I). For example, in Dindigul, Bellary and Bidar branches of WWF (I), the LIC Social Security Schemes are not offered because the members do not want it. In Adiramapattinam, Narasapur and Bhimavaram branches, the premiums for the LIC-JBY schemes are much higher. It is ₹ 167 in Adiramapattinam, ₹ 460 in Narasapur and ₹ 820 in Bhimavaram and for the rest of the branches it is ₹ 100. The difference in premium payments at different branches for the LIC-JBY scheme is due to high claims in these branches.

Initially, the LIC commenced its life insurance programme for the WWF (I) members in 1983. The annual premium was ₹ 3 and the amount of claim in case of natural death only was ₹ 1,000. Later, in 1990, the premium was revised to ₹ 25 and the claim was increased to ₹ 5,000. The watershed moment came in the year 2000, when the then ruling Government at the Centre announced the social security schemes for the workers in the unorganized sector. Then, the LIC Social Security (LIC-SS) Scheme and the LIC Janashree Bheema Yojana (JBY) scheme came into vogue.

***LIC Social Security Scheme (LIC-SS)***

This scheme was started in the year 2000. This policy provides life and disability cover to all its members. The insured needs to be a member of ICNW. The annual premium is ₹ 25. If the member does not pay the premium, it is automatically deducted from the savings account if a minimum balance of ₹ 50 is available. The target group is women members between the ages 18–60 years. The premium is not deducted if the premium of ₹ 100 for the LIC Janashree BheemaYojana scheme is paid. The policy holder receives ₹ 12,500 and ₹ 25,000 in case of partial and complete disability, respectively. The nominee or the legal heir of the policy holder receives ₹ 5,000 in case of natural death and ₹ 25,000 in case of accidental death of the insured.

### *LIC Janashree Bheema Yojana Scheme (LIC-JBY)*

The JBY scheme was started in the year 2000. The annual premium is ₹ 100. The benefits are more attractive than the (LIC-SS) social security scheme. In case of natural death of the member, the nominee gets ₹ 20,000 and ₹ 50,000 in case of accidental death. In case of partial disability, ₹ 25,000 is paid and in case of total disability ₹ 50,000 will be paid. The unique feature of this scheme is that scholarship benefits are offered for school-going children studying in 9th, 10th, 11th and 12th standards. Each family will receive a scholarship amount for two children of up to ₹ 1,200 in a year. However, evidence of two premium payments should be produced and the beneficiary students should have an excellent academic record. The LIC releases scholarship payouts based on their administrative norms.

### *Royal Sundaram Health Insurance Scheme*

In order to address the health needs of the women members holistically, an insurance scheme in association with the Royal Sundaram Alliance Pvt. Ltd. was started in 2001. Members enrolled in the Health Insurance Scheme are entitled to hospitalization benefits for admission to a private hospital. In case of maternity, ₹ 3,000 can be claimed. Maternity benefits are allowed up to two children. In case of cataract surgery, a maximum of ₹ 3,000 in a year can be claimed. For surgery and other illnesses, a maximum of ₹ 7,000 in a year, subject to a maximum of ₹ 5,000 for one admission can be claimed. The premium varies by age of the insured and is ₹ 65 up to 18 years, ₹ 125 for 18–45 years, an amount of ₹ 175 for 45–60 years and an amount of ₹ 210 for 60–75 years.

### *Royal Sundaram Shakthi Security Shield (RSA-SSS)*

On a special request from WWF (I), Royal Sundaram Alliance brought out a scheme exclusively for the benefit of poor women members in 2002. The annual premium is ₹ 34. In case of accidental death of the insured or spouse or parents/guardian an amount of ₹ 25,000 can be claimed. If the member and her husband or parent/guardian die accidentally, the legal heir/nominee of the deceased is entitled for the insurance amount of ₹ 50,000. In case of total disability, i.e., loss of two limbs, the insured gets a claim of ₹ 25,000, whereas for the loss of one limb or one eye ₹ 12,500 can be claimed. The scheme also provides cash relief for the period when the insured is temporarily or totally disabled from engaging in any work. Under such circumstances, ₹ 100 per week subject to a maximum of ₹ 1,500 will be paid. The scheme also has a provision to reimburse hospitalization expenses arising out of an accident – up to a limit of ₹ 1,000. Also, compensation is provided for the loss of or damage to the insured's dwellings and household goods due to natural calamities – up to ₹ 1,000 for dwelling and ₹ 500 for contents.

### Claims

The total number of beneficiaries upto December 2007 in the social security schemes were 15,198. The number of beneficiaries under LIC-JBY scheme were 811 (5.34%), under LIC-SSS were 2,827 (18.60%) and under LIC-JBY scholarship scheme were 6,062 (39.89%). Beneficiaries under Royal Sundaram's Sakthi Health Scheme (RSA-HIS) were 191 (1.26%), out of which 98 benefited under the Maternity scheme, 29 underwent Eye surgery and 64 benefited from claims for other ailments. Under Royal Sundaram Sakthi Security Scheme (RSA-SSS) 5,307 (34.92%) participants benefited, out of which 5,014 were flood victims, 135 fire victims, 77 were tsunami victims and 81 were other personal accident victims.

### Effectiveness of the Social Security Schemes

In order to examine the effectiveness of the social security schemes, a survey was conducted in June-July of 2005 to assess the social security needs of the WWF members, to evaluate the factors which influenced their purchase of a particular insurance policy, to explore the subjectively perceived benefits and costs of social security schemes and to evaluate the limitation of the present social security schemes. A sample of 200 members of the WWF (I) was chosen from the Chennai metropolis covering South, Central and North Chennai. The members were chosen at random on a proportional representation basis. A questionnaire was designed and translated into Tamil, the local language. The WWF's experienced supervisors interviewed the respondents.

The profile of the members surveyed is presented from Table 7.1 to 7.6. Table 7.1 presents the membership in the different social security schemes. 37.5 % of the policy holders are members in LIC-JBY scheme, 6.5% are members of RSA-Shakthi Security Shield, 1% are members of RSA-Health Insurance; 38% are members of any two schemes, 6% are members in all the three schemes and 9.5% are not purchasers of any scheme.

**Table 7.1**

*Membership in the Social Security Schemes of WWF (I)*

| *Social Security Scheme* | *No. of Members* |
|---|---|
| Member in LIC-JBY only | 75 (37.5%) |
| Member in Royal Sundaram Shakthi Security Shield | 13 (6.5%) |
| Member in Royal Sundaram Health Insurance Scheme | 2 (1%) |
| Member in any two schemes | 76 (38%) |
| Member in all three schemes | 12 (6%) |
| Non-policy-holders | 19 (9.5%) |
| Missing | 3 (1.5%) |
| Total | 200 |

Members who opt for two or more schemes clearly indicate a strong preference for insurance cover as well as their ability to pay the premium. The fact that 44 % have opted for two or more schemes indicates a strong preference of a large majority for such social security. A marginally higher proportion of 45% are covered under one of the three social security schemes, indicating once again that 89% of the respondents do desire and opt for social security schemes like these. Only about 10% are not covered under these three schemes, although they too as members of ICNW would be covered for life and disability under the LIC-SSS.

Table 7.2 below presents the age profile of the respondents:

**Table 7.2**

*Age of Purchasers of Social Security*

| *Age (in years)* | *No. of Members* |
|---|---|
| 24–29 | 8 (4%) |
| 30–39 | 80 (40%) |
| 40–49 | 70 (35%) |
| 50–59 | 16 (8%) |
| >60 | 2 (1%) |
| Non-policy-holders | 19 (9.5%) |
| Missing | 3 (1.5%) |
| Total | 200 |

Forty per cent of the policy holders belong to the age group of 30–39 years and 35% belong to the age group 40–49 years. Thus, 75% of the policy holders are in the working and reproductive years. Only 8% belong to the age group 50–59 years. This distribution may also be a reflection of the age composition of the majority of the WWF members who are likely to be in the 30–49 years age group. Women above 60 years are not covered under these insurance schemes.

**Table 7.3**

*Marital Status of Purchasers of Social Security*

| *Marital Status* | *No. of Members* |
|---|---|
| Married | 147 (73.5%) |
| Single | 1 (0.5%) |
| Widowed | 25 (12.5%) |
| Deserted | 4 (2%) |
| Non-policy holders | 19 (9.5%) |
| Missing | 2 (1%) |
| Total | 200 |

As Table 7.3 above indicates, 74% of the social security subscribers are married while 13% are widowed and 2% are deserted.

**Table 7.4**

*Number of Family Members of Purchasers of Social Security*

| *No. of Family Members* | *No. of Members* |
|---|---|
| 0–4 | 83 (41.5%) |
| 5–6 | 79 (39.5%) |
| 7–8 | 10 (5%) |
| >8 | 5 (2.5%) |
| Non-policy holders | 19 (9.5%) |
| Missing | 3 (1.5%) |
| Total | 200 |

From Table 7.4, it is clear that 41.5% of the policy holders have up to four family members, while 39.5% have family members between five and six. Five per cent have family members between seven and eight and 2.5% have more than eight family members. The fact that 48% of the policy holders have family size of five or more members indicates the preference for social security even when family size is large. One would have expected that additional family members may in itself be a kind of security in times of crisis but clearly that is not the case.

**Table 7.5**

*Membership (in Years) in WWF*

| *Membership (in years) in WWF (I)* | *No. of Respondents* |
|---|---|
| < 5 | 92 (46%) |
| 6–10 | 57 (28.5%) |
| 11-15 | 15 (7.5%) |
| 16–20 | 11 (5.5%) |
| > 20 | 1 (0.5%) |
| Non-policy-holders | 19 (9.5%) |
| Missing | 5 (2.5%) |
| Total | 200 |

Forty-six per cent of the policy holders have been members for less than five years, 28.5% have been members for 6–10 years, 7.5% have been members for 11–15 years, 5.5% for 16–20 years and 0.5% for more than 20 years. These social securities are more popular with the new members of WWF than with those who have been long-term members.

**Table 7.6**

*Educational Level of Purchasers of Social Security*

| *Education* | *No. of Respondents* |
|---|---|
| Upto V std. | 85 (42.5%) |
| V–X std. | 78 (39%) |
| XI–XII std. | 12 (6%) |
| Non-policy-holders | 19 (9.5%) |
| Missing | 6 (3%) |
| Total | 200 |

A total of 42.5% of the policy holders have neither no education at all or only up to primary education, 39% have education up to 10th standard and 6% up to 12th standard. The majority of the policy holders have at best only secondary school education.

### Insurance Claims Filed

A total of 123 claims were filed; 99 being first claims filed, 21 being second claims filed and three being third claims filed as shown in Table

7.7 below. The highest number of claims was for scholarship, with over 90 claims being filed. The other claims were for health – 10 claims, for disability – 3 claims and accident – 20 claims. Ninety-six per cent of those who received the amount said it was not sufficient and the shortfall had to be met by borrowing, selling personal assets or withdrawing from savings.

**Table 7.7**

*Total Insurance Claims Filed in the Last Five Years by the Respondents*

| *Claim* | *No. of Claims* |
|---|---|
| I – Claim | 99 |
| II – Claim | 21 |
| III – Claim | 3 |
| | 123* |

* For Health – 10, Disability – 3, Scholarship – 90
Accident (Fire, Tsunami, Flood, etc.) – 20

## Reasons for Joining the Social Security Schemes

The survey revealed that security for life was the main reason for purchasing insurance. Given the list of reasons, respondents were asked which of the reasons prompted them to opt for social security schemes. As Table 7.8 below indicates, 71% of the respondents pointed out that security for life was the reason, 26% attributed the reason to the training sessions and skill meetings of WWF, for 21% it was the need for old-age pension, for 38% it was for future savings, 50% wanted scholarship and 12% said it was for the well-being of their children.

**Table 7.8**

*Reasons for Joining the Social Security Schemes of WWF (I)*

| *Reasons* | *Percent of Responses* |
|---|---|
| Security for life | 71% |
| WWF (I) Training Programmes/Skills | 26% |
| Old-age Security | 21% |
| Savings for Future | 38% |
| Scholarship for Education | 50% |
| Well-being of children | 12% |

The reason "security for life" may be an expected response to the benefits accruing from an insurance scheme. But the fact that half the respondents looked towards social security support for children's education shows both the importance of child's education among women in the informal sector in Chennai as well as the rising private cost of education that makes such social security support necessary. Chennai being a fast growing region, the poorer classes have realized the importance of education for children as a way of upward economic mobility. There are a large number of first-generation college students in the colleges in Chennai and its suburbs, and it is not uncommon for autorickshaw drivers or domestic servants to surprise us by saying that their children are pursuing graduate courses in bio-technology or computers. This is a pointer to the need for social security coverage for children's education in other states and regions that will in course of time follow this path, where the poorer working classes would realize the importance of children's education.

**Perceived Benefits and Costs of Insurance**

Purchasing insurance seems to have a positive impact on the respondents. The survey sought to find out the perceived benefits and costs. Seventy-two per cent of the respondents felt a sense of protection and 56% of the respondents experienced a sense of well-being. On an analysis of the subjective costs, 16% of the respondents said there were frequent quarrels in the household and 10% of the respondents indicated too much time was spent on paying the insurance premium. The respondents revealed that the men folk in the household objected to the fact that even after paying an annual premium of ₹ 100, there was no assurance of benefit when the insured reaches the age of 60 years. Also, often disputes arose over the nominations of family members for the insurance policy. To avoid such discords, the women would hide the passbook from the other members of their family.

**Shortcomings of the Prevalent Social Security Schemes**

The respondents were also asked about the major shortcomings of the present schemes and their suggestions for improvement. The prominent weakness was that insurance coverage was only up to 60 years (75% of responses), followed by need for scholarship from sixth standard onwards and for higher education (35% of responses), coverage for other expenses such as marriage, house construction and repairs, higher education (24%), need for lump sum amount after the age of 60 years (20%), inclusion of adopted or grandchildren for the purpose of scholarship (20%), delay in settlement of claim (11%), lack of annuity after the age of 60 years (12%), full family coverage 6% and credit for reimbursement of hospitalization expenses (4%) (Table 7.9).

**Table 7.9**

*Drawbacks of the Present Social Security Schemes of WWF (I)*

| *Drawbacks* | *% of Responses* |
|---|---|
| Lack of coverage beyond 60 years | 75% |
| Lack of coverage for expenses such as marriage, house construction repairs, etc. | 35% |
| Lack of coverage for higher education | 24% |
| No lump sum amount after the age of 60 years | 20% |
| Exclusion of adopted or grandchildren for scholarship | 20% |
| Delay in settlement of claims | 11% |
| Lack of annuity after age of 60 years | 12% |
| Lack of full family coverage | 6% |
| Lack of credit facilities for hospitalizations | 4% |

*Note:* These percentages are the proportion of respondents who cited the specified reason and therefore do not total 100.

## Suggestions for Improvement

Among the suggestions offered by the respondents as given below in Table 7.10, the most immediate need was the extension of coverage after the age of 60 years (72% of the responses), need for old-age pension (46% of the responses), need for scholarship from sixth standard onwards and for college education (32% of the responses), need for insurance schemes for major expenditure such as marriage, house construction and repairs and higher education (29% of the responses), scholarship for grandchildren or adopted children (24% of the responses), the need for proxies to pay the insurance premium on behalf of the insured (17% of the responses), requirement for full family coverage (11% of the responses) and need for higher claim amount (9% of the responses).

**Table 7.10**

*Improvement of the Present Social Security Schemes of WWF (I)*

| *Suggestions* | *% of Responses* |
|---|---|
| Need for coverage beyond 60 years | 72% |
| Need for coverage at old age | 46% |
| Need for extended scholarship | 32% |
| Need for insurance for major expenses | 29% |
| Need for scholarship for grandchildren or adopted children | 24% |
| Need for representatives to pay insurance premium on behalf of the insured | 11% |
| Need for full family coverage | 11% |
| Need for higher claim amount | 9% |

*Note:* These percentages are the proportion of respondents who cited the specified reason and therefore do not total 100.

In the light of the experiences of WWF (I) as facilitators for the present social security schemes, it is felt that the present schemes are confusing and vague. For instance, the LIC-Social Security Scheme and LIC-Jana Shree Bheema Yojana schemes, both started in the year 2000, have many common characteristics. The only difference between the two schemes is that the benefits are higher in the latter, with a negligible difference in the premium amount. The existence of both these schemes tends to confuse the members. It would be wiser to have just one scheme that offers better benefits. Also, the schemes should not result in discrimination among the beneficiaries. For example, the annual scholarship amount under the LIC-JBY scheme is based on the administrative norms of LIC. The amount disbursed, each year is invariably less than the amount claimed. This leads to unequal distribution of the benefits among beneficiaries, sometimes causing resentment among them. It is also important that the benefits offered should be timely. The scholarship is disbursed by LIC well after the school year has commenced which puts the beneficiaries into a lot of financial hardship. It would help the beneficiaries if the scholarship amounts are distributed well before the deadline for the payment of school fees.

Azad (2006) studied these social security schemes, especially of the linkages of WWF (I) with the two insurers – a government enterprise and a privately owned, and assessed the opportunities involved in such linkages towards a wider coverage of women in the informal sector and also identified different state characteristics that influence different levels of success among informal sector workers organizations' ability to secure labour benefits. Azad observes that the ability to secure benefits is marked by continuous negotiations that is sometimes confrontational and at other times enabling. She notes that for struggles to become successful movements requires knowledge of the larger political, legislative and policy environments.

### Unorganized Sector Workers' Social Security Bill, 2005

This Bill was passed by the Indian parliament in December 2008. It seeks to provide social security to 340 million unorganized sector workers including agricultural workers and migrant workers over the following five-year period. It would provide health, life and disability insurance, old-age pension and group accident insurance scheme. According to this Bill, an "Unorganized Sector Worker" means a person who works for wages or income; directly or through any agency or contractor; or who works on his/her own account or is self-employed; in any place of work including his/her home, field or any public place; and who is not availing of benefits under the ESIC Act and the P.F. Act, individual insurance and pension schemes of LIC, private insurance companies, or other benefits as decided by the Authority from time to time. In India, over 92% – 300 million – work in the unorganized sector and are not eligible for coverage under any of the Worker's Acts for benefits. Though these workers contribute over 60% of the country's GDP, they have no coverage for contingencies such as illness and children's education and for old age. This bill seeks to build a social security system for these unorganized workers. A variety of social security benefits such as health insurance, maternity benefits and pensions will be provided initially with children's education, housing and skill building to be included later. The Bill redefines "worker" so as to include all types of workers, such as self-employed workers as well as casual, contract, home-based, etc. The Union Government may levy a cess or an appropriate tax, or create an appropriate mechanism for collection of contribution from individual employers (or their contractors), or a class of employers, or an industry as a whole in order to partly finance the schemes or projects undertaken.

The initiative taken by the Union Government to provide recognition to the unorganized workers is commendable but the mechanism for the implementation of this Act is vague. For instance, it is not clear if there are special provisions for women. It is also not clear as to how the government will make sure that contributions is made by every employer or contractor, and how erring employers or contractors will be penalized. In such cases, will the workers suffer the consequences?

Also in case of self-employed or home-based workers who do not work for contractors who will contribute? It is also not clear whether the medical insurance will be extended to the family or be restricted to the member only. The details of contributions to be made and payouts to be received are also not very clearly stated.

The Bill envisages a wider role for the civil society initiatives. Known as "facilitating agencies", these civil society initiatives would administer and supervise what is known as "Worker's Facilitation Centres". These Worker's Facilitation Centres would provide direct service to the members by registering them, securing the contribution of members and deliver the benefits to the members. The other functions would be to maintain a database of members, training for skill upgradation, maintain and provide information related to employment and marketing, create public awareness about the social security schemes, collect data of the unorganized workers and undertake such activities as prescribed by the National Social Security Authority.

There are several reservations on the role of the civil society initiatives. The NGOs and CBOs that are civil society initiatives that are already existing and working in the field have their goals and activities already set up and underway. In this context, it is a sweeping assumption that the civil society initiatives, which are under-staffed and burdened with their own activities, will have the requisite infrastructure to undertake the huge responsibilities under the proposed bill. It is not clear in the proposed Bill as to whether the present LIC social security schemes would be continued or would be replaced by new schemes.

**Conclusion**

The analysis thus far reveals that women, in general, have an awareness and desire for social security and also experience a feeling of security and well-being when they do have such coverage. The drawbacks of the present schemes are however many. The most immediate need is for extended coverage – for health insurance, pension and expenditure (for marriage, housing and education) – beyond the age of 60 years. As life expectancy is increasing even among the poorer classes, old age social security becomes very important for these classes as dependency among the younger members of the family would be burdensome with rising health costs. Older women are more likely to suffer neglect if they can not earn their living. There is a great need for extended scholarship benefits for education, major family expenditures, full family medical coverage, inclusion of grandchildren or adopted children in the list of beneficiaries.

The scope of the proposed 2005 Social Security Bill can be widened to provide for periods of unemployment in urban and rural areas, and also for major expenditures such as education, housing, loss due to natural calamities. The Bill should also cover unpaid workers like housewives and those receiving kind wages in some feudal kinds of work arrangements that are still prevalent in parts of the country. The social security schemes should also be gender-sensitive considering that 96% of the women workers are in the informal sector. Women also run a risk of more health-related problems. The insurance scheme should take into consideration those diseases that have a high incidence among women of all ages. The child care needs should also be addressed. Maternity benefits in addition to unemployment benefits, especially when women are out of work after childbirth and other health problems should be addressed. Arunachalam (2005b) has argued that social security should encompass occupational safety measures, not only concentrating on the promotional aspect which might be an incentive to workers, but it must also be a measure of protection to the worker. When a worker dies, the family has to be taken care of, children's education has to be looked after, in case both parents die, in calamities such as tsunami or due to HIV/AIDS arrangements for adoption of these children have to be taken care of as a protective measure. Such provision must be made mandatory on the employer. But the draft social security bill did not seek any of these benefits, she observed.

Disaster relief in case of natural calamities is very important. An example of the social security offered by the WWF (I) movement itself is demonstrated by the relief and rehabilitation efforts it provided to its tsunami-affected members. The very next day after the disaster in December 2004, WWF (I) volunteers rushed to the affected areas and distributed relief measures and offered comfort to the affected members. Relief and rehabilitation measures worth well over ₹ 10 million were distributed by WWF (I) to its tsunami-affected members.

Clearly, such assistance in times of disaster is only one dimension of the security cover that WWF (I) provides to its members. The more sustained and enduring coverage is the very activity of microcredit lending that constitutes the core activity of WWF (I) which provides livelihood security for women informal sector workers. As part of its livelihood security objective, WWF (I) also engages in skills training wherever needed. For instance, with the demand for tobacco products decreasing on account of the curbs and ban on smoking on health grounds, WWF (I) engaged in retraining the beedi workers of Vellore to help them move into alternative occupations. Similarly, when there was a slump in the demand for silk products of Kanchipuram weavers, WWF (I) initiated a skills retraining programme to enable weavers to create new design patterns to stimulate demand. Thus, WWF (I) seeks to provide a broad and holistic social protection package in which the empowerment process is built-in as a continuous process.

Such an approach to social protection is possible only within similar organizational structures dedicated to social movement objectives. Any attempts by the state to provide social security benefits to the informal sector workers even through the intermediary organizations like Workers Facilitation Centres are only likely to be scheme-based programmes with the intermediaries overseeing its implementation. Clearly, the informal sector workers who lack social security benefits ought to get these benefits and there is an argument for implementing schemes effectively. For women and marginalized sections though, such an approach and objective would still fall short if it is also not simultaneously embedded within an empowerment framework. The state that is committed to social security and social justice ought to encourage and identify NGOs and CBOs that are part of the social movement process to be associated with such service delivery as the social security schemes, giving them at the same time the autonomy to structure their domains of intervention to serve the transformative and empowerment agendas.

Arunachalam (2005b) has noted that it is time for the government and other international agencies to formulate strategies to enable the replication of such efforts as WWF (I) so as to scale up their financial services to reach more and more of the unreached. She notes, "Scaling up includes reaching the unreached (enhancing access) and also financial deepening of the already reached poor (newer financial products and the like). All the daring experiments of microfinance practices are only the task of civil society initiatives and their networks so far, and they have remained the real torch bearers of this industry" (cited from the note dated March 13th).

## Notes

1. Life Insurance Corporation of India (LIC), established in 1956, is a wholly owned corporation of the Government of India.
2. Royal Sundaram Alliance Pvt. Ltd. is a joint venture between Sundaram Finance and Royal and SunAlliance of the UK.

# 8

# Gender, Democracy and Decentralized Governance*

It is increasingly being realized that strengthening and deepening democracy both at grassroots and other levels is crucial to the strengthening of a rights regime that has become an essential political instrument to buffet the risks and vulnerabilities of market-led development under neoliberal globalization. One aspect of such strengthening is to include members of excluded groups as elected representatives in the political set up of democratic governance in order to ensure their participation in decision-making for an inclusive political and development process. Pande (2003) has argued that mandated political representation of disadvantaged minorities and excluded groups provide them with policy influence and has shown that such reservation for scheduled castes (SCs) and scheduled tribes (STs) in the Indian states has increased targeted transfers to these groups which benefit from the mandate. The same could be hoped for mandated reservations for women as well. Women's representation in elected bodies of the legislatures have in general been below par; in fact in some developed countries women gained even their right to vote in elections after much struggle and quite late in the 20th century. Women in postcolonial societies that embarked on democratic political systems fared better in gaining their franchise and election to legislative bodies as their participation in anti-colonial nationalist movement enabled them to come on to the political stage. Thus, in India, women's right to vote and participate in the political process was granted quite easily without much struggle unlike the suffragette movement in Europe (Roy, 2005). Many women in the decades after independence and even

* This is a revised and expanded version of the paper published in *Journal of Grassroots Governance*, December, 2008.

in the present time have played significant roles in the political life of the country and their names are only all too familiar.

However, over the years, women's representation in the elected legislative bodies both at the Centre and the states, has not grown relatively to the desired extent. As awareness of women's subordinate status increased in the society, the women's movement in the country supported the demand for one-third representation of women in the legislative bodies (Sharma, 2000). While accepted in principle by the political powers, the legislative enactment to make it into a law has been stalled for long by various political parties whose political arithmetic indicated that such a move would likely bring in more upper caste women as representatives and thereby marginalize backward caste women with its associated implications for caste-based vote bank politics. Thus, in the debates, the issue of women empowerment was overtaken by the caste-electoral politics. But as the bill has been passed by the Rajya Sabha (the upper house of the parliament), it is hoped that at some time in future it will become a law, once the Lok Sabha (the lower house of the parliament) approves it.

Undoubtedly increased representation of women in legislative bodies will enhance the political power of women, increase their role in decision-making and enhance their status and power. But from the debates that are stalling the bill, it can also be surmised that elected women representatives are more likely to be lending support to issues along the party and caste lines than along the gender or issue basis, and to that extent it is not a foregone conclusion that such a move would contribute to the enhancement of women's power and status across the board. By no means are women a homogenous group and there are bound to be differences among them, some organized along party lines. The political parties are also predominantly male-dominated. Mandated reservation of seats in the legislatures for women would make it necessary for the political parties to field women candidates for the reserved seats, thus enhancing their position within their parties as well.

The three-tier system of decentralized democratic structure below the state level, namely, the district, block and village called Zilla Parishad, Panchayat Samiti and Gram Panchayat which is a village-level elected council of members with the Gram Pradhan as its head, known as the Panchayati Raj Institutions (PRIs), has been in vogue since the early 1950s. The 73rd and 74th constitutional amendments passed in

1992 reserved one-third of seats in these local elected bodies (Gram Panchayats and Nagar Palikas) to women. The 73rd amendment provided that one-third of the seats in all Panchayat Councils as well as one-third of the Pradhan positions must be reserved for women. Seats and Pradhan positions were also reserved for the disadvantaged minorities in India, SCs and STs, in the form of mandated representation proportional to each minority's population share in each district. With this amendment, elections to these PRIs have become more regular. Between 1993 and 2003, all the major states but two (Bihar and Punjab) had at least two elections and the mandated representation of women has caused a manifold increase in women leaders at the grassroots.

As states have the power to bring in amendments in their state laws to increase women's representation to 50%, some states such as Bihar, Uttarakhand, Himachal Pradesh and Chhattisgarh have already introduced 50% reservation for women in panchayats. Rajasthan has also recently done so in the latest 2010 panchayat elections and the state of Kerala too has announced the same. In Uttarakhand, women have an overwhelming 55% representation in panchayats as many of them contested from non-reserved seats and won. The UPA government at the centre had cleared a proposal to bring in an amendment to the earlier 73rd amendment to increase the reservation for women in panchayats to 50% in August 2009. With this proposed amendment, the number of elected women's representatives at the grassroots level is expected to rise to more than 14 lakhs. At present, women account for 36.8% of the total of 28.1 lakhs elected panchayat representatives (*Times of India*, August 28, 2009).

Highlighting the nature of systemic exclusion and discrimination that women face in the development process, this chapter argues that gender-sensitive grassroots governance under the present system of PRIs is possible only if women gain "voice" and "rights" (World Bank, 2001). It also requires that synergies be built with community-based organizations (CBOs), non-governmental organizations (NGOs) and social movements.

## Importance of Grassroots Governance

Grassroots governance is increasingly being recognized as an important requisite for the fulfilment of development agendas and goals. In the decade of the 80s, it was considered politically correct for development intellectuals to assume a critical vantage point in debates on development issues and policies, and to pose the question "development for whom?" All policies came under the scanner of that morally loaded question and only those considered politically naïve would bypass that question. The intervening years have enhanced the collective wisdom to an extent that we now realize that posing that question critically does not necessarily imply positive outcomes on the ground. Even carefully framed policies meant for the masses, for the poor and for the common man do not reach those in need. Hence, many more questions of development practice need to be addressed before development could become a reality for the poor. It is in this context that "inclusive development", "participatory democracy" and "grassroots governance" as ideas for development practice have assumed importance.

For development to be "inclusive", it has to bring into the mainstream of development all groups and communities without marginalizing them from the development process and the outcomes. Unfortunately though, the processes of capitalist development bring about both inequalities as well as marginalization. While inequality is an outcome and a status, marginalization is the process that results in such an outcome. In the name of modern development, life forms and livelihoods undergo changes and traditional occupations, and means of livelihood are lost forever. Modern development by its exclusivist tendencies has resulted in inequality and marginalized sections of the population both in economic and social development. Social structural factors such as caste, gender, ethnicity and so on have furthered the exclusivist tendencies of modern development. For development both economic and social to be "inclusive", such that development does not bypass any section of the society, or that the development of one group does not lead to the underdevelopment of some others, development practices must be oriented to an "inclusive" approach. Such an inclusive approach is possible only if development practice is participatory. Top-down bureaucratic approaches to development and market-led development can be made to become "inclusive" in their effects, only if at the grassroots these approaches are buffeted by a participatory approach.

Top-down bureaucratic approaches became the most significant approach with planned economic development. Development schemes such as the various poverty alleviation and employment programmes like food-for-work were conceived as part of plan schemes and delivered through the bureaucracy through district, block and village level development officers. Although the importance of village-level governance through panchayats was recognized very early on, inspired by the Gandhian ideals of decentralized democracy anchored in self-governing village panchayats, their roles in participatory development were not adequately recognized, which led over time to an increasing top-down approach in development planning and practice. Mukerji (2008: 42) observes that "the period between the passing of the Indian Constitution by the Constituent Assembly in 1950 and the passage of the Constitution (Seventy-third) Amendment Act (1992) has been marked by a tortuous dialectic in the form of contestations between the forces of participatory and parliamentary democracy". It was this dialectic that led to the formalization of the third tier of government at the grassroots level in 1992. It has been noted by many that this constitutional amendment was indeed not the outcome of grassroots demand through a process of struggle or mass movement, but rather the acknowledgement by policymakers of the lacuna in the development administration. There are three components to the PRI process of grassroots governance, namely the electoral process, the decision-making process and the service delivery. Deepening democracy at the grassroots could enable the process of "inclusive" development if and only if the three components of PRI are set up to work efficiently.

Evaluations of various development programmes have over the years highlighted the facts of corruption, siphoning of funds and appropriation of benefits by the undeserving groups, willful neglect of the very poor and marginalized sections, except in the rare instances of committed elected governments, and an efficient and committed development bureaucracy coming together and acting in tandem. This accounts in part for regional variations in the performance of development programmes. It is now not wide off the mark to note that development programmes perform better in the southern states than in the Hindi belt of north India. Vested-interest groups generally seek to corner development benefits such that the ones most deserving, the deprived are neglected and marginalized. Especially in rural areas, rural power structures are correlated with asset ownership, resource control and caste or the placement in the social stratification. Instituting the PRI process of grassroots governance thus faces tremendous hurdles and is expectedly fraught with contestations and struggles.

Marginalization and exclusion does not arise only with respect to the development programmes of the state. Even the market-led development process leads to marginalization and exclusion. Small landholders are often rendered landless when either big farmers increase their scale of operations or as is increasingly the case when corporate farming becomes established. Communities engaged in traditional occupations such as rural artisans and weavers have been compelled to give up their traditional occupations when newer commodities that are factory made are substituted for the traditional products. Tribal groups who had customary rights over forests and grazing lands and their products have been pushed back or forced to join the ranks of landless labourers when market forces such as the setting up of industrial plants in lands occupied by tribal groups are forcibly acquired from them under the modernization agenda. Exploitative use of natural resources by multinational and other commercial interests resulting in depletion and making such resource-dependent livelihoods unviable have exacerbated the marginalization of many traditional communities. The social exclusion of stigmatized groups such as scheduled castes, now called as Dalits, and the different tribal groups resulted in their exclusion from the development process by and large, both on account of their low command over assets and resources, and their lack of social power. In fact, all these forces have now galvanized the affected social groups to prevent these tendencies of marginalization and exclusion by their attempts to claim both "voice" and "rights" in the development process.

Recently, there have been numerous controversies such as the Narmada dam oustees and their rehabilitation, the farmers whose lands were appropriated by the Tata Singur plant, the projects of the various SEZs now put on hold and many more that seem to be cropping up with increasing regularity. In most of these instances, corporate and multi-national companies, and big capital are pitted against the livelihood interests of members of the marginalized communities. While grassroots governance that brings about a democratic and participatory approach could counter some of these tendencies of marginalization and exclusion, and make development more inclusive, it is in itself not sufficient as the role of the state in the federal polity could either favour the interest of capital or be supportive of marginalized groups. Grassroots democratic and participatory government could equally change the outlook of the federal states in their favour, as some of the results of recent social movements seem to suggest at least on issues such as environmental concerns, land grab, displacement and rehabilitation. An inclusive development is one in which social justice becomes an integral part of the economic growth and development.

**Women as Excluded Others**

Much has been written by now to show that women are marginalized and excluded from the development process. The reasons for such exclusion have been attributed to the widely upheld social ideology that women are primarily homemakers even though the large mass of poor women is economically active. Women's reproductive roles of child bearing and nurturing functions are seen to further confine women to the realm of domesticity. These ideological constructs of women have also obscured the fact that women in no way constitute a homogenous group; the social fault lines that run through the society makes women as much into a heterogeneous category as it does the men. Some groups of women therefore suffer greater exclusion such as Dalits, tribal women, poorer women, women of lower castes and so on. Many women combine both their roles as homemakers and are economically active as well, even if the official statistics sometimes do not reveal so, contributing to the invisibility of women's work. Such invisibilizing tendencies in conjunction with the patriarchal blinkers of men and of the women who have by and large internalized patriarchal ideologies operate as much at the level of development policy and practice as it does in both the household and society at large.

While development policy may have become more gender sensitive and strive not to exclude women on account of the growing awareness and activism at national and international levels, development practice at the grassroots level, the point at which it affects women by exclusion or inclusion has not significantly changed. A massive and radical change at the grassroots that can prevent not only women but others as well to become the "excluded others" from the development process requires multi-pronged efforts of both state and non-state actors, and in which education as well as the economic empowerment of women become important factors. The growth and spread of social activism through grassroots NGOs in the last two decades, social movements as well as enabling development policies like the 73rd and 74th constitutional amendments for local self-governance and women's participation in such governance as well as policies of poverty alleviation and employment generation such as the National Rural Employment Guarantee Act (NREGA), the Self-Help Groups

(SHGs), microcredit lending and so on, are all efforts that provide opportunities towards an inclusive development.

Let us now examine how and why women belong to the category of "excluded others", by first examining the processes of exclusion and marginalization of women viewed as a homogeneous category and then of women as a heterogeneous group. The invisibility of women's work on account of the patriarchal ideologies certainly cause their discrimination in the labour market which accounts for their lower wages, lower skill attainments, fewer entrepreneurial opportunities and confinement to jobs in the lower rungs, often in the informal sector. Labour market discrimination is complemented with and is partly the outcome of patriarchal discrimination within families and households. Women face discrimination in terms of household tasks and the often rigid sexual division of labour leaves them with less leisure to acquire skills, education, participation in community activities and so on. Girls face discrimination on account of the same patriarchal ideology of women being homemakers and are often denied educational opportunities that are at par with their male siblings. Lack of property rights and the consequent low command over household assets along with patriarchal dominance deny most women a fair share in household decision-making. Even when women do earn cash incomes by way of employment, this does not always enhance her decision-making power or autonomy, and more often women are denied the control over even their earned incomes. All these facets of discrimination result in women being excluded from measures and means that could enhance their well-being.

This is most starkly brought out in the aggregate statistics on indices of human development such as education and health. Gender disparities do exist, even if in some regions, classes and communities, these gaps may be decreasing over time. The pervasive disparities and gaps as indicated in statistics clearly suggest that these tendencies of discrimination and exclusion operate at the level of daily existence, the family/household and the work sphere. These tendencies have inhibiting effects on their public and community roles as well.

Different categories of women face discrimination and exclusion in different ways. If girls are deprived of education, adolescent and young women face curtailment in their movement in an attempt to control their sexuality, and do not often enjoy the freedom of interacting with people which denies them the chance of coming to learn of the various opportunities in the world. If married, women face exclusion on account of their reproductive role and as homemakers, there is further exclusion within the family based on age and status hierarchies as well. Especially among young married women in rural areas, one often hears them say that they enjoy greater freedom after marriage than before. But daughters-in-law bear a greater burden in the division of household chores and in many parts of rural north India at least have to abide by the norms of veiling and seclusion. While single unmarried women among the poorer classes are not so common, as the status of singleness is unviable economically, poor women also face a greater likelihood of sexual harassment in case they remain single. Female heads of household left to fend for themselves and their children also face severe discrimination much like the single women. Older widows too face neglect and are often on their own trying to subsist, doing some odd work to earn a living. No doubt there are caste and class differences both in the nature and intensity of discrimination and exclusion that women face. Dalit women face far more discrimination even in the hands of upper caste women. But it is in general true to conclude that women do form a part of the "excluded others".

Development programmes such as the numerous poverty alleviation and employment programmes, health, education and social security programmes often bypass many of these categories of women, unless specific attempts are made to reach out to them. This is on account of the patriarchal biases operating on numerous fronts both within and outside the family. It has been widely acknowledged that many poverty alleviation programmes that needed the deserving poor to be first identified ignored female-headed households completely, and poor and destitute widows find it difficult to access social security schemes like old-age pension. Similarly, patriarchal biases within the family have succeeded largely in ignoring women's health, thus giving it very low priority. Even the state's health policies have insufficiently focused only on maternal and child health programmes, thereby viewing women primarily in their child-bearing and nurturing roles. It can be concluded that top-down development policy approaches in which the service delivery is attempted through a bureaucratic administration that is insufficiently sensitized to the ways in which grassroots power structures including that of patriarchal power operates, has not succeeded in including women in the development process.

Market-led development processes have also marginalized women of various categories and communities. Especially since in rural areas poor women bear a greater burden of household survival through various kinds of subsistence activities such as collection of forest produce, fuel and fodder in addition to waged work on others' fields or non-waged work on own farms if they are from slightly better off households, the marginalization of women by the market-led development processes have severely impacted on the subsistence and survival strategies of poor women and their households. When rural artisans and those in traditional occupations lose their livelihood on account of the development of the modern economy, the men and women not only join the ranks of wage labourers but lose their traditional skills and knowledge. Women's knowledge of agrarian system, food processing, water management and so on are rendered obsolete and is not even taken cognizance of. As modern methods of farming are introduced, women are often excluded from acquiring the knowledge of modern farming techniques. Resource depletion on account of market-led development such as ground water depletion has severely affected many rural women who now have to expend more time and effort in water collection. Many caste groups and ethnic communities that had earlier served rural communities through their wares and services now stand marginalized, and the women of these marginalized communities remain further marginalized on account of the new and older norms of patriarchal power affecting their lives.

An inclusive development approach can only be based on a participatory approach that is based on democratic grassroots governance. Only such an approach can attempt to counter the multiple forces of marginalization and exclusion at work and bring women, especially rural women, into the mainstream of development.

**Panchayats, Grassroots Governance and Women**

The project of democratic decentralization in India is not complete and is still evolving. Democratic decentralization of governance envisages a three-tier system of elected representatives to help in governance at the local level in rural and urban areas. In rural areas, the three tiers are the Gram Panchayat (the body of elected representatives at the village level), Panchayat Samitis (the body of elected representatives at the block level) and Zilla Parishad (the body of elected representatives at the district level). The landmark 73rd constitutional amendment made way for one-third reservation of seats in panchayats for women, both in general category and in the reserved scheduled caste category. Women could be elected on either of these two categories. Mukerji (2008) has highlighted through a study of the panchayat elections in Punjab and West Bengal in 2008 of the various lacunae and loopholes in the electoral system and has suggested improvements to achieve the desired result of democratic decentralization. He like many others before him has found the widespread problem of women being used as "proxy" candidates. This argument of women being used as "proxy" candidates however true it may be, has been used by a large number of people to question the validity of seat reservation for women.

This stand unfortunately does not question why "proxy" cases occur and is so widespread, nor how the situation can be changed. It also does not recognize that a single amendment or a few years experience down the line does not exhaust the possibility of moving towards a more efficient and perfect system of democratic decentralization in which women function as equal partners in development in the long run. The amendment, encapsulating a long-term vision, has conferred on women the legitimate status to become equal partners in development. Despite the criticism, the amended system of representation in the Gram Panchayats has allowed many thousands of women to become grassroots leaders for the first time (Dogra, 2001). It could also be argued that even in the case of "proxy" candidates in which the male members of the household are the *de facto* panchayat members, it is heartening that male members prevailed upon the female members of the family in agreeing to put them up as "proxy", thereby giving their women some public roles, however symbolic and devoid of the real decision-making power, which they otherwise would not have done.

Equally, and infrequently overlooked, is the possibility of the fact that entry through the "proxy" woman route has enabled groups that had never acquired or had power in the village before to do so now. In one of my fieldwork situations, I came across one such proxy, a young Muslim woman as village *pradhan* in Lahoorpur village in Allahabad district. In her own admission, it was her husband, a shoe shop owner who conducted her affairs and she just put her signature or thumb impression wherever she was asked to do. But her self-esteem grew, when even researchers like me had to call on her before I conducted my study in her village. Most importantly, the Muslims were only a small minority, and even her family was not residing in the village habitat itself but outside the village near the main road, nor did they own any land in the village where the dominant landholding caste was the Kurmis.

The probability of all elected women in a Gram Panchayats being proxy candidates is likely to be anyway lower than of a single elected woman being so. It is quite possible that by functioning together with others on the panchayat, they do learn something over time. The more important issue though is the fact of high illiteracy among women, and many of the elected women are illiterates. Education and training become essential for elected women.

The question of being a "proxy" raises the more fundamental question of patriarchal dominance and women's low status and power in decision-making in the household. Once again it is necessary to look at the optimistic side to argue that even proxiness could in slow degrees give the individual woman more decision-making power in the family, for by granting her some public visibility and role, there is the unintended consequence of giving the woman a little more voice even within the family. Thus, public roles and private roles are intertwined and mutually reinforcing. In the case of non-proxy woman candidates, the empowerment processes could in fact be hastened.

The other problems that equally merit some concern are situations when a woman wishes to contest for the panchayat election but is dissuaded or prevented by her spouse and family members saying that her role is primarily to take care of the family and not be concerned with community affairs as yet another instance of patriarchal domination. In some cases, a woman desirous of contesting the election may be prevented from doing so, not by her family members, but by others in the village, supposedly on caste, class and other grounds. Often such attempts at dissuading women are more violent than non-violent acts of persuasion, reflecting how brute the power realities are at the village level. Even elected women representatives are debarred from holding office by family and other social forces of domination. This is more so in the case of Dalit women candidates, where it is often accompanied by caste violence. However, it is perhaps still true to say that while all these problems are prevalent, the new system of representation has thrown up a large number of women grassroots leaders, whose functioning however questionable now on grounds of efficiency could be improved over time.

Equally it is true that as the same set of elected representatives are not likely to prevail indefinitely, and newer and newer grassroots leaders are likely to emerge, there may be an anxiety that this inefficient and undesirable feature of "proxy candidacy" is likely to prevail in the long run. This clearly suggests that greater awareness needs to be created among all rural women about patriarchal and social domination.

The problem of the illiteracy of elected women and lack of knowledge about rules, regulations and functioning of PRIs can be solved, at least to some extent, through functional literacy programmes and carefully designed training programmes which are already underway in many states. But the issue of sensitizing women at large on issues of patriarchal and social domination is more difficult as the multiple and intertwined layers of domination and resistance have to be cognized, understood and transformed. Social movements including that of the women's movement has now well understood that such transformative agendas require concerted collective action which in turn feeds into transformative visions and agendas at the level of the individual as well. Individual imaginations of transforming society have to be turned into a collective imagination, if it is not to be ensnared by power and engulfed with fear.

The question to be raised here is whether the existing system of PRIs allows for the possibility of recognizing these issues of patriarchal and social domination, and of the ways of transforming them. Mukerji (2008) has noted that even the electoral system for PRIs varies from state to state. Whereas in some states contestants for the Gram Sabha election are not conducted along party lines, and individuals are merely allotted symbols for the voters to identify as in Punjab, in yet others it is along party lines as in West Bengal. The implications of party and non-party contestation for women in Gram Panchayats elections have to be clearly understood.

Although in the evolution of a democratic polity with an electoral system for over 60 years women have identified with parties, voted for parties and constituted a sizeable segment of the membership in many political parties, parties in their preoccupation with electoral gains and power have not significantly concerned themselves with local-level development issues in the ways they ought to have and have belied the hopes of the citizens. Many parties do not even have grassroots cadres and women party workers have more often been used instrumentally towards the party's goals rather than allow women to raise issues of development that they think are important at the local and national levels, nor have they been given the space and encouragement to raise gender concerns. Male grassroots cadres of some political parties are even notorious for intimidating women in their local areas. Had it been otherwise it would be difficult to explain as to why the Women's Reservation Bill granting one-third seat reservation in the central and state legislatures was languishing for so long, especially when the country boasts of its record of having a woman prime minister, a woman president, women chief ministers and many women elected legislators in central and state legislatures.

There are strong arguments for both party and non-party contestation of Gram Panchayat elections. One argument in favour of party contestation is that it is an anomaly in the democratic structure if it does not allow for party contestation when it does so at all other levels – the Panchayat Samitis, Zilla Parishads, state and central legislatures. However, a gender perspective on grassroots governance would weigh more in favour of non-party contestation at the Gram Panchayat level for it removes one more force of power that women have to negotiate with, at least until such time that most women can begin to function effectively without any fear and with self-confidence.

What perhaps hinders women most is the functioning of traditional panchayats alongside the newly elected panchayats. Traditional panchayats have overwhelmingly acted to discipline women and bind them everywhere with rigid social norms and disciplines. In north India, these traditional panchayats, also including caste panchayats that cover not one village but a set of villages in a region, have on many occasions even killed young girls and couples for choosing to marry outside of the caste or from the proscribed groups. Even in states where the courts have declared traditional panchayats as illegal, as in Tamil Nadu, they still do function. The existence of traditional panchayats indicates that grassroots governance has been prevalent since time immemorial, but it has only practiced gendered exclusion and was a grassroots mechanism to ensure the systemic reproduction of social and gender hierarchies and caste domination everywhere.

The newly elected tiers of decentralized democratic governance is in fact a social and political contestation with the traditionally dominant forces that had everywhere kept women in subjugation and denied them a voice in matters concerning them, even if their actions constituted violation of human rights. In an interesting internet news report, Gautham (2007) writes how the traditional panchayats also called Katta Panchayats practiced gendered exclusion in the distribution of post-tsunami aid in the coastal villages of Tirunelveli district in Tamil Nadu in 2004–2005. Women by and large, especially the Dalit women, were excluded from receiving any aid because their names were omitted on the argument that males were the heads of households thereby excluding single, deserted, divorced women and also the widows, and also on the ground that they were not boat owners and were not paying annual taxes to the traditional panchayats even when the women played numerous economic roles in supporting the fishing economy of the villages and had lost their homes and livelihoods in the tsunami. Such social and gendered exclusion had in the past forced the villagers to shun the traditional panchayats and to turn towards the Christian churches for assistance.

Women therefore have much at stake in ensuring that the democratically elected PRIs function satisfactorily in terms of the ways in which the electoral system functions, in the decision-making process in the panchayats, and in service delivery. A satisfactory level of performance of the PRIs can be ensured only if women have both voice in decision-making and rights. Women have to be pro-active at all levels to ensure that they gain voice and rights to enhance their capabilities in the democratic functioning of PRIs.

**Women, Voice and Rights**

Women's representation in the Gram Panchayats under the 73rd amendment was indeed meant to give women both "voice" and "rights". But mere representation alone will not help in realizing that goal. Even if the electoral system for Gram Panchayats gets improved over time such that the situation of proxy candidacy gets somewhat corrected, women's voice may not be articulated or heard nor will they be able to realize their rights. There should be an overall awareness of the multiple roles that different classes of women perform and especially of their crucial roles in the maintenance of household food security. It is now widely acknowledged by researchers that women's roles in subsistence among the very poor households are crucial and vary over the year depending on the seasonal availability of different kinds of food, some even obtained through collection in fields, forests and water sources. Within each village, the arenas of women's concern have to be delineated and a consensus among women should evolve. Women's decision-making powers over issues in these arenas should be enhanced formally by restructuring the process of decision-making that gives women of different classes a greater say in whatever issues concern their lives. There should also be attempts to ensure that women of different classes do not work at cross-purposes because their interests vary. For instance, upper caste/class women cannot ask that restrictions be imposed on how resources in the village commons are used, or defend themselves and their male members when questioned on the illegal appropriation of the village commons, if women of lower caste/class use these resources for food, fuel, fodder and livelihood.

Dogra (2001) after observing the manner in which women elected to Gram Panchayats function in many parts of North India, observed that they bring to sharp focus issues of gender bias, poor sanitation, alcoholism, wasteful expenditure and corruption, and that women in panchayats are not sufficiently concerned and active in the areas of education, health, SHGs, watershed management, pastures, forestry and food security. In all these issues, women of all classes have indeed very high stakes as these have a direct bearing both on their own and their family's well-being and survival. Not only should women in panchayats be trained to take up these issues, but also the decision-making processes too will have to be reoriented at the ground level so that their voice prevails. Chattopadhyay and Duflo (2004a and 2004b) in their experimental study based on evidence gathered from the two districts in West Bengal and Rajasthan show that women elected representatives in the panchayats invest more in local public goods that are relevant to the needs of women such as water and roads in West Bengal and water in Rajasthan. They invest less in goods that are less relevant to their needs such as non-formal education centres in West Bengal and roads in Rajasthan. In Birbhum district of West Bengal where they had data on investments in hamlets populated by SCs, STs, and the general population within each village, Chattopadhyay and Duflo (2004a and 2004b) show that SC Pradhans invest a larger share of public goods on SC hamlets than do the non-SC Pradhans. They argue that fears regarding decentralization are unfounded and that local leaders seem to have some effective control over decisions even when they are women or SCs. They further argue that the oft-heard anecdotal evidence regarding women being entirely controlled by their husbands when in office should not be given too much weight. They conclude that reservation of electoral seats and changing elector identity through reservation is an effective tool to safeguard the interests of the weaker groups. They note, "given the difficulty of targeting public transfers to specific groups in an otherwise decentralized system, reservation may be a tool to ensure not only adequate representation but also adequate delivery of local public goods to disadvantaged groups" (Chattopadhyay and Duflo, 2004a, p. 986).

Generally, it has been found that when a *Gram Pradhan* is a woman, the involvement of women in the affairs of the Gram Panchayat increases significantly. Topalova (2003) found that not only was the quality of water provided better in the Gram Panchayats that are reserved for women, and that women are somewhat less likely to demand bribes, but that villagers are less likely to be satisfied about the quality of water when the Gram Panchayats are reserved for women, despite receiving objectively better service. She concluded that it suggests that women tend to be considered as worse policy-makers even when they are objectively better. Equally it could be interpreted that with a woman Gram Panchayat, women are better able to express their expectations of good governance, whereas their voices are suppressed by male representatives. It is the demand for good and better governance that makes women complain about the quality of water even when it is objectively better as a way of pushing up the bar on governance standards.

The general belief that women representatives are less corrupt has been criticized as a "myth-making" process that espouses an instrumental justification for bringing women into the public realm of governance by interested agencies such as the World Bank, observes Goetz (undated). According to her, women elected leaders probably do not have the same set of opportunities as men to engage in illicit or illegal acts because they are not part of the male patronage and power networks. She has also noted that women who have held reserved seats at Village, Block and District levels are not backed by parties when they attempt to run again in the next election when the seat is de-reserved, and thus they are unable to build up local political capital and skills. Chathukulam and John (2000) observed from their study among women panchayat representatives of Kerala that women who were not supported by parties found it difficult to adjust to their roles as "the local party committees of leftist parties, dominated by males, alternated as institutionalized sites of patriarchal power" (ibid.: 73). Women generally did not like partisan considerations to enter the field of panchayat work. They also noted that none of the elected women members showed any enthusiasm to contest elections another time as most alleged party domination and sexist attitudes of male members. With their roles in the domestic sphere, women found the opportunity cost of involvement in politics to be quite high, notwithstanding their improved awareness of development issues and enhancement of their communication skills through training. This suggests that this empowerment process as grassroots leaders is more ephemeral and not likely to be long lasting.

There is by now a well-acknowledged literature on planning for gender needs (Moser, 1989). Two sets of needs have to be cognized and planned for in development practice to empower women, these are "practical gender needs" and "strategic gender needs". Practical gender needs refer to those that would advance poor women's interests on practical issues that would alleviate drudgery, oppression, domestic violence and promote well-being in everyday life. Addressing practical gender needs is important for women but that alone cannot address the problem of systemic gender exclusion. Strategic gender needs are those needs of women that would enhance their capabilities to address the issues arising out of systemic exclusion. Strategic gender needs also vary between different categories of women. While education will help women to secure better jobs than that of a casual labourer, education for empowerment such as legal literacy will help them become aware of their rights, ways and means of securing their rights and of how not to remain cowed down by the fear of police and law courts. Gender training for women in panchayats should enable them to identify the set of practical and strategic needs in their village communities through participatory research techniques.

In recent years, more and more development programmes are trying to build into the programmes both gender budgeting and social audit (Goetz and Jenkins, 1999). Gender budgeting seeks not only financial allocation towards women in all development programmes, but attempts to monitor the expenditure such that it is possible to measure the quantum of money spent towards women's benefit in every single instance at all levels. This is to ensure mainstreaming women in the development process to promote inclusive development, and to enable communities to control the performance and outcome of these programmes so that there is continuous monitoring and evaluation by the communities that are the intended beneficiaries. With the power provided by the recently enacted RTI Act (Right to Information Act), it is now possible for individuals and communities to interrogate the bureaucracy and the state for negligence, indifference, delays, corruption and other malpractices. These legal instruments and bureaucratic mechanisms to ensure transparency and accountability help to promote inclusive development and democratic decentralization only when they are also backed by a bundle of legally enforceable rights.

The emerging discourse of rights-based development is progressively expanding the notion of universal human rights, which while it may appear to have a homogenizing effect across cultures and communities also transposes social and economic rights outside the pale of national-level political process into universally valid rights. As capitalist globalization extends its predatory fangs into village communities destroying the ecological balance and the livelihoods of people, non-state actors can seek to defend the exploited communities only within a well-articulated rights regime. Gender training for women in panchayats should help them to understand these issues and enable them to both demand and subject themselves to the communities' demands for transparency and accountability in governance and participate effectively in gender budgeting at their level by demanding greater devolution of financial powers and finances for a gender inclusive local development.

**Building Synergy with CBOs and NGOs**

Apart from the elected panchayats, there are other community-based organizations (CBOs) that are run along the same lines as the panchayats with elected members. Here too, women must take an active interest and contest for decision-making positions so as to serve women's interests. For instance, many states and village communities have Joint Forest Management (JFM) committees at the village level, which has representatives from the state as well as elected community representatives. These are sometimes called "Van Panchayats". It is necessary to make it mandatory in all the states to have elected women representatives in all these auxillary CBOs as well. If there are women representatives in the Van Panchayat, they will be able to highlight, if adequate awareness is brought about through training given to them, the crucial importance of forest produce and their roles in providing family subsistence and ensure that their access to these resources are not restricted. Similarly, many villages have Water Users Associations, sometimes called "Paani Panchayats" that address the issues of the distribution of drinking water. Here too, women's representation must be made mandatory and in fact women should constitute the majority representation in these committees as the supply of drinking and home-use water is everywhere considered women's responsibility. Here too, the representation must adequately take care of caste and class issues, as it is all too well-known that even upper caste women participate in reproducing systemic exclusion by prohibiting SC women from drawing water from wells and pumps used by the upper castes. Elected women in the Gram Panchayats should be trained to build a synergy with these CBOs, ensure women's participation in these CBOs and seek collectively to raise women's voice on all matters that affect them. There are other CBOs where women are generally bypassed as these are considered "male" domains, such as irrigation committees, marketing committees, seed procurement committee, etc. All these supposedly male domains have to be critically examined and deconstructed by the community women and a place for women in all these male domains have to be secured. The elected women in Gram Panchayats should be trained along these lines as well, so that they will be able to work along with their community women in making their presence felt and voices heard on all these matters as well.

Attempts are also being made to introduce new CBOs that focus on addressing issues such as health along gender lines. For instance, NIPCCD (New Delhi) has been involved in a programme of experimenting with "Kishori Panchayats" which are (Adolescent Girls Forum) that sensitizes adolescent girls on health-related issues and representative members of this forum also participate in VCC (Village Coordination Committee) meetings to bring their health concerns to the fore. E-Panchayats is yet another new innovative venture to promote grassroots e-governance through the use of ICT technologies that is being tried out in some regions. Women elected members, some of whom are likely to be illiterate will be ignored from acquiring skills in the use of ICT. Care should be taken that they too are given sufficient functional and computer literacy, especially the younger women. The essence of democratic decentralization is to inculcate the democratic spirit and enable grassroots governance. Rural women should be made to understand what this spirit entails in terms of overcoming systemic exclusion and the importance of gaining rights and voice in decision-making.

It is now well-known that cases of litigation in a village hang on for years, as there is no speedy settlement at the village level. Land disputes predominate among these cases. Nyaya Panchayats with women representation should be set up in all villages for speedy justice and the amicable settlement of certain disputes. Not only should women be represented in the Nyaya Panchayats and given powers of adjudication even in such purportedly "male" matters such as land disputes, there should also be a separate wing of the Nyaya Panchayat comprising women only to function as a family court at the village level that will concern itself with family disputes including domestic violence. It is really when the Nyaya Panchayats take off enfolding within it the all-women family courts can the dominance and disciplinary powers of the traditional panchayats be curtailed and superseded.

Self-Help Groups (SHGs) are another set of CBOs that hold remarkable potential for building synergies with PRIs for better grassroots governance. The growth of SHGs, especially among rural women to enhance their incomes and livelihood by entrepreneurial initiatives through a system of microcredit lending has generated enthusiasm among women to become economically empowered. Such SHG initiatives facilitated by NGOs rather than through the government development programmes have in most instances a broader agenda than just income generation. They try in varied ways to encompass other aspects of social and economic empowerment. As SHGs are another avenue to promote grassroots leaders, the SHGs members by showing a greater degree of awareness on issues pertaining to exclusion and empowerment could work conjointly with the elected women members of the Gram Panchayat. But such synergies have to be conscientiously built up through various gender training programmes for women in panchayats and in the CBOs, of how to strategically create opportunities out of everyday situations to advance their gender interests in matters of grassroots governance.

Social movements are yet another community-based initiative with which the elected representatives will have to work, especially as rural social movements are generally concerned with issues affecting the rural masses. Elected women panchayat members are likely to identify themselves solely as agents of the state and distance themselves from the social movements that engulf their communities. Social movements are increasingly taking up issues of displacement and rehabilitation arising out of development projects such as dams and factories, and ecological issues. Panchayats should sensitize the community as well as put pressure on the state to solve these issues. Women panchayat members should gain knowledge of these issues and encourage solving them. Social movements have done much in recent years to place the issues of public accountability and transparency in governance at the centre stage. The social audit mechanisms that are now in place for the NREGA (National Rural Employment Guarantee Act) was conceived and experimented by a rural NGO from Rajasthan and put forth as a demand to the state under the leadership of social activist Aruna Roy (Jenkins and Goetz, 1999). News reports from Rajasthan itself have indicated that in some villages, the panchayats were against the social audit and placed hurdles in its conduct. Such situations can occur when state-level political patronage nurtures and promotes muscle power and money power in the panchayats. Also, with the deepening of the democratic spirit, people at the grassroots are increasingly going to redefine and expand the idea of grassroots governance that will likely be at variance with that designed by the state, which in the future may lead to both a struggle and restructuring of the system.

Many NGOs exist in rural areas or operate in rural areas for the welfare and upliftment of the people usually with some specific area of focus such as education, health, microcredit, Dalit empowerment and so on. Some are specifically oriented to women's welfare and empowerment. These NGOs also serve as nurturing ground for grassroots leaders, and women often pick up experience of grassroots collective action while being associated with these NGOs. One such NGO is the Working Women's Forum (India) headquartered in Chennai and working in many areas in the three southern states of Tamil Nadu, Andhra Pradesh and Karnataka (Kalpagam and Rajagopalan, 2006).

Using microcredit as a point of entry, WWF (I)'s approach of group formation and group lending has promoted grassroots leadership among women who with the self-confidence gained through WWF (I) association and activities have shown remarkable ability to undertake grassroots level collective action. Table 8.1 shows the grassroots initiative of WWF (I) since 2005, although in its 29 years of existence, numerous such initiatives have been regularly undertaken. Many group leaders of WWF (I) have successfully contested in the elections of the Gram panchayats as well, and have on occasions even taken the panchayats to task on various issues that concern them such as pasture land, water, housing and alcoholism. Such kinds of social activism should be promoted and synergies should be built between them and the Gram panchayats to ensure both gender-sensitive grassroots governance, and one that can effectively counter systemic gender exclusion, discrimination and oppression.

Regional variations in women's participation in panchayats are also a reflection of the effects of political mobilization both by the women's movement and by other social and political movements. Lele (2008) has shown how the rural women's movement in Maharashtra has succeeded in mobilizing and creating awareness among women elected members of the panchayats. This stresses the importance of prior political mobilization of women for the success of the panchayat representation by women. Such political mobilization could be along various trajectories and through a process of building synergies with CBOs, NGOs and social movements.

**Table 8.1**

*Details on Grassroots Initiatives by WWF (I)*

| | |
|---|---|
| The crisis management in WWF is handled with great care. To drive home the point an example of crisis management handled both internally and externally in WWF/ICNW is with regard to the tsunami killer wave that hit the Marina coast of Chennai, the eastern coast of Tamil Nadu and few coastal areas of Andhra Pradesh on December 26, 2004 where nearly 2000 members of WWF were worst affected in Tamil Nadu and Andhra Pradesh.<br>WWF/ICNW quickly volunteered to organize one-day counselling as advocacy workshop to the representatives of the fishing families who were in trauma and gave them expert advice through oceanography experts and marine engineers, assuring that the tsunami doesn't come as often but only in 50–80 years.<br>Later on June 28, 2005 a function was organized where His Excellency the Governor of Tamil Nadu was invited as the chief guest to distribute rehabilitation measures of boats/nets and other requirements worth ₹ 1,17,57,667.00 through resources that was received from various national/international humanitarian foundations by WWF to assist tsunami victims. | 28th June 2005 |
| With the humanitarian assistance, the housing requirements - new houses and repairs of the damaged houses have been undertaken in not only 17 villages of eastern coastal areas of Tamil Nadu where the WWF member live but also in Chennai Marina Coast with fishing colonies. Nearly 140 houses were repaired and new houses have been constructed.<br>In Narsapur, Andhra Pradesh, a fishing market was built for the fishing community which was inaugurated by Dr Jaya Arunachalam President Working Women's Forum (India). | 11th September 2005 |
| Demanding 33?% reservation for the women in the parliament, 8,000 members of WWF and the President took out a rally and submitted the petition signed by one lakh members, to the Governor of Tamil Nadu on September 5, 2005 to protest over the delay in passing of the Women's Reservation Bill in the Parliament. The content of the petition was a message to the politicians not to find new strategy and divide women on the basis of caste and religion. | 5th September 2005 |
| National Commission for Enterprises in the Unorganized Sector set up by Government of India as a watchdog invited President, WWF on March 13, 2006 to testify and share the experiences/achievement of WWF in enhancing socio-economic status of women workers and to testify the same. The Commission stressed to focus on the nature of enterprises, size, scope/magnitude of unorganized labour force, constraints faced by small enterprises, lack of access to material, backward/forward linkages towards better facilitation to the unorganized poor to carry on micro-enterprises. As a result, a feasibility study about the weavers from Varanasi and Kanchipuram was handed to WWF. | 13th March 2006 |

| | |
|---|---|
| As a result an exchange programme between the weavers was organized from the North, i.e. Varanasi and the South, i.e. Kanchipuram. | 29th September 2006 |
| A grievance petition signed by 20,000 women workers with regards to Social Security Bill not being presented in the Parliament was sent to the Prime Minister, UPA Chair Person, Central Labour Minister and Deputy Chairman, Planning Commission, Government of India. | June 6, 2007 |
| A Petition requesting for a bore pump with a hand pump-set in the area of Thottapalayam, Pillaiyarkoil Street, Vellore was sent to the district Collector and the Municipal Commissioner. | 18th October 2007 |
| A grievance petition from 36 women employees of TANSI Unit in Ooty who were retrenched from the services was sent to WWF which was later forwarded to the Governor of Tamil Nadu, Chief Minister of Tamil Nadu, Leader of Opposition, Local Administration Minister and Minister of Rural Industries. | 3rd March 2008 |
| Working Women's Forum (India) Submitted a Memorandum representing views/suggestions of the members with reference to Women's Reservation Bill to the Department of Standing Committee on Personnel, Public Grievances Law and Justice – Regarding the Constitution (108) Amendment Bill 2008. | 24th May 2008 |
| The ground work to identify pressing issues that affect poor women adversely in three districts (Dharmapuri, Bidar and Bellary) were taken up. Later, the three-day material development workshop was organized in Chennai.<br>The highlight of such workshop is mainly awareness and consciousness raising where solutions are collectively found. The various events in the workshop include lectures, pictorial charts, role-play, puppet show, skit and folk song, mostly visual demonstrations. | 10, 11 & 12 March 2008 |
| As a follow up measure to the macro Material Development Workshop organized in Chennai on March 10–12, 2008. Six micro-workshop were conducted from July 22–29, 2008 in the backward districts of Bidar and Bellary (Karnataka) to disseminate information to the poor women on various issues lying dormant in their areas and on August 31–September 2, 2008 in Dharmapuri in Tamil Nadu not only to create awareness on the most pressing issues, but also to inculcate in them income generating activities, gender equality whereby enabling them to realize their potential as human beings. The workshop serves twin purposes, i.e. to empower women to acquire the means and ability to participate in the main stream of economic and social development, as well as in the decision that affect their lives and those of their families. The solutions to their existing problems were conveyed through pictorial charts in vernacular. Apart from handling social problems, their economic concern too were given major emphasis. In this perspective, the food and chemical processing products were demonstrated to the poor women enabling them to prepare these products in groups and market in the local areas and neighbourhood to sustain their livelihood. | July 22–29 2008 and August 31 – September 2, 2008 |

| | |
|---|---|
| A grievance petition signed by 50 families residing in Thiruvatravar Nagar, Perungudi for the irregular drinking water supply was sent to the Corporation Commissioner, Chennai, the President Perungudi Panchayat and the Area Engineer, X-B Chennai Metropolitan Water Supply and Sewage Board. | April 19, 2008 |
| Grievances of 15 members who were displaced from their hutments just because they have constructed their hutments on government (porambokku) land in Adiramapattinam was sent to the Chief Minister of Tamil Nadu and the District Collector. | May 26, 2008 |
| National Union of Working Women fought several cases for the rights of women. In these five years, the NUWW handled 29 cases relating to dowry, seven land dispute cases, three money lending cheating cases, five counselling cases where women who had differences with their spouse were solved, five cases relating to business activities and four cases relating to vacate the house premises. Apart from this, nearly 405 families were facilitated with the drinking water supply – in Velachery (212), Kallukuttai (74) and Padi Pudhu Nagar (119) and one case relating to inter-caste marriage. | |

## Conclusion

Gender-sensitive grassroots governance under the present system of democratic decentralization through the PRIs can become possible and effective only if elected women members are made aware of the systemic gender exclusion and of how the process of development further marginalizes them. Such an understanding has to be further bolstered by a critical mass of grassroots support by the community women who could collectively transform the nature of grassroots governance. But it is necessary to build collaborative ties and cooperative relations with CBOs, NGOs and social movements for the process of democratic decentralization and grassroots governance to be really effective in its transformative agendas.

# 9

# Perspectives for a Grassroots Feminist Theory*

In the current milieu of the social sciences where new theoretical approaches and concepts of Western social theory invade our reflective spaces – and women's studies is no exception to it – there is a justified defensive reaction among some Indian feminist scholars that we will not only have our national agendas for feminist work hijacked by western interests, but even the theories and paradigms that are borrowed or imitated from Western social sciences and that inform our work may prove to be irrelevant to our concerns and completely divorced from the experiences of women at the grassroots. I am not one of those who accept this criticism completely as I believe that Western social theory can enrich our analysis significantly. But I do recognize that such a criticism touches the chords of many feminist scholars that even if they do not completely abandon their baggage of borrowed paradigms, they nevertheless concede the validity of the criticism by merely acknowledging the need for relevance and often without examining the theoretical and philosophical presuppositions of such a critique.

Three strands of reactionary criticism have permeated the contemporary discursive field in the era of globalization. These are inimical in some senses to women's studies desiring to bring changes in gender relations at the societal level along progressive and egalitarian lines. First, there is a naive and uncritical Western or American culture bashing that has been popular with the self-styled culture police of today. Secondly, there is an increasing number of male interlocutors of Indian feminism with rather suspect motives, often drawing support from the first set of culture police – whom I prefer to call as the "Hamara

* An earlier version of this was published in *Economic and Political Weekly*, Vol. XXXVII, No. 47, November 23, 2002.

Sanskriti Group". It is a common refrain among this group of male interlocutors to question the "Indian-ness" of the Indian women's movement, only to be dismissive of the concern for egalitarianism. Thirdly, there are the fuzzy thinkers on indigenous social science who while being skeptical of Western social science categories aspire to reconstruct social science which is purportedly more contextually relevant and based on indigenous categories of thought, but nevertheless seem never able to constructively work towards building such alternatives. If a well-meaning criticism of the received paradigms of Western feminist theory and the alternative of a grassroots feminist theory is to be reflected upon seriously, then it is important to carefully navigate through these inimical discourses or risk being reduced to their positions. This chapter is an attempt to initiate such an exercise not so much by posing the question of relevance, but by examining the theoretical and philosophical presuppositions of a grassroots feminist theory.

## Arguments Against Western-Culture Bashers

Let me first consider the issues at stake in the uncritical Western or American culture bashing that has been popular with the self-styled culture police of today. The most common storyline of this critique is that the exposure to Western media, particularly through television channels has led to the internalization of Western cultural norms to the detriment of traditional Indian values and this particularly affects family life which is the most cherished Indian cultural value for the culture police. Apart from the materialism and consumerism that the West has come to signify, it also stands for breakdown of family relations, high divorce rates, lesbian and gay relationships, dating, public kissing, children talking sex, Valentine's day celebrations, skimpy clothes, show biz and models. This is in many ways a reverse Orientalism that Edward Said has critically examined regarding how the West represents the rest. Here cultural particularity is sought to be projected and defended against a supposedly universal (read Western) culture. This kind of civilization critique (zivilisationskritik) that was once made popular by German "kultur" discourses finds recent echoes in the defense of "Asian values" by many authoritarian regimes in the countries of south-east Asia as well.

The problem with this kind of positioning is to attribute to the West a cultural homogeneity that it certainly lacks in the increasingly multicultural world of immigrants, diasporic populations and hybridities. Moreover, it does not recognize the plurality of opinions and lifestyles even in this imagined homogeneous group of Western Anglo-Saxon Protestant (Wasp) populations, for if there are groups that support abortions, and gay and lesbian marriages there are equally vociferous religiously inspired groups that oppose these social and legal changes. Yet, the remarkable aspect of the West is the awareness that even such fundamental institutions such as marriage are subject to on-going social changes and that moral and ethical judgements of these changes can only be validated from the standpoint of individual and social freedom. It would be downright silly on our part to attribute immorality on the part of the legislators and the judges who legalize domestic partnerships outside of marriages (live-in-couples) or those legalizing same-sex partnerships in the USA, though it is necessary on their part to take cognizance of alternative opinions in the society and to ensure its proper articulation. What is commendable though of the West is the tolerance that is cherished in their liberal public sphere and the discourse of democracy that such liberalism sustains in the West. Such discursive practices in the West influence the constitution, functioning and participation in their public institutions. All this is either absent or exists in distorted and perverted forms in India, but strangely these are invisible to the Western-culture bashers for whom the West signifies only cultural degeneration. Such epistemic and political vantage point occupied by the American-culture bashers hardly enables them to recognize the historicity of modernity and the creative assimilation in cultural transformations in India and elsewhere. If certain forms of Western lifestyle shock us today and if it poses a threat to our values, our earlier generations too must have felt the same sense of shock and threat when some middle-class Indian women broke free from the confines of their homes to partake of modern education that colonial modernity so persuasively offered it, or more recently when educated women began to take up employment in modern sectors of the economy. In other words, seeing the West in purely derogatory ways may be a tit-for-tat gesture after centuries of Western political and economic superiority over the others, but is nevertheless an impoverishing perspective.

I have taken up a position of defence against Western-culture bashers for the present purpose of working towards a contextually relevant grassroots feminist theory so as to underline the importance of incorporating into the framework how the forces of modernity impinge at the grassroots in terms of transformation of desires, needs and resources. While acknowledging that modernity impacts across social groups in an uneven manner and that it percolates rather slowly to groups way down in the socio-economic hierarchy, it does reach out to all at least in two distinctly important ways. First is to draw grassroots groups and individuals into the sphere of social exchange, however unequal the terms of exchange may be and second, to bring them within the fold of modern polity as participants in politics even if their citizenship rights exist in severely restricted forms. Cultural changes associated with modernity at the grassroots level are never an imitative adoption of Western cultural mores, rather these are generally changes made possible by the twin processes of modern exchange relations and a modern polity, and are generally in the direction in which the individuals and communities adapting to these cultural changes perceive the change as promoting a sense of freedom that was hitherto unavailable to them. The promise of unlimited freedom may be a seductive trick of Western modernity as modern power itself constitutes modern freedom through the institution of rights and law. Modern subjectivity is everywhere moulded and shaped by this desire for modern freedom although the nature of that freedom so ardently desired by moderns may vary across cultures. Modern democracy today has a universal value. In this context then, one must be wary of Western-culture bashing for often what is hidden in this critique is the attack against this desire for freedom. Especially for women, this hidden attack is an attempt to keep them under control and put them in their place by patriarchal forces.

**Facing the Challenge of "Hamara Sanskriti"**

The second set of inimical discourses that we need to bring to critical attention is the "Hamara Sanskriti" group comprising predominantly of male interlocutors of Indian feminism with rather suspect motives, often drawing support from the first set of culture police. It is a common refrain among this group of male interlocutors to question the "Indian-ness" of the Indian women's movement, only to be dismissive of the concern for egalitarianism. This group of feminist bashers view Indian culture as fixed and unchanging, in which an upper caste middle class idea of culture, often the culture that the interlocutor is familiar with, serves to substitute as the "national" culture to which all are imagined to conform. Eliding the diversities of culture within the national society, this group explains away all obvious gender inequalities as preferred, sanctioned and immutable cultural arrangements meant to accord a complementarity between the sexes and to ensure harmony in family life. Systemic and structured inequalities between the sexes as well as unequal opportunities are not so much cultural arrangements as they are the outcome of social processes.

No doubt, it is only a modernist epistemology that allows us to perceive these as social processes and not perhaps as cultural arrangements, but such a modernist perspective also renders possible forms of intervention, bureaucratic or otherwise, that could reverse these unfavourable outcomes. Our feminist bashers are neither prepared to take cognizance of these inequalities or the conditions for the possibilities of change; hence the Indian women's movement is perceived as Western or Western-inspired feminism ill-suited to our culture, nor is the women's movement's concern for egalitarianism conceded any merit. Ask them what the feminist movement stands for and they will tell you that it stands for sexual freedom, family-destroying tendencies such as sharing of housework between spouses, women's economic independence, their choice to have or not to have sex and children, support for lesbianism and so on. They would hardly mention issues such as imbalances in sex ratios, high female illiteracy, feminization of poverty, gender discrimination in labour markets, violence against women, and other kinds of systemic and social gender inequalities which the Indian women's movement has highlighted.

A grassroots feminist theory that can challenge the onslaught of this group of interlocutors needs to highlight the inequalities and oppressive social and gender relations within a framework that captures both diversities and dynamics of cultural processes and retains the authenticity of grassroots women's experiences. Such an approach would make clear that cultural arrangements are indeed not immutable and the process of challenging social, economic and cultural relations that does not accord dignity to women at the grassroots could in itself make modern freedom desirable to those seen as occupying the fringes of modernity. A grassroots feminist theory that privileges a discourse of the "local" has in this context a greater potential to challenge traditionalist male chauvinism than one that fails to buy critical purchase from this conceptual innovation.

## Fuzzy Thinking on Indigenous Social Science

Of late, the voices calling for an indigenous social science have become shrill and sharp. There are many different ways in which the need for indigenous social science is articulated. For some it is just doing contextually relevant social science, which position is reasonable and acceptable although one may want to question the credentials of those who espouse contextually irrelevant social science. Another manner in which the issue is posed, and quite problematically I must say, is to substitute indigenous categories of thought for Western categories of thought. It may be relevant here to note that social sciences has broadly two goals and corresponding set of methodologies. One is explanation of social phenomenon in terms of causes and effects, and the other seeks to understand social phenomenon preserving the authenticity of experience. A concern for explanation in terms of causes and effects has as its corollary the purpose of shaping social processes in desired ways through interventions. In such situations of purposive management of social phenomenon, the representation of objects and entities in discursive practices has no doubt to satisfy the needs of intervention. It is not difficult to imagine contexts where indigenous conceptions and indigenous discursive practices are mismatched with the techniques of intervention, as for instance, a conception of poverty not as material deprivation but as a necessary affliction caused by divine wrath on account of one's actions in past lives would be ill-suited for poverty eradication programmes that define poverty in statistical terms of unmet needs. More and more interventions in the modern world such as techniques of modern economic management would find indigenous conceptions of exchange, service, poverty, wealth and so on, not only ill-suited but even contextually irrelevant as commodity relations and markets transform pre-capitalist relations everywhere.

The other motivation for the social science is to understand social phenomenon keeping intact the authenticity of the experiences of the actors. Here, the need for indigenous conceptions appear quite persuasive especially since it is widely believed that the authenticity of experience is best captured if understanding is based on the so-called "natives point of view", or in our context, the actors point of view. Hermeneutics method that has been so successful in the interpretive approaches in ethnography has no doubt been seductive in persuading the reader to believe that experiences of the actors, from their point of view, have been used in the narrative accounts of their culture. But as the recent postmodernist critiques of ethnography have highlighted, such persuasive attempts of interpretive approaches are indeed problematic as it ignores how power construes the dialogical setting of the ethnographer and the subjects of his inquiry. Even granting that the researcher is critical and reflective enough to capture only the "native's point of view", the researcher's attempt to translate that point of view to an audience other than those studied entails a move away from their point of view if only to make their experience comprehensible to others outside their group. The need for inter-group communication of experience has to reckon that more and more groups are articulating their experience in the same language of progress, development and statistics. The fuzzy thinkers who enthusiastically espouse the promotion of indigenous social science hardly consider these epistemological issues. The point that is being argued here is not the demise of relativism and the complete conquest by universalism, but that relativist discourses in social science seeking to highlight cultural particularities have themselves to be conducted within universalist frameworks of knowledge.

## II

Let us now examine the stakes of these arguments for a grassroots feminist theory. Especially since feminism seeks to valorise women's experience, it is important to explore ways of articulating women's experiences. Here I think it is necessary to explore the relationship between language, speech, categories and experience. Does experience stand independently of these? It is often said that language fails to capture experience fully and that cultural categories by which people live their lives constitute their experience. Yet we do know that across all cultures there is a common denominator of emotions that expresses human experience. Few across cultures would feel joyous at the loss of a loved one, although what they would feel happy about, be it wealth, success, fame, spiritual peace, etc., would vary even with individuals in a culture. While indigenous categories become necessary to articulate some aspects of experience in their cultural particularity, we still have to encounter the issue of cultural translation to make that experience in its cultural particularity comprehensible to other cultures. The crucial issue we however face in articulating women's experiences is that in almost all patriarchal cultures, there is a cultural censorship and hence silence over articulating certain aspects of women's experience, these censorship rules known only to members socialized in that culture which others may be able to learn through some effort. A grassroots feminist theory should no doubt be sensitive to the ways of articulating women's experience in their cultural particularity both through the use of appropriate indigenous categories that best constitute and represent certain experiences even as it is sensitive to letting the silences speak and be heard. It is equally important for a grassroots feminist theory to provide explanatory insights into the processual dynamics of systemic gender inequalities at the grassroots. Such explanatory analysis requires undoubtedly the use of universalist frameworks as well as universalist concepts and categories. The categories by which people in a particular culture live their lives are not the categories that will enable us to understand social phenomenon and cause-effect relationships.

However, we do need to be clear about what we mean by "grassroots" given that it is a much-used term and is bound to have multiple meanings. In what follows, we clarify the term "grassroots" as relevant to our analysis.

**Grassroots: Multiple Meanings**

The term "grassroots" as used in the women's studies movement is often used in various senses and it is necessary to explicitly state them. Often grassroots refer to "women out there", implicitly meaning all those poor women in the villages and urban slums. In this sense, there is a clear distinction between "elite women" who are "here" and the "grassroots women who are out there". Notice that in this sense many subtle distinctions are made, and these are more subjective distinctions that a community of women's studies scholars seems to agree inter-subjectively. These distinctions are elite/grassroots, non-poor/poor, urban/rural, here/out-there (often signifying metropolitan proximity to power and decision-making, and peripheral distancing from power and decision-making). Not only does the community of scholars has its definitions at stake here, but also the increasing number of NGOs working in the field have their own meanings of the notion "grassroots". Not only do they refer to the women they work with as "grassroots women", but even the organizations are called "grassroots", adding another layer of meaning to the term, namely, "decentralized" or institutional structures closer to the grassroots women.

This naturalistic adjective "grassroots" appears to have instituted itself in development language primarily to signify the distance between those whom development interventions sought to reach on account of the hierarchically layered structures of bureaucracy, which structures the developmental state has come to rely upon to distribute its developmental goods. In its general connotation, the term has come to signify those deprived of power and effective resources and hence those who possess only a circumscribed and constrained agency in their institutional transactions.

The other idea that the notion of "grassroots" evokes is its close association with the "local". The "local" stands for all that bestows meanings, identities, a sense of belonging or dwelling in a place, resources, a sense of purpose, etc. For the people distanced from institutional sources of power and decision-making, the sense of the "local" carries far greater significance in everyday life than other possible supra-local forms of belonging such as the "nation" or the "global". A grassroots feminist theory has to incorporate these two essential dimensions in its theoretical and analytical constructions. In attempting to do so, a grassroots feminist theory will call attention to the inadequacies of much feminist thinking that have been motivated by the well-known slogan of the global women's movement – "Think Globally, Act Locally". Merely thinking globally will not result in effective local actions, if one does not also simultaneously learn to *think locally* as well. Learning to think locally means understanding both the forms of disempowerment as well as the forms of significance that the "local" or "grassroots" bestows.

**Privileging the "Local"**

The attempt to privilege a discourse of "local" has far-reaching implications for understanding the role of culture and cultural change in our grassroots framework. A cultural critique that privileges the "local" can be empowering, democratic and respectful of diversity. Such an endeavour requires us to invest the "local" with new meanings and extend its critical purchase. The "local" represents the terrain of accessibility, of meanings, of resources and of practices for the majority in the majority world. The dialectic of the global-local processes is not merely reshaping the local but rapidly shrinking it as well. Such shrinking of the "local" means an associated decline in the values that the "local" entails. These are values of collectivism and avoidance of excessive individualism, a spirit of community and reciprocity, a less rapacious man-nature interaction, markets embedded in local social relations, religious influence over cultural values and an ethnicity contained within a local cosmopolitanism. These co-exist with the values of a liberal democracy inspired by the twin ideals of nation-state and capitalist development.

The suggestion to privilege the "local" is a careful choice over either the "indigenous" or the "ethnic". A set of contingent forces and factors that bring together a group of people in materiality and sociality constitute the "local". Such people share a common local culture, but all do not share all the aspects of a common local culture. Anthropology so far has fought shy of such a definition of culture that does not make it an ideational unity. Such a concept of culture is not possible in the case of "indigenous" and "ethnic" where the categories themselves are posited in terms of ideational unities. The advantage of such a notion of culture is that it enables us to distance from the question of origins or leads us into essentialisms and so renders possible a new way of understanding "tradition".

"Tradition" is a resource for communities. Hence, it should not be seen negatively as co-terminus with superstition or irrationality. Rather tradition is to be understood as discursive practices embedded in local communities and that constitutes cultural practices of these communities. So long as these cultural practices survive the changes ushered in by modernity, these discursive practices also continue in however transformed a form they may be. But when these cultural practices do die out, these discursive practices have no functional coexistence in the communities and so are transposed into the communities' memories lingering often in the form of myths or folklore. Our focus on the "local" rather than on "indigenous" or "ethnic" enables us to view tradition as discursive practices that are not insulated; rather they interact and intersect with other traditions thus constituting them and in turn being constituted by them. It is the porousness of cultural boundaries between communities that constitutes the "local", that unlike the "indigenous" which by assuming insularity beckons us to an originary moment. Equally, "ethnic" would be inappropriate in a context where every single community in a local context can lay claim to being "ethnic" on grounds of some perceived cultural difference with the others.

The "local" is here taken to be the experiential site of the majority despite the operation of global forces and despite the fact that the site of the local is rapidly changing. Of late, scholars' engagement with globalization has compelled them to reflect on the "local" as well. Appadurai, for instance, argues that the poor and powerless can participate actively in shaping practices of imagination called for by globalization, but that "the task of producing locality ... is increasingly a struggle in the wake of globalising forces" (1996: 189). He argues that people can recover agency through a process of "indigenization" that was deployed in resisting colonialism. Bauman (1998) concedes to the widely held view that globalization exacerbates social differentiation and inequality and in so doing fixes some people in space and restricts their access to the globally circulating capital and culture that others enjoy. Bauman notes that getting localized while others get globalized "is a sign of social deprivation and degradation" (1998: 2), while Robertson (1995) observes that this localization being imposed produces a loss of agency and freedom and hence creates passive local viewers out of global actors.

These reflections on the "local" suggest that the "local" is being increasingly problematized by the social scientists. The "local" is produced through a set of discursive and non-discursive practices. Analogous to the way, "pre-modern" carried with it a stigma of being outside of "modern", so too does the "local" carry the stigma of being outside of the "global". Such stigmatization also implies loss of agency and freedom to those confined to the local. The attempt at privileging the "local" is an attempt to foreground it in social scientific discourses so as to overcome this attitude as well as the loss of agency. Especially for a "third world" feminist analysis that is already overburdened with the agendas of recovering women's agency and resisting the myriad stigmas that taunt women in general, a sensitivity to "thinking locally" can be an effective strategy of empowerment to face the challenges of globalization. Some Western feminist scholars have sought to argue that the "local" is also actively involved in shaping the "global" and so are deploying agency in new ways.

We should also be cautious of the fact that the discourse of the "local" could be used in disempowering ways. Briggs (2001) highlights how public health authorities in Venezuela in managing cholera epidemic there in the 90s deployed the discourse of the "local" through cultural reasoning by focussing on the particular features of the "local" culture which made the people susceptible to cholera infection, while the "local" people "focussed their accounts of the epidemic on national and regional political institutions, transnational commerce, and international conflict" (Briggs, 2001: 677). Briggs goes on to warn us that globalization and growing social inequality are posing many challenges to the nation-state; one such challenge is that institutions are charged with the responsibility of "generating ideologies and practices that construct inequality in ways that transfer responsibility from the state and corporations onto the shoulders of the growing ranks of the poor" (ibid.: 687). The discourses of the "local" could thus serve as a legitimizing rhetoric of culture for new social inequalities. Yet, it is equally true that it is only from the discursive site of the "local" that discourse of human rights can be deployed by the subaltern majority populations everywhere to challenge the new inequalities imposed by globalization.

Privileging the "local" should reinforce the resilience of local cultures and cultural diversities against their imminent fragility and non-sustainability in the face of the sweeping changes brought in by globalization. While the cliche "Think Globally, Act Locally" has gained enormous popularity with NGOs worldwide for the sake of global solidarity, we wish to impart a new dimension to that discourse by insisting that in all instances "acting locally" would also necessitate "thinking locally". A grassroots feminist theory should help us to learn to *think locally.*

**Gender Needs at the Grassroots**

Understanding gender needs at the grassroots requires fine tuning our assessments of the needs of men and women of different classes and groups at the local level. We already noted that the local represents the terrain of accessibility, of meanings, of resources and of practices for the majority in the majority world. The local is also associated in people's minds at the local level with a set of values such as collectivism and avoidance of excessive individualism, a spirit of community and reciprocity, a less rapacious man-nature interaction, markets embedded in local social relations, religious influence over cultural values, and an ethnicity contained within a local cosmopolitanism and so on. These values not only co-exist with modern political values and capitalist exchange values, but are also forced to confront and contest a new set of value-regime in the making that is associated with globalization and neoliberalism. Although not completely a matter of choice, people at the grassroots associate themselves with one set of values even as they are in the state of transition accommodating to other new values as well. Thinking locally of gender needs requires us to keep in mind this dialectic of value regimes, for people's perception of needs is determined by the values that inform their lifestyles. Generational differences in the perception of needs may in fact arise on this score of differing sets of values, and the assessment of gender needs at the grassroots ought to be sensitive to that as well.

In the 1980s, gender and development studies profited much by the distinction made by the perceptive feminist scholar, Maxine Molyneux, between strategic gender interests and practical gender interests. While strategic gender interests referred to those interests that would significantly alter gender and power relations, and contribute to women's empowerment through effective patriarchal bargains with state and men, practical gender interests took care of the immediate interests of women that no doubt enhanced their well-being, but did not significantly alter the gender and power relations. Techniques of gender planning that were subsequently developed drew much insight from this distinction. Such techniques of gender planning are no doubt the reflection of global thinking and so far the techniques evolved through that process were made to have the desired effects at the grassroots. However in assessing gender needs at the grassroots, it would be useful to carry this distinction of needs and see how it could be modified by "thinking locally" with the concepts "strategic gender needs" and "practical gender needs".

Strategic gender needs that will alter gender and power relations in the direction of greater equality has to concern itself with what is happening to the terrain of the local itself as well as the corresponding changes in values. Practical gender needs in the local episteme would relate to those needs that would contribute to well-being that could be made attainable at every configuration of the local, that is, practical gender needs are tempered by local feasibility. Thus, gender needs are configured not simplistically in terms of what women desire or need which they did not hitherto have vis-à-vis men. Then, every man and woman is likely to spell out a different need list as his or her individual preference. Rather, we see gender needs as those which women and men require for empowerment and well-being, and mediated by changes that are constantly being effected in the terrain of the local. It is now easy to see why approaches evolved out of global thinking, as for instance the Human Development Index would be an inadequate tool to assess gender needs at the grassroots as it renders invisible the particularities of the local changes, the way we have conceptualized "local" not merely as a regional site.

Let us for a moment imagine that the "local" is changing on account of globalization and let us figure out the likely directions in which changes are likely to be effected and their consequences for gender needs. We had already noted that the local represents the terrain of accessibility, of meanings, of resources and of practices for the people at the grassroots. In a situation of change occasioned by global forces, the degree of accessibility of the local is diminished as more and more of the local in terms of its resources and values get colonized by global forces. By global forces it is meant not only an increasing commodification of social relations but one in which market relations become more of supra-local relations which restrict effective participation only to those possessing the capabilities to participate in supra-local activities. The majority of women in the third world countries are constrained in terms of their poverty, family roles, working lives, education, skills, etc., to be effective participants in these supra-local affairs thus confining them more and more to an increasingly shrinking local in which not only is accessibility getting more difficult but where resources, practices and meanings undergo transformation. Not only material resources but non-material resources such as traditional knowledge which local communities hitherto possessed become more and more restricted, local practices that once flourished on these knowledge systems correspondingly change or give way to modern practices and most significantly a new set of meanings reflecting the increasing commodification of social relations begin to contest with the older set of meanings. For the people at the grassroots, the changes that are brought onto the terrain of the local also brings about a change in their perspective of social relations as older ties based on status get transformed by contractual social relations. Local actors increasingly view social relations and opportunities in game-theoretic terms. Those with more information and the ability to play smartly secure better outcomes in the changing scenario. The distributions of all kinds of information, both traditional and modern, as well as the resources are skewed in local communities such that women are in general unable to secure better outcomes than men in such transactions do. At any moment, there are always people who are still more firmly rooted in the older situations of the local, those who have not adapted to the changing local scenario, whose aspirations are defined by the older conditions and those for whom the appeal of the changes backed by information and resources make changes desirable at least at the individual level.

It is thus clear that in rethinking strategic gender needs we ought to take into account these changing factors at the local. If women are losing on account of the shrinking of the local and the changes in the local situational context, and are also failing to make gains on account of the newer changes that global forces have set in, then we need to reconsider the "strategic needs" for women's empowerment. The important point to note is that strategic gender needs in a grassroots framework cannot be stipulated without taking cognizance of what is happening at the local and their impact on both men and women. Strategic gender empowerment as a corollary cannot therefore merely enable women to overcome patriarchal relations of domination of men over women. In fact, the gender and development paradigms that Indian feminist scholars have rightly emphasized so far sought to locate gender inequalities and gender oppression in their structural context. However, a greater emphasis was placed on the macro-structural context arising in part from global thinking and the failure to recognize the importance of "thinking locally". My plea for "local thinking" is not to effect a shift in focus from a macro-structural context to a micro-structural one, which need not actually entail "local thinking" but could be just carrying over global thinking at more decentralized or disaggregated levels of analysis. The approach suggested here is to integrate analysis of changing culture, values and economy at the local and to recognize that the perceptions of strengths and weaknesses by people at the grassroots are in many ways determined by their cognizance of the changes at the local. Most often macro-structural context and changes are beyond the realm of cognition of grassroots people, but they can better understand the local context guided by the immediacy of their experiences.

Practical gender needs arising out of local thinking is of course easier to understand. It refers to those perceived needs of women taking into account the local situational context that will enhance their well-being which in so doing will impact positively on the attainment of strategic gender needs as well. For even under whatever context of changes at the local level, there is a consensus among all that certain minimum level of well-being such as freedom from hunger, poverty, ill health, poor nutrition, improper shelter, water and sanitation facilities is due to all. As a matter of fact, my suggestion to evolve strategic gender needs and practical gender needs through a process of local thinking is not as academic or abstract as it sounds. All grassroots level organizations working for gender empowerment do to a certain extent evolve their mission and tasks at least partly through the process of thinking locally. My attempt here has been merely to unite the myriad of such efforts and activities within a unified framework of thought.

### Understanding Grassroots Transactional Matrix

A grassroots feminist theory that seeks to provide an understanding of the processes toward the attainment of gender empowerment ought to pay special attention to the nature of self-other relations that local conditions bind women to. This calls for an understanding of both the nature of the "self" and of the "other". It has often been noted that self-other interactions at the grassroots is not a rigid and bounded one, as one would expect of a contractual society with a strong sense of individualism, since values of both individualism and communitarianism co-exist. Rather, depending on the context, the "self" is at times expansive to include a range of "others". Age and generational differences also account for differences in the nature of the "self". Many grassroots activists working for gender empowerment have often reported that when women talk about themselves, it is never about themselves but about a number of others whose lives are enmeshed with theirs. Yet, women are also involved in many contractual relations where notions of expansive self would be inappropriate. For an understanding of gender empowerment process, it is necessary to have an understanding of the transactional matrix of women. By transactional matrix, I refer to the set of human relations that encompass women's life. These include those of her spouse, the immediate family, children, kin groups, employers, neighbours, government functionaries, community and so on. It is necessary to understand how patriarchal relations of domination in one relation impact on other transactional relations. It is only a meaningful assumption that women do not exercise a uniform degree of agency in each transactional relation. It is possible that patriarchal domination in one relation is severely constricting but not so in other relations.

Grassroots women's ability to access goods and services that are potentially available to them would be an important factor in our transaction matrix. Classifying the sites of accessibility as those that pertain to the market, state, community and household, the transactional analysis on accessibility should inquire into the constraints and possibilities of such access to goods and services in these sites. It can be reasonably assumed that the degree of accessibility differ both within the four sites of markets, state, community and household, but also differs between women conditioned by such factors as skills, literacy, age, caste, assets, etc. One of the very significant causes of the weak agency of most grassroots women is the non-availability of institutional sources of power that will help to channel more goods and services to them. Especially their distance from decision-making agencies of the state means that they are always only at the receiving end, which they are not always fortunate to actually receive, as they are never actively able to access what is potentially available to them.

A transactional analysis is therefore necessary to understand how women's interactions with agents and institutions could be strengthened to be able to secure for them a greater agency. Agency can be reckoned and realized by agents only if they are able to recognize the limits of the realms over which they can leverage and meaningfully act upon. While it is well recognized among social scientists that "structure" constitutes/constrains "agency", thereby meaning that the limits of agency are set by structural constraints, there is much less importance given to how agents perceive structure, for the agent's ability to exercise agency is dependent only on her perceptions of the structure. Structure at any point in time no doubt represents the embedded outcomes of the cumulated actions of the aggregate of agents; and if structure determines an agent's action, it is only to the extent to which the agent perceives the structure. Multiplicity of agents thus leads to varying perceptions of the same objective structure and hence diverse sets of actions among agents. Transactional analysis introduced into action and participatory research with the grassroots women enables them to both perceive the structure as well as ensure a congruence of perceptions among a community of women.

Considerations for a grassroots feminist theory outlined so far would undoubtedly provide both a greater rationale as well as a greater clarity to both the efforts of democratic decentralization and women's participation in grassroots democratic governance. Feminist efforts should however not stop at just political democratization though even that in the Indian context is far from being complete, but should direct their efforts at social democratization as well. Such efforts would bear greater results if we accept the importance of learning to "think locally". In the following, we will examine, by a process of "thinking locally" the relations between democratization, governance and empowerment.

## Democracy, Governance and Empowerment

Everybody believes that grassroots activism among women, of whatever kind, is meant to empower them. Empowerment has been understood broadly as enhancing capabilities so as to enable women to take greater control over their lives and to transform dependencies leading to their subordination by ensuring them greater autonomy. The means for empowerment are greater information or knowledge and greater access to resources. Grassroots initiatives in development have generally acknowledged the need for interventions that are based crucially on an awareness of and sensitivity to local conditions. Thus, epistemologies based on local knowledge such as participatory research techniques and so on sought to mitigate the brutality of external top-down interventions in grassroots women's lives by incorporating their experiences and opinions in strategic interventions; indeed making them the agents rather than the targets of interventions. Such approaches though sensitive to incorporating local knowledge and to some extent critical of "global" thinking did not go far enough in promoting "local" thinking. This may in part have been due to the rather late foregrounding in paradigmatic frames of the "global", a position that was occupied till recently by the "state". Grassroots initiatives generally criticized state-directed bureaucratic development interventions as being overly centralized and though they succeeded in part in ensuring decentralization were unable to conceptually integrate the goals of governance, empowerment and democracy in the modern societies.

Drawing insights from Triantafillou's extension of Foucault's ideas of governmentality in the context of development, we note that governance is not limited to the actions of the state, "but entails the entire set of techniques, knowledges and strategies for acting, notably through indirect means, on the conduct of *others* under a range of different authorities, and the practices for acting upon the *self by the self*" (Triantafillou and Nielsen, 2001: 66). If modernity is an "attitude of the mind" that causes the individual to be engaged in reflexive activity to discover and produce the truth about themselves through a constant dialogue with different bodies of expert knowledge and that provides the individual with techniques both to interpret and carry out her conduct and that of others, then it is clear that modernity involves more than the creation of a modern state as it also involves the creation of a modern society and a modern subjectivity as well. Practices of citizenship that emerge in the modern nation-state shape modern subjectivity through new techniques to ensure particular conduct. It is in this sense of shaping practices and the formation of new subjectivity that is willed by the subjects themselves that links up democracy, governance and empowerment.

The strategies of women's empowerment through grassroots initiatives attempts to bring before women at the grassroots level specific developmental rationalities such as progress, social change and individual and community well-being, and bodies of knowledge on health, education, etc., such that by engaging in certain actions they can reshape their subjectivity voluntarily in the direction of improvement. Whatever may be the intended and unintended effects of such grassroots interventions (and indeed there is now a voluminous literature on this), these no doubt serve as techniques of normalization by imparting in women appropriate desires, norms and capacities to function as capable and empowered citizens. Triantafillou rightly notes that "the making of the capable subject with increased room for choice is preconditioned on her subjection to rituals that conform to a modern mode of being" (Triantafillou and Nielsen, 2001: 83).

The normative agendas for the "capable" subject has for long been premised on their identification with supra-local entities such as the nation and state. In the evolving modern society, there was no intermediary level of identification for individuals between the loyalty to the family and patriotism to the nation. This was in part due to "global thinking" promoted by the nation-state. The attempt to foreground "local thinking" will in course of time bring in a new sphere of identification, namely that sphere which is the site of resources, meanings and practices for the majority. Such an intermediary sphere of the "local" would be particularly relevant as global forces seek to conquer and reshape the "local". The "capable subject of majority" in this present age is not the traditional woman guarding the domestic realm or the patriotic woman identifying herself with the nation symbolically represented as "Mother India" or the one carrying the tags of hyphenated and hybrid identities, but one who learns to think locally and learns to defend and cherish that which provides her the resources, meanings and practices. Viewed in this perspective, women's participation in democratic decentralization through their representation in the panchayats is just the beginning of new challenges that modernity has forced on us.

# References


Abraham, K. (2009). "The names in your address book: Are mobile phone networks effective in advocating for women rights in Zambia?" In Buskens, I. and Webb, A. (Eds) *African Women and ICTs: Investigating Technology, Gender and Empowerment*. London: Zed Press.

Agarwal, B. (1990). "Social security and the family: Coping with seasonality and calamity in rural India", *Journal of Peasant Studies* 17(3): 341–412.

Agarwal, B. (1997). "Bargaining and gender relations: Within and beyond the household", *Feminist Economics* 3(1): 1–51.

Alampay, E.A. (2005). "Beyond access to ICTs: Measuring capabilities in the information society", *International Journal of Education and Development using ICT* (Online) 2(3): 4–22.

Aminuzzaman, S., Baldersheim, H. and Jamil, I. (2003). "Talking back! Empowerment and mobile phones in rural Bangladesh: A study of the Village Phone Scheme of Grameen Bank", *Contemporary South Asia* 12(3): 327–348.

Anand, A. (2002). "ICTs: Empowering women, assisting development", *Gender, Technology & Development* 6(1): 121–127.

Antony, P. and Gayathri, V. (2008). "Ricocheting gender equations: Women workers in the call centre industry". In Saith, A., Vijayabaskar, M. and Gayathri, V. (Eds) *ICTs and Indian Social Change: Diffusion, Poverty, Governance*. New Delhi: Sage.

Antrobus, P. (1989). "The empowerment of women". In Gallin, R., Arnoff, M. and Ferguson, A. (Eds) *The Women and International Development Annual*. Boulder, CO: Westview Press Inc.

Appadurai, A. (1996). *Modernity at Large: Cultural Dimensions of Globalisation*. Minneapolis: University of Minnesota Press.

Arunachalam, J. (2005a). *Women's Equality: A Struggle for Survival*. New Delhi: Gyan Publishing House.

Arunachalam, J. (2005b). “Problems and issues of the unorganized sector workers placed before The National Commission for Enterprises in the Unorganized Sector”. Note dated 13 March.

Arunachalam, J. (2006). “Micro-insurance: A mitigating tool to protect the poor from the vicious circle of poverty”, Mimeographed.

Arunachalam, J. and Landwehr, B. (eds). (2003). *“Structuring a movement and spreading it on”: History and growth of the Working Women’s Forum (India)-1978–2003.* Frankfurt & London: IKO-Verlag fur Interkulturelle Kommunikation.

Arunachalam, S. (2002). “Reaching the unreached: How can we use ICTs to empower the rural poor in the developing world through enhanced access to relevant information?” *68th IFLA Council and General Conference,* August 18–24. Glasgow, Scotland.

Azad, M. (2006). *Social Insurance Provision for Women in the Urban Informal Sector: Interpreting the Successful Strategy of Working Women’s Forum, India.* Masters Thesis in City Planning submitted to the Department of Urban Studies and Planning, Massachusetts Institute of Technology, Cambridge, Massachusetts.

Azad, N. (2007). “Towards an engendered poverty paradigm in SAARC”. In Arunachalam, J. and Kalpagam, U. (Eds) *Rural Women in South Asia.* Jaipur: Rawat Publications.

Bakesha, S., Nakafeero, A. and Okello, D. (2009). “ICTs as an agent of change: A case of grassroots women entrepreneurs in Uganda”. In Buskens, I. and Webb, A. (Eds) *African Women and ICTs: Investigating Technology, Gender and Empowerment.* London: Zed Press.

Banerjee, N. (1999). “How real is the bogey of feminization?” In Papola, T.S. and Sharma, A.N. (Eds) *Gender and Employment in India.* pp. 299–317. New Delhi: Vikas Publishing House.

Bantebya-Kyomuhendo, G. (2009). “The mobile pay phone business: A vehicle for rural women’s empowerment in Uganda”. In Buskens, I. and Webb, A. (Eds) *African Women and ICTs: Investigating Technology, Gender and Empowerment.* London: Zed Press.

Bardhan, P. (2001). “Social justice in the global economy”, *Economic and Political Weekly,* February 3: 467.

Bauman, Z. (1998). *Globalisation: The Human Consequences.* Columbia University Press: New York.

Best, M.L. and Kumar, R. (2008). “Sustainability failure of rural telecenters: Challenges from the Sustainable Access in Rural India (SARI) Project”, *Information Technologies and International Development* 4(4): 31–45.

Best, M.L. and Maier, S.G. (2007). "Gender, culture and ICT use in rural south India", *Gender, Technology & Development* 11(2): 137–155.

Bhalla, G.S. and Hazell, P. (2003). "Rural employment and poverty strategies to eliminate rural poverty within a generation", *Economic and Political weekly*, August 16. pp. 3473–3484.

Bhatnagar, S. (2000). "Social implications of information and communication technology in developing countries: Lessons from Asian success stories", *The Electronic Journal on Information Systems in Developing Countries* 1(4): 1–9.

Bhatnagar, S. and Schware, R. (2000). *Information and Communication Technology in Development: Cases from India.* New Delhi: Sage.

Bloch, M. and Bloch, J.H. (1980). "Women and the Dialectics of nature in eighteenth century French thought". In MacCormack, C.P. and Strathern, M. (Eds) *Nature, Culture and Gender.* Cambridge: Cambridge University Press.

Breman, J. (1996). *Footloose Labour: Working in India's Informal Economy.* Cambridge: Cambridge University Press.

Breman, J. (1999). "The study of industrial labour in post-colonial India - The informal sector: A concluding review", *Contributions to Indian Sociology* (n.s.) 33(1–2): 407–431.

Bremen, J. (2004). *The Making and Unmaking of an Industrial Working Class.* New Delhi: Oxford University Press.

Bremen, J. and Patel, P. (2004). *Working in the Mill no More.* New Delhi: Oxford University Press.

Briggs, C.L. (2001). "Modernity, cultural reasoning, and the institutionalisation of social inequality: Racialising death in a Venezuelan cholera epidemic", *Comparative Studies in Society and History*: 665–700. Vol. 43, Part 4.

Burra, N., Deshmukh-Ranadive, J. and Murthy, R.K. (2005). *Micro-credit, Poverty and Empowerment.* New Delhi: Sage.

Buskens, I. and Webb, A. (eds) 2009. *African women and ICTs: Investigating Technology, Gender and Empowerment.* London: Zed Press.

Carr, M., Chen M. and Jhabvala, R. (eds) (1997). *Speaking Out: Women's Economic Empowerment in South Asia.* New Delhi: Vistaar Publications.

Castells, M. (2006). *The Rise of the Network Society.* Oxford: Blackwell.

Cecehini, S. and Scott, C. (2003). "Can information and communication technology applications contribute to poverty reduction? Lessons from rural India", *Information Technology for Development* 10: 73–84.

Chadha, G.K. (1999). "Non-farm employment in rural areas: How well can female workers compete?" In Papola, T.S. and Sharma, A.N. (Eds) *Gender and Employment in India*. pp. 139–177. New Delhi: Vikas Publishing House.

Chadha, G.K. and Sahoo, P.P. (2002). "Post-reform setbacks in rural employment", *Economic and Political Weekly*, May 25. Vol. 37, ISS 21, pp. 1988–2003.

Chathukulam, J. and John, M.S. (2000). "Empowerment of women panchayat members: learning from Kerala (India)", *Asian Journal of Women's Studies* 6(4): 66–101.

Chattopadhyay, R. and Duflo, E. (2004a). "The impact of reservation in the panchayati raj: Evidence from a nationwide randomized experiment', *Economic and Political Weekly*. Vol. 39, ISS 9, pp. 979–986.

Chattopadhyay, R. and Duflo, E. (2004b). "Women as policy makers: Evidence from a randomized policy experiment in India", *Econometrica* 72(5), September: 1409–1443.

Chaudhuri, M. (2010). "Nationalism is not what it used to be, can feminism be any different: A view from India", *Nivedini* 16, November/ December: 120–145.

Chen, M.A. (1983). "The working women's forum: Organizing for credit and change". *Seeds* 6: 1–20.

Chen, M.A. (1998). *Widows in India: Social Neglect and Public Action*. New Delhi: Sage.

Chhachhi, A. (1999). "Gender, flexibility, skill and industrial restructuring: The electronics industry in India", *Gender, Technology & Development* 3(3): 329–360.

Comfort, K. and Dada, J. (2009). "Women's use of cell phones to meet their communication needs-A study of rural women from northern Nigeria". In Buskens, I. and Webb, A. (Eds) *African Women and ICTs: Investigating Technology, Gender and Empowerment*. London: Zed Press.

Dankelman, I. (2010). *Gender and Climate Change: An Introduction*. London: Earthscan.

Datar, C. and Pawar, P. (2008). "Micro-credit and income generation activities for the poorest: Insights from Vadgaonlakh". In Kalpagam, U. and Arunachalam, J. (Eds) *Rural Women and Development in India: Issues and Challenges*. Jaipur: Rawat Publications.

Deepak, P. and Bhamidipaty, A. (2007). "Optimizing on mobile usage cost for the lower income group: Insights and recommendation". In Baranauskas, C. et al. (Eds) *INTERACT 2007*, LNCS 4662, Part I: 339–342.

Deshmukh, J.R. (2008). "Gender concerns in the right to food: Theoretical explorations". In Kalpagam, U. and Arunachalam, J. (Eds) *Rural Women and Development in India: Issues and Challenges.* Jaipur: Rawat Publications.

Deshpande, S. and Deshpande, L.K. (1999). "Gender-based discrimination in the urban labour market". In Papola, T.S. and Sharma, A.N. (Eds) *Gender and Employment in India.* pp. 223–248. New Delhi: Vikas Publishing House.

Dev, M.S. (2000a). "Economic liberalisation and employment in South Asia I & II", *Economic and Political Weekly* XXXV(1–3), Jan 8 & 15: 40–51 & 135–146.

Dev, M.S. (2000b). "Economic reforms, poverty, income distribution and employment", *Economic and Political Weekly* XXXV(10), March 4–10: 823–835.

Dev, S.M.P., Gayathri, V. and Mamgain, R.P. (2002). "Social and economic security in India", *International Labour Review.* Vol. 141, ISS 1–2, pp. 175–198.

Dewan, R. (2005). "Gender Budget Perspectives on Macro and Meso Policies in Small Urban Manufacturies in Greater Mumbai". Discussion Paper Series-12, April, HDRC, UNDP, New Delhi.

Dewan, R. and Prabhu, S. (eds) 2009. *Macroeconomics and Gender.* New Delhi: Zubaan.

Dogra, B. (2001). "Women justify reservation policy in panchayats", *Good News India,* August, http//www.goodnewsindia.com/pages/content/transitions/panwomen.html

Donner, J. (2005). "The use of mobile phones by microentrepreneurs in Kigali, Rwanda: Changes to social and business networks', Submitted to *Wireless Communication and Development: A Global Perspective Annenberg Research Network on International Communication Workshop,* October 7–8 (Available on the internet)
http://www.mitpressjournals.org/doi/abs/10.1162/ibid.2007.3.2.3

Donner, J. (2006). "Internet use (and non-use) among urban microenterprises in the developing world: an update from India", Paper prepared for AOIR 7.0, Brisbane, Australia, September.

Donner, J. (2007). "Customer acquisition among small and informal business in urban India: Comparing face to face and mediated channels", *The Electronic Journal on Information System in Developing Countries* 32(3): 1–16.

Dreze, J. and Sen, A. (1991). "Public action for social security: Foundation and strategy". In Ahmad, Dreze, Hills and Sen (eds), *Social Security in Developing Countries,* Oxford: Oxford University Press.

Dwyer, D. and Bruce, J. (eds) (1988). *A Home Divided: Women and Income in the Third World.* Stanford: Stanford University Press.

Elijah, O.A., and Ogunlade, I. (2006). "Analysis of the uses of information and communication technology for gender empowerment and sustainable poverty alleviation in Nigeria", *International Journal of Education and Development using ICT* (Online) 2(3): 45–69.

Elson, D. (1994). "Structural adjustment with gender awareness", *Indian Journal of Gender Studies* 1(2), July-December. pp. 149–167.

Faulkner, W. and Lie, M. (2007). "Gender in the information society: Strategies of inclusion", *Gender, Technology and Development* 11(2): 157–177.

Fernandez-Kelly, P. and Wolf, D. (2001). "A dialogue on globalization", *Signs* 26(4), *Globalization and Gender,* Summer: 1243–1249.

Foley, P. (2004). "Does the internet help to overcome social exclusion?" *Electronic Journal of E-Government,* http://www.ejeg.com/volume-2/volume2-issue2/v2-i2foley-139–146.pdf. *Frontline.* (2000). "Conflict in Chilka", *Frontline,* July 16: 44–45.

Gautham, S. (2007). *India Together,* April 27, http//www.indiatogether.org/2007/apr/soc-kattarule.html.

Ghosh, J. (2009). *Never Done and Poorly Paid: Women's Work in Globalising India.* New Delhi: Women Unlimited.

Ginneken, W. van (1998). *Social Security for all Indians.* International Labour Office. Oxford University Press.

Ginneken, W. van (1999). "Social security for the informal sector: A new challenge for the developing countries", *International Social Security Review.* Vol. 52, 49–69.

Goetz, A.M. (undated). "Political Cleaners: How Women are the New Anti-Corruption Force. Does the Evidence Wash?"

Goetz, A.M. and Jenkins, R. (1999). "Accountability to women in development spending-experiments in service-delivery audits at the local level". Paper presented at the UNDP Conference *Gender, Poverty and Environment-Sensitive Budget Analysis,* June, New York.

Gothoskar, S. (1997). "Women, work and health: An interconnected web-case of drugs and cosmetics industries", *Economic and Political Weekly, Review of Women's Studies* XXXII(43), 25 October. WS 45–WS52.

Gothoskar, S. (2000). "Teleworking and gender", *Economic and Political Weekly* XXXV(26), June 24: 2293–2298.

Guhan, S. (1994). "Social security options for developing countries", *International Labour Review*, Vol. 133, 35–53.

Gurumurthy, A. (2006). "Promoting gender equality? Some development-related uses of ICTs by women", *Development in Practice* 16(6): 611–615.

Hafkin, N. (2002). "Gender issues in ICT policy in developing countries: An overview". *United Nations Division for the Advancement of Women* (DAW), October .

Heeks R., Arun S. and Morgan, S. (2004). *Researching ICT-based enterprise for women in developing countries: An enterprise perspective.* Project report IDPM, University of Manchester, UK.

Hensman, R. (2004). "Globalisation, women and work: What are we talking about?" *Economic and Political Weekly*, March 6: 1030–1034.

Hirway, I. (1996). "Economic reforms and gender issues in India", *The Indian Journal of Labour Economics* 39(3), July-September. pp. 577–589.

Huyer, S. and Carr, M. (2002). "Information and communication technologies: A priority for women', *Gender, Technology and Development* 6(1): 85–100.

Jain, D. (1996). "Valuing work: Time as a measure", *Economic and Political Weekly* 31(43), October 26: WS 46-WS 57.

Jayawardene, K. (1986). *Feminism and Nationalism in the Third World.* London: Zed Press.

Jenkins, R. and Goetz, A.M. (1999). "Accounts and accountability: theoretical implications of the right-to-information movement in India", *Third World Quarterly* 20(3): 603–622.

Jeyaranjan, J. and Swaminathan, P. (1999). "Resilience of gender inequalities: Women and employment in Chennai", *Economic and Political Weekly* 34(16/17), April 17–30: WS2-WS11.

Jhabvala, R. (1998). "Social security for unorganised sector", *Economic and Political Weekly* 33(22), May 30–June 5: L7-L11.

Jhabvala, R. (1999). "Interventions in the labour market: The case of SEWA". In Papola, T.S. and Sharma, A.N. (Eds) *Gender and Employment in India.* pp. 412–426. New Delhi: Vikas Publishing House.

Jhabvala, R. and Sinha, S. (2002). "Liberalisation and the Woman Worker", *Economic and Political Weekly,* May 25, pp. 2037.

Jhabvala, R. and Subrahmanya, R.K.A. (2000). *The Unorganised Sector: Work Security and Social Protection.* New Delhi: Sage.

Jhabwala, R. and Sinha, S. (2001). "Social security for women workers in the unorganised sector", *The Indian Journal of Labour Economics* 44(4): 577.

Kabeer, N. (1994). *Reversed Realities: Gender Hierarchies in Development Thought.* London: Verso.

Kabeer, N. (2001). "Conflicts over credit: Re-evaluating the empowerment potential of loans to women in rural Bangladesh", *World Development* 29(1), January: 63–84.

Kabeer, N. (2002). *Safety Nets and Opportunity Ladders: Addressing Vulnerability in South Asia.* Working Paper 159, Overseas Development Institute, London.

Kalpagam, U. (1994). *Labour and Gender: Survival in Urban India.* New Delhi: Sage.

Kalpagam, U. (2009). "Global trading of carbon emissions and India", *Man & Development,* March: 47–66.

Kalpagam, U. and Rajagopalan, S. (2006). "A social platform for women workers: The case of Working Women's Forum (India)". In Arunachalam, J. and Kalpagam, U. (Eds) *Development and Empowerment: Rural Women in India.* pp. 120–144. Jaipur: Rawat Publications.

Kalpana, K. (2005). "Shifting trajectories in microfinance discourse", *Economic and Political Weekly* 40(51), Dec 17–23: 5400–5409.

Kantor, P. (1997). "Informal sector: lifting the shroud", *Economic and Political Weekly* XXXII(40), Oct 4, pp. 2512–2514.

Kapadia, K. (1999). "Gender ideologies and the formation of rural industrial classes in South India today", *Contributions to Indian Sociology* (n.s.) 33(1 & 2): 329–352.

Katz, E. (1997). "The intra-household economics of voice and exit", *Feminist Economics* 3(3): 25–46.

Kelkar, G., Shrestha, G. and Veena, N. (2002). "IT industry and women's agency: Explorations in Bangalore and Delhi, India", *Gender, Technology and Development* 6(1): 63–84.

Keniston, K. (2002). "Grassroots ICT Projects in India: Some Preliminary Hypotheses". *ASCI Journal of Management* 31. pp. 1–9.

Kingdon, G.G. (1999). "Labour-force participation, returns to education and sex-discrimination". In Papola, T.S. and Sharma, A.N. (Eds)

*Gender and Employment in India*. pp. 249–277. New Delhi: Vikas Publishing House.

Knorringa, P. (1999). "Artisan labour in the Agra footwear industry: continued informality and changing threats", *Contributions to Indian Sociology* (n.s.) 33(1 & 2): 303–328.

Kothari, A. (1999). "To save the sanctuaries", *Frontline*, July 30: 66–70.

Krishnakumar, A. (2000). "Livelihood issues: Handloom sector worries", *Frontline*, April 14: 64–70.

Krishnakumar, R. (1999). "A landmark proposal", *Frontline*, January 29: 66–72.

Krishnaraj, M. (2003). "Challenges before women's movement in a changing context", *Economic and Political Weekly*, October 25: 4536–4545.

Kumar, R. and Best, M. (2006a). "Impact and sustainability of e-government services in developing countries: Lessons learned from Tamil Nadu, India", *The Information Society* 22(1): 1–12.

Kumar, R. and Best, M. (2006b). "Social impact and diffusion of telecenter use: A study from the Sustainable Access in Rural India Project", *The Journal of Community Informatics* 2(3).

Kundu, A. (1999). "Trends and pattern of female employment: A case of organized informalisation". In Papola, T.S. and Sharma, A.N. (Eds) *Gender and Employment in India*. pp. 52–70. New Delhi: Vikas Publishing House.

Kundu, A. (2000). "Globalising Gujarat: Urbanisation, employment and poverty", *Economic and Political Weekly* XXXV(35 & 36), Aug 26-Sept 2: 3172–3182.

Larson, M.J. (2002). "Transforming power relationships and building capacity for ecological security". In Masika, R. (ed.) *Gender, Development and Climate Change*. London: Oxfam.

Lele, M.K. (2008). "Contesting power in panchayats". In Kalpagam, U. and Arunachalam, J. (Eds) *Rural Women and Development in India: Issues and Challenges*. pp. 219–237. Jaipur: Rawat Publications.

Lundberg, A. (2001). *Experience and Identity*. Dept. of History, Lund, Sweden

MacCormack, C.P. (1980). Nature, culture and gender: A critique". In MacCormack, C.P. and Strathern, M. (Eds) *Nature, Culture and Gender*. Cambridge: Cambridge University Press.

Madon, S. (2004). "Evaluating the development impact of e-governance limitations: An exploratory framework". *The Electronic Journal on Information System in Developing Countries* 20(5): 1–13.

Mahadevia, D. (1998). "Informalisation of employment and incidence of poverty in Ahmedabad", *The Indian Journal of Labour Economics* 41(3): 515–530.

Mahalingam, S. (2000). "Changing the rules of the game", *Frontline*, April 28: 16–18.

Mazumdar, I. (2007). *Women Workers and Globalization: Emergent Contradictions in India*. Kolkata: Stree Publications.

Menon, P. (1999). "A looming crisis", *Frontline*, February 12: 38–40.

Menon, P. (2000). "Hungry in Anantapur", *Frontline*, July 7: 43–45.

Menon, P. (2010). "Need to regulate microfinance institutions: AIDWA", *The Hindu*, November 12: 15.

Merchant, C. (1980). *The Death of Nature: Women, Ecology and the Scientific Revolution*, New York: Harper Collins.

Mies, M. (1986). *Patriarchy and Accumulation on a World Scale*. London: Zed Press.

Mitter, S. (2000). "Teleworking and teletrade in India", *Economic and Political Weekly* XXXV(26), June 24: 2241–2252.

Mitter, S. (2004). "Globalization, ICTs, and economic empowerment: A feminist critique", *Gender, Technology and Development* 8(1): 5–30.

Mitter, S. and Sen, A. (2000). "Can Calcutta become another Bangalore? Looking for windows of opportunity in international telework", *Economic and Political Weekly* XXXV(26), June 24: 2263–2268.

Molyneux, M. (1986). "Anthropological perspectives on women's collective actions", Special Issue, *IWAC Bulletin*, New York.

Moser, C. (1989). "Gender planning in the third world: Meeting practical and strategic gender needs", *World Development* 17(11), pp. 1799–1825.

Moser, C.O.N. (1993). *Gender Planning and Development: Theory, Practice and Training*. London: Routledge.

Mukerji, P.N. (2008). "Panchayat elections and grassroots democracy (comparative study of the May 2008 elections in West Bengal and Punjab)", *Man & Development* XXX(3), September: 41–54.

Mukhopadhyay, M. and Meer, S. (2004). *Creating Voice and Carving Space: Redefining Governance from a Gender Perspective*. New Delhi: Zubaan.

Mukhopadhyay, S. (1999). "Locating women within informal sector hierarchies". In Papola, T.S. and Sharma, A.N. (Eds) *Gender and Employment in India*. pp. 206–220. New Delhi: Vikas Publishing House.

Murthy, R. (2001). *Building Women's Capacities: Interventions in Gender Transformation*. New Delhi: Sage.

Nachiappan, S., Soundara Rajan, S.N., Shanthi, N. and Sudha, C. (2008). "Bridging the digital divide: The case of Working Women's Forum (India)", *Journal of International Women's Studies,* November, e-journal website: http//www.bridgew.edu/SoAS/JIWS/

NCEUS (2008). *Report on Conditions of Work and Promotion of Livelihoods in the Unorganised Sector.* New Delhi: Academic Foundation.

Ndubisi, N.O. and Kahraman, C. (2005). "Malaysian women entrepreneurs: Understanding the ICT usage behaviours and drivers", *Journal of Enterprise Information Management* 18(6): 721–739.

Note on unorganized sector worker's social security Bill, 2005 – internet.

NSSO (2006). Employment and Unemployment Situation in India 2004–05 (Part I), NSS 61st Round, July 2004–June 2005 Report No. 515, GoI, New Delhi.

Oommen, M.A. (2000). "Globalization and poverty in India: Some explanatory hypotheses", *Man and Development* XXII(3), September: 17–36.

Ortner, S. (1972). "Is female to male as nature is to culture?" *Feminist Studies* 1(2), Autumn: 5–31.

Pal, J. (2008). "Computers and the promise of development: Aspiration, neoliberalism and 'technolity' in India's ICTD enterprise". Paper Presented at *Confronting the Challenge of Technology for Development: Experiences from the BRICS,* May29–30, University of Oxford.

Panchamukhi, P.R. (2000). "Social impact of economic reforms in India", *Economic and Political Weekly* XXXV(10), March 4–10: 836–847.

Pande, R. (2003). "Can mandated political representation increase policy influence for disadvantaged minorities", *American Economic Review* 93: 1132–1151.

Papanek, H. (1979). "The "Work" and "Non-Work" of Women", *Signs* 4(4), Summer: 775–781.

Patel, V. (2010). "Gender audit of budgets in India - 2001–02 to 2009–10", *Nivedini* 16, November/ December: 146–172.

Patnaik, P. (1997). "On the concept of efficiency", *Economic and Political Weekly* XXXII(43), October 25. pp. 2807–2183.

Patnaik, U. (1996). "Export-oriented agriculture and food security in developing countries and India", *Economic and Political Weekly*, Special number. Vol. 31, ISS 35/37 pp. 2429–2450.

Patnaik, U. (2007). "Neoliberalism and rural poverty in India", *Economic and Political Weekly* XLII(38), July 28-August 3: 3132–3150.

Phadke, S. (2003). "Thirty years on: Women's studies reflects on the women's movement", *Economic and Political Weekly* XXXVIII(43), Oct 25–31: 4567–4576.

Quota for Women in panchayats to be raised to 50%. *The Times of India*, Aug 28, 2009.

Rajalakshmi, T.K. (1997). "A global forum of fishworkers", *Frontline*, Dec 26. pp. 13–26.

Rajalakshmi, T.K. (1999). "The woes of a workforce", *Frontline*, April 23: 119–120.

Rao, N. (1996). "Empowerment through organisation: Women workers in the informal sector", *Indian Journal of Gender Studies* 3(2), July-December. pp. 171–196.

Robertson, R. (1995). *Globalisation: Social Theory and Global Culture*. London: Sage.

Roy Chowdhury, S. (2004). "Globalisation and labour", *Economic and Political Weekly*, January 3: 105–108

Roy, A. (2000). "Breaking the shackles: Kol tribal labourers", *Economic and Political Weekly* XXXV(6), Feb 5–11: 425–426.

Roy, A. (2005). *Gendered Citizenship: Historical and Conceptual Explorations*. Hyderabad: Orient Longman.

Saith, A. (2008). "ICTs and poverty alleviation: Hope or hype?" In Saith, A., Vijayabaskar. M. and Gayathri, V. (Eds) *ICTs and Indian Social Change: Diffusion, Poverty, Governance*. New Delhi: Sage.

Sakthivel, S., and Joddar, P. (2006). "Unorganised sector workforce in India: Trends, patterns and social security coverage", *Economic and Political Weekly* 41(21): 2107–2114.

Sane, I. and Traore, M.B. (2009). "Mobile phones in a time of modernity: The quest for increased self-sufficiency amongst women fishmonger and fish processors in Dakar". In Buskens, I. and Webb, A. (Eds) *African Women and ICTs: Investigating Technology, Gender and Empowerment*. London: Zed Press.

Schenk-Sandbergen. (2008). "The economic impact of re-loaning: An assessment of Working Women's Forum's experience". In Kalpagam, U. and Arunachalam, J. (Eds) *Rural Women and Development in India: Issues and Challenges*. Jaipur: Rawat Publications.

Sen, A.K. (1990). "Gender and co-operative conflicts". In I. Tinker (ed.) *Persistent Inequalities*. Oxford: Oxford University Press.

Sen, Ilina (2008). "Forest-based Communities, Decentralized Food Security Systems and Women", in U. Kalpagam and Jaya Arunachalam (eds)

*Rural Women and Development in India: Issues and Challenges*, Jaipur: Rawat Publications.

Sharma, K. (1991–1992). "Grassroots organisation and women's empowerment: Some issues in the contemporary debate", *Samya Shakti* VI. pp. 28–44.

Sharma, K. (2000). "Power and representation: Reservation for women in India", *Asian Journal of Women's Studies* 6(1): 47–87.

Sharma, R.C. (2003). "Gender, e-commerce and development", *The Electronic Journal on Information System in Developing Countries* 11(3): 1–2.

Sharpe, J. and Spivak, G.C. (2003). "A conversation with Gayatri Chakravorty Spivak: Politics and the imagination", *Signs* 28(2), Winter: 609–624.

Shiva, V. (1989). *Staying Alive: Women, Ecology and Development*. New Delhi: Kali for Women.

——. (2006) *Earth Democracy: Justice, Sustainability and Peace*, London: Zed Press.

——. (2009) Soil not Oil: Environmental Justice in an Age of Climate Crisis.

Singh, N. (2006). "ICTs and rural development in India". SCCIE Working Paper# 06–11, *University of California*, October, Santa Cruz.

Sivaraman, M. (1999). "An experiment in empowerment", *Frontline*, Dec 24: 70–72.

Smith, N. and Harvey, D. (1984/2008). *Uneven Development: Nature, Capital and the Production of Space.* Athens: University of Georgia Press.

Somasundaram, U.V. (2006). *Working Women's Forum: Invisibility to Visibility-Reaching the Other 100 Million Poor.* In Indian Studies in Urban Microfinance, Centre for Micro Finance, Institute for Financial Management and Research, Chennai. Published by CARE INDIA'S Finance.

Soni-Sinha, U. (2006). "Where are the women? Gender, labor, and discourse in the Noida Export Processing Zone and Delhi", *Feminist Economics* 12(3), July: 335–365.

Sparr, P. (1994). *Mortgaging Women's Lives: Feminist Critiques of Structural Adjustment*, London/New Jersey: Zed Books

Special Correspondent (2010b). "Protect minimum wage right of rural job scheme workers", *The Hindu*, Sun, November 7: 8.

Sridhar, V. (1999). "Mills in crisis", *Frontline*, Mar 12: 65–71.

Sridhar, V. (2000). "Livelihood issues", *Frontline*, Apr 28: 19–20.

Sriram, R. and Ganapathy, H. (1997). "The unresolved dilemma: Child care options in agricultural contexts", *Economic and Political Weekly, Review of Women's Studies* XXXII(43), October 25–31. pp. 64–72.

Srivastava, N. (1999). "Striving for a toe-hold: Women in the organised sector". In Papola, T.S. and Sharma, A.N. (Eds) *Gender and Employment in India*. pp. 181–205. New Delhi: Vikas Publishing House.

Staff Reporter (2010a). "Microfinance units under the scanner", *The Hindu*, Sun, November 7: 5.

*Tenth Five Year Plan* 2002–2007. (2002). Governance and Implementation, Vol. 1, Government of India, Planning Commission, Delhi.

Terry, G. (ed.) (2009). *Climate Change and Gender Justice*. London: Oxfam & Practical Action Publishing.

Tewari, M. (2008). "ICTs and poverty reduction: User perspective study of rural Madhya Pradesh, India", *The European Journal of Development Research* 20(3): 448–461.

Thompson, M.R. (2000): "The survival of 'Asian Values' as Zivilisationskritik", *Theory and Society* 29(5): 651–686.

Thorat, S. (1999). "Social security in unorganised sector in India: How secure are the scheduled castes?" *The Indian Journal of Labour Economics*, Vol. 42(3): 451–470.

Topalova, P. (2003). "Women are changing governance in India? The impact of female leadership on household satisfaction, quality of public goods and governance", Mimeo, MIT.

Triantafillou, P. and Nielsen, M.R. (2001). "Policing empowerment: The making of capable subjects", *History of the Human Sciences* 14(2): 63–86.

Umrani, F. and Ghadially, R. (2003). "Empowering women through ICT education: Facilitating computer adoption". *Gender, Technology and Development* 7(3): 359–377.

Unni, J. (1999). "Women workers in agriculture: Some recent trends". In Papola, T.S. and Sharma, A.N. (Eds) *Gender and Employment in India*. pp. 99–121. New Delhi: Vikas Publishing House.

Unni, J. and Bali, N. (2002). "Sub-contracted women workers in the global economy: Case of garment industry in India". In R. Balakrishnan (ed.) *The Hidden Assembly Line: Gender Dynamics of Subcontracted Work in a Global Economy*. Connecticut: Kumarian Press.

Unni, J. and Rani, U. (2000). "Globalisation, information technology revolution and service sector in India". *Keynote Address at the 42nd Annual Conference, The Indian Journal of Labour Economics* 43(4), Oct-Dec: 803–827.

Unni, J. and Rani, U. (2001). "Social protection for informal workers", *The Indian Journal of Labour Economics* 44(4): 565.S.

Unni, J. and Rani, U. (2003). "Social protection for informal workers in India: Insecurities, instruments and institutional mechanisms", *Development and Change* 34(1), January: 127–161.

Urquhart, C.L.S. and Kah, M. (2007). "ICT and poverty reduction: A social capital and knowledge perspective", *Journal of Information Technology* 23(3): 203–213.

Vanamala, M. (2001). "Informalisation and Feminisation of a Formal Sector Industry: A Case Study", *Economic and Political Weekly*, June 30, Vol. 36, No. 26, pp. 2378–2389.

Vijay, G. (1999). "Social security of labour in new industrial towns", *Economic and Political Weekly* 34(39), Sept 25-Oct 1: L10-L18.

Warrier, S.M.V. (2010). "Globalization and women's identities: New forms of work, survival strategies and images of migrant women". In Gupta, S., Basu, T. and Chattarji, S. (Eds) *Globalization in India: Contents and Discontents*. New Delhi: Pearson Education.

World Bank. (2001). *Engendering Development: Through Gender Equality in Rights, Resources, and Voice*. New York: Oxford University Press and World Bank.

# Index